The Road
Less Traveled

A NEW PSYCHOLOGY OF LOVE, TRADITIONAL VALUES AND SPIRITUAL GROWTH

M. SCOTT PECK, M.D.

A TOUCHSTONE BOOK
Published by Simon & Schuster

⅂

TOUCHSTONE
Rockefeller Center
1230 Avenue of the Americas
New York, New York 10020

First Touchstone Edition 1980
Second Touchstone Edition 1998

TOUCHSTONE and colophon are registered trademarks
of Simon & Schuster Inc.

Designed by Dianne Pinkowitz

Manufactured in the United States of America

1 0

Library of Congress Cataloging-in-Publication Data
Peck, Morgan Scott, date.
    The road less traveled.

    (A Touchstone book)
    Includes bibliographical references.
    1. Maturation (Psychology).   2. Psychiatry and religion.
3. Psychoanalysis and religion.   I. Title.
BF637.S4P43   1979   158'.1   79-15410

ISBN 0-671-24086-2
ISBN 0-684-84724-8 (Pbk)
ISBN 0-684-84728-0 (Flexibind)

The author gratefully acknowledges permission to reprint excerpts
from the following:

"Beyond the Norm: A Speculative Model of Self-Realization," by Michael Stark
and Michael Washburn, in *Journal of Religion and Health*, Vol. 16, No. 1 (1977),
pp. 58–59. Used by permission.
"Child Custody Contests in Historical Perspective," by André P. Derdeyn,
in *American Journal of Psychiatry*, Vol. 133, No. 12 (Dec. 1976), p. 1369,
copyright © 1976, the American Psychiatric Association. Reprinted by permission.
The Cloud of Unknowing, translated by Ira Progoff, copyright © 1957 by Ira Progoff.
Used by permission of the Julian Press, a Division of Crown Publishers, Inc.

(*continued on page 318*)

To my parents,
Elizabeth and David,
whose discipline and love
gave me the eyes
to see grace

Contents

10   CONTENTS

III: GROWTH AND RELIGION

IV: GRACE

Introduction

The ideas herein presented stem, for the most part, from my day-to-day clinical work with patients as they struggled to avoid or to gain ever greater levels of maturity. Consequently, this book contains portions of many actual case histories. Confidentiality is essential to psychiatric practice, and all case descriptions, therefore, have been altered in name and in other particulars so as to preserve the anonymity of my patients without distorting the essential reality of our experience with each other.

There may, however, be some distortion by virtue of the brevity of the case presentations. Psychotherapy is seldom a brief process, but since I have, of necessity, focused on the highlights of a case, the reader may be left with the impression that the process is one of drama and clarity. The drama is real and clarity may eventually be achieved, but it should be remembered that in the interest of readability, accounts of the lengthy periods of confusion and frustration inherent in most therapy have been omitted from these case descriptions.

I would also like to apologize for continually referring to God in the traditionally masculine image, but I have done so in the interest of simplicity rather than from any rigidly held concept as to gender.

As a psychiatrist, I feel it is important to mention at the outset two assumptions that underlie this book. One is that I make no distinction between the mind and the spirit, and therefore no distinction between the process of achieving spiritual growth and achieving mental growth. They are one and the same.

The other assumption is that this process is a complex, arduous and lifelong task. Psychotherapy, if it is to provide substantial assistance to the process of mental and spiritual growth, is not a quick or simple procedure. I do not belong to any particular school of psychiatry or psychotherapy; I am not simply a Freudian or Jungian or Adlerian or behaviorist or gestaltist. I do not believe there are any single easy answers. I believe that brief forms of psychotherapy may be helpful and are not to be decried, but the help they provide is inevitably superficial.

The journey of spiritual growth is a long one. I would like to thank those of my patients who have given me the privilege of accompanying them for major portions of their journey. For their journey has also been mine, and much of what is presented here is what we have learned together. I would also like to thank many of my teachers and colleagues. Principal among them is my wife, Lily. She has been so giving that it is hardly possible to distinguish her wisdom as a spouse, parent, psychotherapist, and person from my own.

SECTION I

Discipline

Problems and Pain

Life is difficult.

This is a great truth, one of the greatest truths.* It is a great truth because once we truly see this truth, we transcend it. Once we truly know that life is difficult—once we truly understand and accept it—then life is no longer difficult. Because once it is accepted, the fact that life is difficult no longer matters.

Most do not fully see this truth that life is difficult. Instead they moan more or less incessantly, noisily or subtly, about the enormity of their problems, their burdens, and their difficulties as if life were generally easy, as if life *should* be easy. They voice their belief, noisily or subtly, that their difficulties represent a unique kind of affliction that should not be and that has somehow been especially visited upon them, or else upon their families, their tribe, their class, their nation, their race or even their species, and not upon others. I know about this moaning because I have done my share.

Life is a series of problems. Do we want to moan about them or solve them? Do we want to teach our children to solve them?

Discipline is the basic set of tools we require to solve life's problems. Without discipline we can solve nothing. With only

* The first of the "Four Noble Truths" which Buddha taught was "Life is suffering."

some discipline we can solve only some problems. With total discipline we can solve all problems.

What makes life difficult is that the process of confronting and solving problems is a painful one. Problems, depending upon their nature, evoke in us frustration or grief or sadness or loneliness or guilt or regret or anger or fear or anxiety or anguish or despair. These are uncomfortable feelings, often very uncomfortable, often as painful as any kind of physical pain, sometimes equaling the very worst kind of physical pain. Indeed, it is *because* of the pain that events or conflicts engender in us all that we call them problems. And since life poses an endless series of problems, life is always difficult and is full of pain as well as joy.

Yet it is in this whole process of meeting and solving problems that life has its meaning. Problems are the cutting edge that distinguishes between success and failure. Problems call forth our courage and our wisdom; indeed, they create our courage and our wisdom. It is only because of problems that we grow mentally and spiritually. When we desire to encourage the growth of the human spirit, we challenge and encourage the human capacity to solve problems, just as in school we deliberately set problems for our children to solve. It is through the pain of confronting and resolving problems that we learn. As Benjamin Franklin said, "Those things that hurt, instruct." It is for this reason that wise people learn not to dread but actually to welcome problems and actually to welcome the pain of problems.

Most of us are not so wise. Fearing the pain involved, almost all of us, to a greater or lesser degree, attempt to avoid problems. We procrastinate, hoping that they will go away. We ignore them, forget them, pretend they do not exist. We even take drugs to assist us in ignoring them, so that by deadening ourselves to the pain we can forget the problems that cause the pain. We attempt to skirt around problems rather than meet them head on. We attempt to get out of them rather than suffer through them.

This tendency to avoid problems and the emotional suffering inherent in them is the primary basis of all human mental illness. Since most of us have this tendency to a greater or lesser degree, most of us are mentally ill to a greater or lesser degree, lacking complete mental health. Some of us will go to quite extraordinary lengths to avoid our problems and the suffering they cause, proceeding far afield from all that is clearly good and sensible in order to try to find an easy way out, building the most elaborate fantasies in which to live, sometimes to the total exclusion of reality. In the succinctly elegant words of Carl Jung, "Neurosis is always a substitute for legitimate suffering."*

But the substitute itself ultimately becomes more painful than the legitimate suffering it was designed to avoid. The neurosis itself becomes the biggest problem. True to form, many will then attempt to avoid this pain and this problem in turn, building layer upon layer of neurosis. Fortunately, however, some possess the courage to face their neuroses and begin—usually with the help of psychotherapy—to learn how to experience legitimate suffering. In any case, when we avoid the legitimate suffering that results from dealing with problems, we also avoid the growth that problems demand from us. It is for this reason that in chronic mental illness we stop growing, we become stuck. And without healing, the human spirit begins to shrivel.

Therefore let us inculcate in ourselves and in our children the means of achieving mental and spiritual health. By this I mean let us teach ourselves and our children the necessity for suffering and the value thereof, the need to face problems directly and to experience the pain involved. I have stated that discipline is the basic set of tools we require to solve life's problems. It will become clear that these tools are techniques of suffering, means by which we experience the pain of problems in such a way as to work them through and solve them

* *Collected Works of C. G. Jung*, Bollingen Ser., No. 20, 2d ed. (Princeton, N.J.: Princeton Univ. Press, 1973), trans. R. F. C. Hull, Vol II, *Psychology and Religion: West and East*, 75.

successfully, learning and growing in the process. When we teach ourselves and our children discipline, we are teaching them and ourselves how to suffer and also how to grow.

What are these tools, these techniques of suffering, these means of experiencing the pain of problems constructively that I call discipline? There are four: delaying of gratification, acceptance of responsibility, dedication to truth, and balancing. As will be evident, these are not complex tools whose application demands extensive training. To the contrary, they are simple tools, and almost all children are adept in their use by the age of ten. Yet presidents and kings will often forget to use them, to their own downfall. The problem lies not in the complexity of these tools but in the will to use them. For they are tools with which pain is confronted rather than avoided, and if one seeks to avoid legitimate suffering, then one will avoid the use of these tools. Therefore, after analyzing each of these tools, we shall in the next section examine the will to use them, which is love.

Delaying Gratification

Not too long ago a thirty-year-old financial analyst was complaining to me over a period of months about her tendency to procrastinate in her job. We had worked through her feelings about her employers and how they related to feelings about authority in general, and to her parents specifically. We had examined her attitudes toward work and success and how these related to her marriage, her sexual identity, her desire to compete with her husband, and her fears of such competition. Yet despite all this standard and painstaking psychoanalytic work, she continued to procrastinate as much as ever. Finally, one day, we dared to look at the obvious. "Do you like cake?" I asked her. She replied that she did. "Which part of the cake do you like better," I went on, "the cake or the frosting?" "Oh, the frosting!" she responded enthusiastically. "And how do you eat a piece of cake?" I inquired, feeling that I must be the most inane psychiatrist that ever lived. "I eat the frosting first, of course," she replied. From her cake-eating habits we went on to examine her work habits, and, as was to be expected, discovered that on any given day she would devote the first hour to the more gratifying half of her work and the remaining six hours getting around to the objectionable remainder. I suggested that if she were to force herself to accomplish the unpleasant part of her job during the first hour, she would then be free to enjoy the other six. It seemed to me, I said, that one hour of pain followed by six of pleasure was preferable to one hour of pleasure followed by six of pain. She agreed, and, being basically a person of strong will, she no longer procrastinates.

Delaying gratification is a process of scheduling the pain and pleasure of life in such a way as to enhance the pleasure by meeting and experiencing the pain first and getting it over with. It is the only decent way to live.

This tool or process of scheduling is learned by most children quite early in life, sometimes as early as age five. For instance, occasionally a five-year-old when playing a game with a companion will suggest that the companion take first turn, so that the child might enjoy his or her turn later. At age six children may start eating their cake first and the frosting last. Throughout grammar school this early capacity to delay gratification is daily exercised, particularly through the performance of homework. By the age of twelve some children are already able to sit down on occasion without any parental prompting and complete their homework before they watch television. By the age of fifteen or sixteen such behavior is expected of the adolescent and is considered normal.

It becomes clear to their educators at this age, however, that a substantial number of adolescents fall far short of this norm. While many have a well-developed capacity to delay gratification, some fifteen- or sixteen-year-olds seem to have hardly developed this capacity at all; indeed, some seem even to lack the capacity entirely. These are the problem students. Despite average or better intelligence, their grades are poor simply because they do not work. They skip classes or skip school entirely on the whim of the moment. They are impulsive, and their impulsiveness spills over into their social life as well. They get into frequent fights, they become involved with drugs, they begin to get in trouble with the police. Play now, pay later, is their motto. So the psychologists and psychotherapists are called in. But most of the time it seems too late. These adolescents are resentful of any attempt to intervene in their life style of impulsiveness, and even when this resentment can be overcome by warmth and friendliness and a nonjudgmental attitude on the part of the therapist, their impulsiveness is often so severe that it precludes their participation in the process of psychotherapy in any meaningful way. They miss their appointments. They avoid all important and painful issues. So usually the attempt at intervention fails, and these children drop out of school, only to continue a pattern of failure that frequently lands them in disastrous marriages, in accidents, in psychiatric hospitals or in jail.

Why is this? Why do a majority develop a capacity to delay gratification while a substantial minority fail, often irretrievably, to develop this capacity. The answer is not absolutely, scientifically known. The role of genetic factors is unclear. The variables cannot be sufficiently controlled for scientific proof. But most of the signs rather clearly point to the quality of parenting as the determinant.

The Sins of the Father

It is not that the homes of these unself-disciplined children are lacking in parental discipline of a sort. More often than not these children are punished frequently and severely throughout their childhood—slapped, punched, kicked, beaten and whipped by their parents for even minor infractions. But this discipline is meaningless. Because it is undisciplined discipline.

One reason that it is meaningless is that the parents themselves are unself-disciplined, and therefore serve as undisciplined role models for their children. They are the "Do as I say, not as I do" parents. They may frequently get drunk in front of their children. They may fight with each other in front of the children without restraint, dignity or rationality. They may be slovenly. They make promises they don't keep. Their own lives are frequently and obviously in disorder and disarray, and their attempts to order the lives of their children seem therefore to make little sense to these children. If father beats up mother regularly, what sense does it make to a boy when his mother beats him up because he beat up his sister? Does it make sense when he's told that he must learn to control his temper? Since we do not have the benefit of comparison when we are young, our parents are godlike figures to our childish eyes. When parents do things a certain way, it seems to the young child the way to do them, the way they should be done. If a child sees his parents day in and day out behaving with self-discipline, restraint, dignity and a capacity to order their own lives, then the child will come to feel in the deepest fibers of his being that this is the way to live. If a child sees his parents day in and day out living without self-restraint or self-discipline, then he will come in the deepest fibers of being to believe that that is the way to live.

Yet even more important than role modeling is love. For even in chaotic and disordered homes genuine love is occasionally present, and from such homes may come self-disciplined children. And not infrequently parents who are professional people—doctors, lawyers, club women and philanthropists—who lead lives of strict orderliness and decorum but yet lack love, send children into the world who are as undisciplined and destructive and disorganized as any child from an impoverished and chaotic home.

Ultimately love is everything. The mystery of love will be examined in later portions of this work. Yet, for the sake of coherency, it may be helpful to make a brief but limited mention of it and its relationship to discipline at this point.

When we love something it is of value to us, and when something is of value to us we spend time with it, time enjoying it and time taking care of it. Observe a teenager in love with his car and note the time he will spend admiring it, polishing it, repairing it, tuning it. Or an older person with a beloved rose garden, and the time spent pruning and mulching and fertilizing and studying it. So it is when we love children; we spend time admiring them and caring for them. We give them our time.

Good discipline requires time. When we have no time to give our children, or no time that we are willing to give, we don't even observe them closely enough to become aware of when their need for our disciplinary assistance is expressed subtly. If their need for discipline is so gross as to impinge upon our consciousness, we may still ignore the need on the grounds that it's easier to let them have their own way—"I just don't have the energy to deal with them today." Or, finally, if we are impelled into action by their misdeeds and our irritation, we will impose discipline, often brutally, out of anger rather than deliberation, without examining the problem or even taking the time to consider which form of discipline is the most appropriate to that particular problem.

The parents who devote time to their children even when it is not demanded by glaring misdeeds will perceive in them subtle needs for discipline, to which they will respond with gentle urging or reprimand or structure or praise, administered with thoughtfulness and care. They will observe how their children eat cake, how they study, when they tell subtle falsehoods, when they run away from problems rather than face them. They will take the time to make these minor corrections and adjustments, listening to their children, responding to them, tightening a little here, loosening a little there, giving them little lectures, little stories, little hugs and kisses, little admonishments, little pats on the back.

So it is that the quality of discipline afforded by loving parents is superior to the discipline of unloving parents. But this is just the beginning. In taking the time to observe and to think about their children's needs, loving parents will frequently agonize over the decisions to be made, and will, in a very real sense, suffer along with their children. The children are not blind to this. They perceive it when their parents are willing to suffer with them, and although they may not respond with immediate gratitude, they will learn also to suffer. "If my parents are willing to suffer with me," they will tell themselves, "then suffering must not be so bad, and I should be willing to suffer with myself." This is the beginning of self-discipline.

The time and the quality of the time that their parents devote to them indicate to children the degree to which they are valued by their parents. Some basically unloving parents, in an attempt to cover up their lack of caring, make frequent professions of love to their children, repetitively and mechanically telling them how much they are valued, but not devoting significant time of high quality to them. Their children are never totally deceived by such hollow words. Consciously they may cling to them, wanting to believe that they are

loved, but unconsciously they know that their parents' words
do not match up with their deeds.

On the other hand, children who are truly loved, although
in moments of pique they may consciously feel or proclaim
that they are being neglected, unconsciously know themselves
to be valued. This knowledge is worth more than any gold.
For when children know that they are valued, when they
truly feel valued in the deepest parts of themselves, then they
feel valuable.

The feeling of being valuable—"I am a valuable person"—
is essential to mental health and is a cornerstone of self-
discipline. It is a direct product of parental love. Such a conviction must be gained in childhood; it is extremely
difficult to acquire it during adulthood. Conversely, when
children have learned through the love of their parents to feel
valuable, it is almost impossible for the vicissitudes of adulthood to destroy their spirit.

This feeling of being valuable is a cornerstone of self-discipline because when one considers oneself valuable one will
take care of oneself in all ways that are necessary. Self-discipline is self-caring. For instance—since we are discussing the
process of delaying gratification, of scheduling and ordering
time—let us examine the matter of time. If we feel ourselves
valuable, then we will feel our time to be valuable, and if we
feel our time to be valuable, then we will want to use it well.
The financial analyst who procrastinated did not value her
time. If she had, she would not have allowed herself to spend
most of her day so unhappily and unproductively. It was not
without consequence for her that throughout her childhood
she was "farmed out" during all school vacations to live with
paid foster parents although her parents could have taken care
of her perfectly well had they wanted to. They did not value
her. They did not want to care for her. So she grew up feeling
herself to be of little value, not worth caring for; therefore she
did not care for herself. She did not feel she was worth disci-
plining herself. Despite the fact that she was an intelligent
and competent woman she required the most elementary in-

struction in self-discipline because she lacked a realistic assessment of her own worth and the value of her own time. Once she was able to perceive her time as being valuable, it naturally followed that she wanted to organize it and protect it and make maximum use of it.

As a result of the experience of consistent parental love and caring throughout childhood, such fortunate children will enter adulthood not only with a deep internal sense of their own value but also with a deep internal sense of security. All children are terrified of abandonment, and with good reason. This fear of abandonment begins around the age of six months, as soon as the child is able to perceive itself to be an individual, separate from its parents. For with this perception of itself as an individual comes the realization that as an individual it is quite helpless, totally dependent and totally at the mercy of its parents for all forms of sustenance and means of survival. To the child, abandonment by its parents is the equivalent of death. Most parents, even when they are otherwise relatively ignorant or callous, are instinctively sensitive to their children's fear of abandonment and will therefore, day in and day out, hundreds and thousands of times, offer their children needed reassurance: "You know Mommy and Daddy aren't going to leave you behind"; "Of course Mommy and Daddy will come back to get you"; "Mommy and Daddy aren't going to forget about you." If these words are matched by deeds, month in and month out, year in and year out, by the time of adolescence the child will have lost the fear of abandonment and in its stead will have a deep inner feeling that the world is a safe place in which to be and protection will be there when it is needed. With this internal sense of the consistent safety of the world, such a child is free to delay gratification of one kind or another, secure in the knowledge that the opportunity for gratification, like home and parents, is always there, available when needed.

But many are not so fortunate. A substantial number of children actually are abandoned by their parents during childhood, by death, by desertion, by sheer negligence, or, as in the case of the financial analyst, by a simple lack of caring. Others, while not abandoned in fact, fail to receive from their parents the reassurance that they will not be abandoned. There are some parents, for instance, who in their desire to enforce discipline as easily and quickly as possible, will actually use the threat of abandonment, overtly or subtly, to achieve this end. The message they give to their children is: "If you don't do exactly what I want you to do I won't love you any more, and you can figure out for yourself what that might mean." It means, of course, abandonment and death. These parents sacrifice love in their need for control and domination over their children, and their reward is children who are excessively fearful of the future. So it is that these children, abandoned either psychologically or in actuality, enter adulthood lacking any deep sense that the world is a safe and protective place. To the contrary, they perceive the world as dangerous and frightening, and they are not about to forsake any gratification or security in the present for the promise of greater gratification or security in the future, since for them the future seems dubious indeed.

In summary, for children to develop the capacity to delay gratification, it is necessary for them to have self-disciplined role models, a sense of self-worth, and a degree of trust in the safety of their existence. These "possessions" are ideally acquired through the self-discipline and consistent, genuine caring of their parents; they are the most precious gifts of themselves that mothers and fathers can bequeath. When these gifts have not been proffered by one's parents, it is possible to acquire them from other sources, but in that case the process of their acquisition is invariably an uphill struggle, often of lifelong duration and often unsuccessful.

Problem-Solving and Time

Having touched upon some of the ways in which parental love or its lack may influence the development of self-discipline in general, and the capacity to delay gratification in particular, let us examine some of the more subtle yet quite devastating ways in which difficulties in delaying gratification affect the lives of most adults. For while most of us, fortunately, develop sufficient capacity to delay gratification to make it through high school or college and embark upon adulthood without landing in jail, our development nonetheless tends to be imperfect and incomplete, with the result that our ability to solve life's problems is still imperfect and incomplete.

At the age of thirty-seven I learned how to fix things. Prior to that time almost all my attempts to make minor plumbing repairs, mend toys or assemble boxed furniture according to the accompanying hieroglyphical instruction sheet ended in confusion, failure and frustration. Despite having managed to make it through medical school and support a family as a more or less successful executive and psychiatrist, I considered myself to be a mechanical idiot. I was convinced I was deficient in some gene, or by curse of nature lacking some mystical quality responsible for mechanical ability. Then one day at the end of my thirty-seventh year, while taking a spring Sunday walk, I happened upon a neighbor in the process of repairing a lawn mower. After greeting him I remarked, "Boy, I sure admire you. I've never been able to fix those kind of things or do anything like that." My neighbor, without a moment's hesitation, shot back, "That's because you don't take the time." I resumed my walk, somehow disquieted by the gurulike simplicity, spontaneity and definitiveness of his response. "You don't suppose he could be right, do you?" I asked myself. Somehow it registered, and the next time the opportunity presented itself to make a minor repair I was able to remind myself to take my time. The parking brake was stuck on a patient's car, and she knew that there was something one could do under the dashboard to release it, but she didn't know what. I lay down on the floor below the front seat of her car. Then I took the time to make myself comfortable. Once I was comfortable, I then took the time to look at the situation. I looked for several minutes. At first all I saw was a confusing jumble of wires and tubes and rods, whose meaning I did not know. But gradually, in no hurry, I was able to focus my sight on the brake apparatus and trace its course. And then it became clear to me that there was a little latch preventing the brake from being released. I slowly studied this latch until it became clear to me that if I were to push it upward with the tip of my finger it would move easily and would release the brake. And so I did this. One single motion, one ounce of pressure from a fingertip, and the problem was solved. I was a master mechanic!

Actually, I don't begin to have the knowledge or the time to gain that knowledge to be able to fix most mechanical failures, given the fact that I choose to concentrate my time on nonmechanical matters. So I still usually go running to the nearest repairman. But I now know that this is a choice I make, and I am not cursed or genetically defective or otherwise incapacitated or impotent. And I know that I and anyone else who is not mentally defective can solve any problem if we are willing to take the time.

The issue is important, because many people simply do not take the time necessary to solve many of life's intellectual, social or spiritual problems, just as I did not take the time to solve mechanical problems. Before my mechanical enlightenment I would have awkwardly stuck my head under the dashboard of my patient's car, immediately yanked at a few wires without having the foggiest idea of what I was doing, and then, when nothing constructive resulted, would have thrown up my hands and proclaimed "It's beyond me." And this is precisely the way that so many of us approach other dilemmas of day-to-day living. The aforementioned financial analyst was a basically loving and dedicated but rather helpless mother to her two young children. She was alert and concerned enough to perceive when her children were having some sort of emotional problem or when something was not working out in her child-raising. But then she inevitably took one of two courses of action with the children: either she made the very first change that came to her mind within a matter of seconds—making them eat more breakfast or sending them to bed earlier—regardless of whether such a change had anything to do with the problem, or else she came to her next therapy session with me (the repairman), despairing: "It's beyond me. What shall I do?" This woman had a perfectly keen and analytical mind, and when she didn't procrastinate, she was quite capable of solving complex problems at work. Yet when confronted with a personal problem, she behaved as if she were totally lacking in intelligence. The issue was one of time. Once she became aware of a personal problem, she felt so discomfited that she demanded an immediate solution, and she was not willing to tolerate her discomfort long enough to analyze the problem. The solution to the problem represented gratification to her, but she was unable to delay this gratification for more than a minute or two, with the result that her solutions were usually inappropriate and her family in chronic turmoil. Fortunately, through her own perseverance in therapy she was gradually able to learn how to discipline herself to take the time necessary to analyze family problems so as to develop well-thought-out and effective solutions.

We are not talking here about esoteric defects in problem-solving associated only with people who clearly manifest psychiatric disturbances. The financial analyst is everyman. Who among us can say that they unfailingly devote sufficient time to analyzing their children's problems or tensions within the family? Who among us is so self-disciplined that he or she never says resignedly in the face of family problems, "It's beyond me"?

Actually, there is a defect in the approach to problem-solving more primitive and more destructive than impatiently inadequate attempts to find instant solutions, a defect even more ubiquitous and universal. It is the hope that problems will go away of their own accord. A thirty-year-old single salesman in group therapy in a small town began to date the recently separated wife of another group member, a banker. The salesman knew the banker to be a chronically angry man who was deeply resentful of his wife's leaving him. He knew that he was not being honest either with the group or with the banker by not confiding his relationship with the banker's wife. He also knew that it was almost inevitable that sooner or later the banker would learn about the continuing relationship. He knew that the only solution to the problem would be to confess the relationship to the group and bear the banker's anger with the group's support. But he did nothing. After three months the banker found out about the friendship, was predictably enraged, and used the incident to quit his therapy. When confronted by the group with his destructive behavior the salesman said: "I knew that talking about it would be a hassle, and I guess I felt that if I did nothing, maybe I could get away with it without the hassle. I guess I thought that if I waited long enough the problem might go away."

Problems do not go away. They must be worked through or else they remain, forever a barrier to the growth and development of the spirit.

The group made the salesman aware in no uncertain terms that his tendency to avoid problem-solving by ignoring a problem in the hope that it would go away was in itself his major problem. Four months later, in the early autumn, the salesman fulfilled a fantasy by rather suddenly quitting his sales job and starting his own furniture-repair business, which would not require him to travel. The group deplored the fact that he was putting all his eggs in one basket and also questioned the wisdom of making the move with winter coming on, but the salesman assured them he would make enough to get by in his new business. The subject was dropped. Then in early February he announced that he would have to quit the group because he could no longer pay the fee. He was dead broke and would have to start looking for another job. In five months he had repaired a total of eight pieces of furniture. When asked why he hadn't started looking for a job sooner, he replied: "I knew six weeks ago that I was running through my money fast, but somehow I couldn't believe that it would come to this point. The whole thing just didn't seem very urgent, but, boy, it's urgent now." He had, of course, ignored his problem. Slowly it began to dawn on him that until he solved his problem of ignoring problems he would never get beyond step one—even with all the psychotherapy in the world.

This inclination to ignore problems is once again a simple manifestation of an unwillingness to delay gratification. Confronting problems is, as I have said, painful. To willingly confront a problem early, before we are forced to confront it by circumstances, means to put aside something pleasant or less painful for something more painful. It is choosing to suffer now in the hope of future gratification rather than choosing to continue present gratification in the hope that future suffering will not be necessary.

It may seem that the salesman who ignored such obvious problems was emotionally immature or psychologically primitive, but, again, I tell you he is everyman and his immaturity and primitiveness exist in us all. A great general, commander of an army, once told me, "The single greatest problem in this army, or I guess in any organization, is that most of the executives will sit looking at problems in their units, staring them right in the face, doing nothing, as if these problems will go away if they sit there long enough." The general wasn't talking about the mentally weak or abnormal. He was talking about other generals and senior colonels, mature men of proven capability and trained in discipline.

Parents are executives, and despite the fact that they are usually ill-prepared for it, their task can be every bit as complex as directing a company or corporation. And like the army executives, most parents will perceive problems in their children or in their relationship with their children for months or years before they take any effective action, if they ever do. "We thought maybe he would grow out of it," the parents say as they come to the child psychiatrist with a problem of five years' duration. And with respect for the complexity of parenting, it must be said that parental decisions are difficult, and that children often do "grow out of it." But it almost never hurts to try to help them grow out of it or to look more closely at the problem. And while children often "grow out of it," often they do not; and as with so many problems, the longer children's problems are ignored, the larger they become and the more painful and difficult to solve.

Responsibility

We cannot solve life's problems except by solving them. This statement may seem idiotically tautological or self-evident, yet it is seemingly beyond the comprehension of much of the human race. This is because we must accept responsibility for a problem before we can solve it. We cannot solve a problem by saying "It's not my problem." We cannot solve a problem by hoping that someone else will solve it for us. I can solve a problem only when I say "This is *my* problem and it's up to me to solve it." But many, so many, seek to avoid the pain of their problems by saying to themselves: "This problem was caused me by other people, or by social circumstances beyond my control, and therefore it is up to other people or society to solve this problem for me. It is not really my personal problem."

The extent to which people will go psychologically to avoid assuming responsibility for personal problems, while always sad, is sometimes almost ludicrous. A career sergeant in the army, stationed in Okinawa and in serious trouble because of his excessive drinking, was referred for psychiatric evaluation and, if possible, assistance. He denied that he was an alcoholic, or even that his use of alcohol was a personal problem, saying, "There's nothing else to do in the evenings in Okinawa except drink."

"Do you like to read?" I asked.

"Oh yes, I like to read, sure."

"Then why don't you read in the evening instead of drinking?"

"It's too noisy to read in the barracks."

"Well, then, why don't you go to the library?"

"The library is too far away."

"Is the library farther away than the bar you go to?"

"Well, I'm not much of a reader. That's not where my interests lie."

"Do you like to fish?" I then inquired.

"Sure, I love to fish."

"Why not go fishing instead of drinking?"

"Because I have to work all day long."

"Can't you go fishing at night?"

"No, there isn't any night fishing in Okinawa."

"But there is," I said. "I know several organizations that fish at night here. Would you like me to put you in touch with them?"

"Well, I really don't like to fish."

"What I hear you saying," I clarified, "is that there are other things to do in Okinawa except drink, but the thing you like to do most in Okinawa is drink."

"Yeah, I guess so."

"But your drinking is getting you in trouble, so you're faced with a real problem, aren't you?"

"This damn island would drive anyone to drink."

I kept trying for a while, but the sergeant was not the least bit interested in seeing his drinking as a personal problem which he could solve either with or without help, and I regretfully told his commander that he was not amenable to assistance. His drinking continued, and he was separated from the service in mid-career.

A young wife, also in Okinawa, cut her wrist lightly with a razor blade and was brought to the emergency room, where I saw her. I asked her why she had done this to herself.

"To kill myself, of course."

"Why do you want to kill yourself?"

"Because I can't stand it on this dumb island. You have to send me back to the States. I'm going to kill myself if I have to stay here any longer."

"What is it about living in Okinawa that's so painful for you?" I asked.

She began to cry in a whining sort of way. "I don't have any friends here, and I'm alone all the time."

"That's too bad. How come you haven't been able to make any friends?"

"Because I have to live in a stupid Okinawan housing area, and none of my neighbors speak English."

"Why don't you drive over to the American housing area or to the wives' club during the day so you can make some friends?"

"Because my husband has to drive the car to work."

"Can't you drive him to work, since you're alone and bored all day?" I asked.

"No. It's a stick-shift car, and I don't know how to drive a stick-shift car, only an automatic."

"Why don't you learn how to drive a stick-shift car?"

She glared at me. "On these roads? You must be crazy."

Neuroses and Character Disorders

Most people who come to see a psychiatrist are suffering from what is called either a neurosis or a character disorder. Put most simply, these two conditions are disorders of responsibility, and as such they are opposite styles of relating to the world and its problems. The neurotic assumes too much responsibility; the person with a character disorder not enough. When neurotics are in conflict with the world they automatically assume that they are at fault. When those with character disorders are in conflict with the world they automatically assume that the world is at fault. The two individuals just described had character disorders: the sergeant felt that his drinking was Okinawa's fault, not his, and the wife also saw herself as playing no role whatsoever in her own isolation. A neurotic woman, on the other hand, also suffering from loneliness and isolation on Okinawa, complained: "I drive over to the Non-Commissioned Officers' Wives Club every day to look for friendship, but I don't feel at ease there. I think that the other wives don't like me. Something must be wrong with me. I should be able to make friends more easily. I ought to be more outgoing. I want to find out what it is about me that makes me so unpopular." This woman assumed total responsibility for her loneliness, feeling she was entirely to blame. What she found out in the course of therapy was that she was an unusually intelligent and ambitious person and that she was ill at ease with the other sergeants' wives, as well as with her husband, because she was considerably more intelligent and ambitious than they. She became able to see that her loneliness, while her problem, was not necessarily due to a fault or defect of her own. Ultimately she was divorced, put herself through college while raising her children, became a magazine editor, and married a successful publisher.

Even the speech patterns of neurotics and those with character disorders are different. The speech of the neurotic is notable for such expressions as "I ought to," "I should," and "I shouldn't," indicating the individual's self-image as an inferior man or woman, always falling short of the mark, always making the wrong choices. The speech of a person with a character disorder, however, relies heavily on "I can't," "I couldn't," "I have to," and "I had to," demonstrating a self-image of a being who has no power of choice, whose behavior is completely directed by external forces totally beyond his or her control. As might be imagined, neurotics, compared with character-disordered people, are easy to work with in psychotherapy because they assume responsibility for their difficulties and therefore see themselves as having problems. Those with character disorders are much more difficult, if not impossible, to work with because they don't see themselves as the source of their problems; they see the world rather than themselves as being in need of change and therefore fail to recognize the necessity for self-examination. In actuality, many individuals have both a neurosis and a character disorder and are referred to as "character neurotics," indicating that in some areas of their lives they are guilt-ridden by virtue of having assumed responsibility that is not really theirs, while in other areas of their lives they fail to take realistic responsibility for themselves. Fortunately, once having established the faith and trust of such individuals in the psychotherapy process through helping them with the neurotic part of their personalities, it is often possible then to engage them in examining and correcting their unwillingness to assume responsibility where appropriate.

Few of us can escape being neurotic or character disordered to at least some degree (which is why essentially everyone can benefit from psychotherapy if he or she is seriously willing to participate in the process). The reason for this is that the problem of distinguishing what we are and what we are not responsible for in this life is one of the greatest problems of human existence. It is never completely solved; for the entirety of our lives we must continually assess and reassess where our responsibilities lie in the ever-changing course of events. Nor is this assessment and reassessment painless if performed adequately and conscientiously. To perform either process adequately we must possess the willingness and the capacity to suffer continual self-examination. And such capacity or willingness is not inherent in any of us. In a sense all children have character disorders, in that their instinctual tendency is to deny their responsibility for many conflicts in which they find themselves. Thus two siblings fighting will always blame each other for initiating the fight and each will totally deny that he or she may have been the culprit. Similarly, all children have neuroses, in that they will instinctually assume responsibility for certain deprivations that they experience but do not yet understand. Thus the child who is not loved by his parents will always assume himself or herself to be unlovable rather than see the parents as deficient in their capacity to love. Or early adolescents who are not yet successful at dating or at sports will see themselves as seriously deficient human beings rather than the late or even average but perfectly adequate bloomers they usually are. It is only through a vast amount of experience and a lengthy and successful maturation that we gain the capacity to see the world and our place in it realistically, and thus are enabled to realistically assess our responsibility for ourselves and the world.

There is much that parents can do to assist their children in this maturation process. Opportunities present themselves thousands of times while children are growing up when parents can either confront them with their tendency to avoid or escape responsibility for their own actions or can reassure them that certain situations are not their fault. But to seize these opportunities, as I have said, requires of parents sensitivity to their children's needs and the willingness to take the time and make the often uncomfortable effort to meet these needs. And this in turn requires love and the willingness to assume appropriate responsibility for the enhancement of their children's growth.

Conversely, even above and beyond simple insensitivity or neglect, there is much that many parents do to hinder this maturation process. Neurotics, because of their willingness to assume responsibility, may be quite excellent parents if their neuroses are relatively mild and they are not so overwhelmed by unnecessary responsibilities that they have scant energy left for the necessary responsibilities of parenthood. Character-disordered people, however, make disastrous parents, blissfully unaware that they often treat their children with vicious destructiveness. It is said that "neurotics make themselves miserable; those with character disorders make everyone else miserable." Chief among the people character-disordered parents make miserable are their children. As in other areas of their lives, they fail to assume adequate responsibility for their parenting. They tend to brush off their children in thousands of little ways rather than provide them with needed attention. When their children are delinquent or are having difficulty in school, character-disordered parents will automatically lay the blame on the school system or on other children who, they insist, are a "bad influence" on their own children. This attitude, of course, ignores the problem. Because they duck responsibility, character-disordered parents serve as role models of irresponsibility for their children. Finally, in their efforts to avoid responsibility for their own lives, character-disordered parents will often lay this responsibility upon their children: "You kids are driving me nuts," or "The only reason I stay married to your father [mother] is because of you kids," or "Your mother's a nervous wreck because of you," or "I could have gone to college and been a success if it weren't for having to support you." In such ways these parents in effect say to their children, "You are responsible for the quality of my marriage, my mental health and my lack of success in life." Since they lack the capacity to see how inappropriate this is, the children will often accept this responsibility, and insofar as they do accept it, they will become neurotic. It is in such ways that character-disordered parents almost invariably produce character-disordered or neurotic children. It is the parents themselves who visit their sins upon their children.

It is not simply in their role as parents that character-disordered individuals are ineffective and destructive; these same character traits usually extend to their marriages, their friendships and their business dealings—to any area of their existence in which they fail to assume responsibility for its quality. This is inevitable since, as has been said, no problem can be solved until an individual assumes the responsibility for solving it. When character-disordered individuals blame someone else—a spouse, a child, a friend, a parent, an employer—or something else—bad influences, the schools, the government, racism, sexism, society, the "system"—for their problems, these problems persist. Nothing has been accomplished. By casting away their responsibility they may feel comfortable with themselves, but they have ceased to solve the problems of living, have ceased to grow spiritually, and have become dead weight for society. They have cast their pain onto society. The saying of the sixties (attributed to Eldridge Cleaver) speaks to all of us for all time: "If you are not part of the solution, then you are part of the problem."

Escape from Freedom

When a psychiatrist makes the diagnosis of a character disorder, it is because the pattern of avoidance of responsibility is relatively gross in the diagnosed individual. Yet almost all of us from time to time seek to avoid—in ways that can be quite subtle—the pain of assuming responsibility for our own problems. For the cure of my own subtle character disorder at the age of thirty I am indebted to Mac Badgely. At the time Mac was the director of the outpatient psychiatric clinic where I was completing my psychiatry residency training. In this clinic my fellow residents and I were assigned new patients on rotation. Perhaps because I was more dedicated to my patients and my own education than most of my fellow residents, I found myself working much longer hours than they. They ordinarily saw patients only once a week. I often saw my patients two or three times a week. As a result I would watch my fellow residents leaving the clinic at four-thirty each afternoon for their homes, while I was scheduled with appointments up to eight or nine o'clock at night, and my heart was filled with resentment. As I became more and more resentful and more and more exhausted I realized that something had to be done. So I went to Dr. Badgely and explained the situation to him. I wondered whether I might be exempted from the rotation of accepting new patients for a few weeks so that I might have time to catch up. Did he think that was feasible? Or could he think of some other solution to the problem? Mac listened to me very intently and receptively, not interrupting once. When I was finished, after a moment's silence, he said to me very sympathetically, "Well, I can see that you do have a problem."

I beamed, feeling understood. "Thank you," I said. "What do you think should be done about it?"

To this Mac replied, "I told you, Scott, you do have a problem."

This was hardly the response I expected. "Yes," I said, slightly annoyed, "I know I have a problem. That's why I came to see you. What do you think I ought to do about it?"

Mac responded: "Scott, apparently you haven't listened to what I said. I have heard you, and I am agreeing with you. You do have a problem."

"Goddammit," I said, "I know I have a problem. I knew

that when I came in here. The question is, what am I going to do about it?"

"Scott," Mac replied, "I want you to listen. Listen closely and I will say it again. I agree with you. You do have a problem. Specifically, you have a problem with time. *Your* time. Not my time. It's not my problem. It's *your* problem with *your* time. You, Scott Peck, have a problem with your time. That's all I'm going to say about it."

I turned and strode out of Mac's office, furious. And I stayed furious. I hated Mac Badgely. For three months I hated him. I felt that he had a severe character disorder. How else could he be so callous? Here I had gone to him humbly asking for just a little bit of help, a little bit of advice, and the bastard wasn't even willing to assume enough responsibility even to try to help me, even to do his job as director of the clinic. If he wasn't supposed to help manage such problems as director of the clinic, what the hell was he supposed to do?

But after three months I somehow came to see that Mac was right, that it was I, not he, who had the character disorder. My time *was* my responsibility. It was up to me and me alone to decide how I wanted to use and order my time. If I wanted to invest my time more heavily than my fellow residents in my work, then that was my choice, and the consequences of that choice were my responsibility. It might be painful for me to watch my fellow residents leave their offices two or three hours before me, and it might be painful to listen to my wife's complaints that I was not devoting myself sufficiently to the family, but these pains were the consequence of a choice that I had made. If I did not want to suffer them, then I was free to choose not to work so hard and to structure my time differently. My working hard was not a burden cast upon me by hardhearted fate or a hardhearted clinic director; it was the way I had chosen to live my life and order my priorities. As it happened, I chose not to change my life style. But with my change in attitude, my resentment of my fellow residents vanished. It simply no longer made any sense to resent them for having chosen a life style different from mine when I was completely free to choose to be like them if I wanted to. To resent them was to resent my own choice to be different from them, a choice that I was happy with.

The difficulty we have in accepting responsibility for our behavior lies in the desire to avoid the pain of the consequences of that behavior. By requesting Mac Badgely to assume responsibility for the structure of my time I was attempting to avoid the pain of working long hours, even though working long hours was an inevitable consequence of my choice to be dedicated to my patients and my training. Yet in so doing I was also unwittingly seeking to increase Mac's authority over me. I was giving him my power, my freedom. I was saying in effect, "Take charge of me. You be the boss!" Whenever we seek to avoid the responsibility for our own behavior, we do so by attempting to give that responsibility to some other individual or organization or entity. But this means we then give away our power to that entity, be it "fate" or "society" or the government or the corporation or our boss. It is for this reason that Erich Fromm so aptly titled his study of Nazism and authoritarianism *Escape from Freedom*. In attempting to avoid the pain of responsibility, millions and even billions daily attempt to escape from freedom.

I have a brilliant but morose acquaintance who, when I allow him to, will speak unceasingly and eloquently of the oppressive forces in our society: racism, sexism, the military-industrial establishment, and the country police who pick on him and his friends because of their long hair. Again and again I have tried to point out to him that he is not a child. As children, by virtue of our real and extensive dependency, our parents have real and extensive power over us. They are, in fact, largely responsible for our well-being, and we are, in fact, largely at their mercy. When parents are oppressive, as so often they are, we as children are largely powerless to do anything about it; our choices are limited. But as adults, when we are physically healthy, our choices are almost unlimited.

That does not mean they are not painful. Frequently our choices lie between the lesser of two evils, but it is still within our power to make these choices. Yes, I agree with my acquaintance, there are indeed oppressive forces at work within the world. We have, however, the freedom to choose every step of the way the manner in which we are going to respond to and deal with these forces. It is his choice to live in an area of the country where the police don't like "long-haired types" and still grow his hair long. He has the freedom to move to the city, or to cut his hair, or even to wage a campaign for the office of police commissioner. But despite his brilliance, he does not acknowledge these freedoms. He chooses to lament his lack of political power instead of accepting and exulting in his immense personal power. He speaks of his love of freedom and of the oppressive forces that thwart it, but every time he speaks of how he is victimized by these forces he actually is giving away his freedom. I hope that some day soon he will stop resenting life simply because some of its choices are painful.*

Dr. Hilde Bruch, in the preface to her book *Learning Psychotherapy*, states that basically all patients come to psychiatrists with "one common problem: the sense of helplessness, the fear and inner conviction of being unable to 'cope' and to change things."† One of the roots of this "sense of impotence" in the majority of patients is some desire to partially or totally escape the pain of freedom, and, therefore, some failure, partial or total, to accept responsibility for their problems and their lives. They feel impotent because they have, in fact, given their power away. Sooner or later, if they are to be

---

* Nowhere, to my knowledge, is the issue of the freedom to choose between two evils more eloquently and even poetically defined than by the psychiatrist Allen Wheelis, in the chapter "Freedom and Necessity" in his book *How People Change* (New York: Harper & Row, 1973). It was tempting to quote the chapter in its entirety, and I recommend it to anyone who desires to explore the issue more fully.

† Cambridge, Mass., Harvard Univ. Press, 1974, p. ix.

healed, they must learn that the entirety of one's adult life is a series of personal choices, decisions. If they can accept this totally, then they become free people. To the extent that they do not accept this they will forever feel themselves victims.

Dedication to Reality

The third tool of discipline or technique of dealing with the pain of problem-solving, which must continually be employed if our lives are to be healthy and our spirits are to grow, is dedication to the truth. Superficially, this should be obvious. For truth is reality. That which is false is unreal. The more clearly we see the reality of the world, the better equipped we are to deal with the world. The less clearly we see the reality of the world—the more our minds are befuddled by falsehood, misperceptions and illusions—the less able we will be to determine correct courses of action and make wise decisions. Our view of reality is like a map with which to negotiate the terrain of life. If the map is true and accurate, we will generally know where we are, and if we have decided where we want to go, we will generally know how to get there. If the map is false and inaccurate, we generally will be lost.

While this is obvious, it is something that most people to a greater or lesser degree choose to ignore. They ignore it because our route to reality is not easy. First of all, we are not born with maps; we have to make them, and the making requires effort. The more effort we make to appreciate and perceive reality, the larger and more accurate our maps will be. But many do not want to make this effort. Some stop making it by the end of adolescence. Their maps are small and sketchy, their views of the world narrow and misleading.

By the end of middle age most people have given up the effort. They feel certain that their maps are complete and their Weltanschauung is correct (indeed, even sacrosanct), and they are no longer interested in new information. It is as if they are tired. Only a relative and fortunate few continue until the moment of death exploring the mystery of reality, ever enlarging and refining and redefining their understanding of the world and what is true.

But the biggest problem of map-making is not that we have to start from scratch, but that if our maps are to be accurate we have to continually revise them. The world itself is constantly changing. Glaciers come, glaciers go. Cultures come, cultures go. There is too little technology, there is too much technology. Even more dramatically, the vantage point from which we view the world is constantly and quite rapidly changing. When we are children we are dependent, powerless. As adults we may be powerful. Yet in illness or an infirm old age we may become powerless and dependent again. When we have children to care for, the world looks different from when we have none; when we are raising infants, the world seems different from when we are raising adolescents. When we are poor, the world looks different from when we are rich. We are daily bombarded with new information as to the nature of reality. If we are to incorporate this information, we must continually revise our maps, and sometimes when enough new information has accumulated, we must make very major revisions. The process of making revisions, particularly major revisions, is painful, sometimes excruciatingly painful. And herein lies the major source of many of the ills of mankind.

What happens when one has striven long and hard to develop a working view of the world, a seemingly useful, workable map, and then is confronted with new information suggesting that that view is wrong and the map needs to be largely redrawn? The painful effort required seems frightening, almost overwhelming. What we do more often than not, and usually unconsciously, is to ignore the new information.

Often this act of ignoring is much more than passive. We may denounce the new information as false, dangerous, heretical, the work of the devil. We may actually crusade against it, and even attempt to manipulate the world so as to make it conform to our view of reality. Rather than try to change the map, an individual may try to destroy the new reality. Sadly, such a person may expend much more energy ultimately in defending an outmoded view of the world than would have been required to revise and correct it in the first place.

Transference: The Outdated Map

This process of active clinging to an outmoded view of reality is the basis for much mental illness. Psychiatrists refer to it as transference. There are probably as many subtle variations of the definition of transference as there are psychiatrists. My own definition is: Transference is that set of ways of perceiving and responding to the world which is developed in childhood and which is usually entirely appropriate to the childhood environment (indeed, often life-saving) but which is *inappropriately* transferred into the adult environment.

The ways in which transference manifests itself, while always pervasive and destructive, are often subtle. Yet the clearest examples must be unsubtle. One such example was a patient whose treatment failed by virtue of his transference. He was a brilliant but unsuccessful computer technician in his early thirties, who came to see me because his wife had left him, taking their two children. He was not particularly unhappy to lose her, but he was devastated by the loss of his children, to whom he was deeply attached. It was in the hope of regaining them that he initiated psychotherapy, since his wife firmly stated she would never return to him unless he had psychiatric treatment. Her principal complaints about him were that he was continually and irrationally jealous of her, and yet at the same time aloof from her, cold, distant, uncommunicative and unaffectionate. She also complained of his frequent changes of employment. His life since adolescence had been markedly unstable. During adolescence he was involved in frequent minor altercations with the police, and had been jailed three times for intoxication, belligerence, "loitering," and "interfering with the duties of an officer." He dropped out of college, where he was studying electrical engineering, because, as he said, "My teachers were a bunch of hypocrites, hardly different from the police." Because of his brilliance and creativeness in the field of computer technology, his services were in high demand by industry. But he had never been able to advance or keep a job for more than a year and a half, occasionally being fired, more often quitting after disputes with his supervisors, whom he described as "liars and cheats, interested only in protecting their own ass." His most frequent expression was "You can't trust a goddamn soul." He described his childhood as "normal" and his parents as "average." In the brief period of time he spent with me, however, he casually and unemotionally recounted numerous instances during childhood in which his parents had let him down. They promised him a bike for his birthday, but they forgot about it and gave him something else. Once they forgot his birthday entirely, but he saw nothing drastically wrong with this since "they were very busy." They would promise to do things with him on weekends, but then were usually "too busy." Numerous times they forgot to pick him up from meetings or parties because "they had a lot on their minds."

What happened to this man was that when he was a young child he suffered painful disappointment after painful disappointment through his parents' lack of caring. Gradually or suddenly—I don't know which—he came to the agonizing realization in mid-childhood that he could not trust his parents. Once he realized this, however, he began to feel better, and his life became more comfortable. He no longer expected things from his parents or got his hopes up when they made promises. When he stopped trusting his parents the frequency and severity of his disappointments diminished dramatically.

Such an adjustment, however, is the basis for future problems. To a child his or her parents are everything; they represent the world. The child does not have the perspective to see that other parents are different and frequently better. He assumes that the way his parents do things is the way that things are done. Consequently the realization—the "reality" —that this child came to was not "I can't trust my parents" but "I can't trust people." Not trusting people therefore became the map with which he entered adolescence and adulthood. With this map and with an abundant store of resentment resulting from his many disappointments, it was inevitable that he came into conflict after conflict with authority figures—police, teacher, employers. And these conflicts only served to reinforce his feeling that people who had anything to give him in the world couldn't be trusted. He had many opportunities to revise his map, but they were all passed up. For one thing, the only way he could learn that there were some people in the adult world he could trust would be to risk trusting them, and that would require a deviation from his map to begin with. For another, such relearning would require him to revise his view of his parents—to realize that they did not love him, that he did not have a normal childhood and that his parents were not average in their callousness to his needs. Such a realization would have been extremely painful. Finally, because his distrust of people was a realistic adjustment to the reality of his childhood, it was an adjustment that worked in terms of diminishing his pain and suffering. Since it is extremely difficult to give up an adjustment that once worked so well, he continued his course of distrust, unconsciously creating situations that served to reinforce it, alienating himself from everyone, making it impossible for himself to enjoy love, warmth, intimacy and affection. He could not even allow himself closeness with his wife; she, too, could not be trusted. The only people he could relate with intimately were his two children. They were the only ones over whom he had control, the only ones who had no authority over him, the only ones he could trust in the whole world.

When problems of transference are involved, as they usually are, psychotherapy is, among other things, a process of map-revising. Patients come to therapy because their maps are clearly not working. But how they may cling to them and fight the process every step of the way! Frequently their need to cling to their maps and fight against losing them is so great that therapy becomes impossible, as it did in the case of the computer technician. Initially he requested a Saturday appointment. After three sessions he stopped coming because he took a job doing lawn-maintenance work on Saturdays and Sundays. I offered him a Thursday-evening appointment. He came for two sessions and then stopped because he was doing overtime work at the plant. I then rearranged my schedule so I could see him on Monday evenings, when, he had said, overtime work was unlikely. After two more sessions, however, he stopped coming because Monday-night overtime work seemed to have picked up. I confronted him with the impossibility of doing therapy under these circumstances. He admitted that he was not required to accept overtime work. He stated, however, that he needed the money and that the work was more important to him than therapy. He stipulated that he could see me only on those Monday evenings when there was no overtime work to be done and that he would call me at four o'clock every Monday afternoon to tell me if he could keep his appointment that evening. I told him that these conditions were not acceptable to me, that I was unwilling to set aside my plans every Monday evening on the chance that he might be able to come to his sessions. He felt that I was being unreasonably rigid, that I had no concern for his needs, that I was interested only in my own time and clearly cared nothing for him, and that therefore I could not be trusted. It was on this basis that our attempt to work together was terminated, with me as another landmark on his old map.

The problem of transference is not simply a problem between psychotherapists and their patients. It is a problem between parents and children, husbands and wives, employers and employees, between friends, between groups, and even between nations. It is interesting to speculate, for instance, on the role that transference issues play in international affairs. Our national leaders are human beings who all had childhoods and childhood experiences that shaped them. What map was Hitler following, and where did it come from? What map were American leaders following in initiating, executing and maintaining the war in Vietnam? Clearly it was a map very different from that of the generation that succeeded theirs. In what ways did the national experience of the Depression years contribute to their map, and the experience of the fifties and sixties contribute to the map of the younger generation? If the national experience of the thirties and forties contributed to the behavior of American leaders in waging war in Vietnam, how appropriate was that experience to the realities of the sixties and seventies? How can we revise our maps more rapidly?

Truth or reality is avoided when it is painful. We can revise our maps only when we have the discipline to overcome that pain. To have such discipline, we must be totally dedicated to truth. That is to say that we must always hold truth, as best we can determine it, to be more important, more vital to our self-interest, than our comfort. Conversely, we must always consider our personal discomfort relatively unimportant and, indeed, even welcome it in the service of the search for truth. Mental health is an ongoing process of dedication to reality at all costs.

Openness to Challenge

What does a life of total dedication to the truth mean? It means, first of all, a life of continuous and never-ending stringent self-examination. We know the world only through our relationship to it. Therefore, to know the world, we must not only examine it but we must simultaneously examine the examiner. Psychiatrists are taught this in their training and know that it is impossible to realistically understand the conflicts and transferences of their patients without understanding their own transferences and conflicts. For this reason psychiatrists are encouraged to receive their own psychotherapy or psychoanalysis as part of their training and development. Unfortunately, not all psychiatrists respond to this encouragement. There are many, psychiatrists among them, who stringently examine the world but not so stringently examine themselves. They may be competent individuals as the world judges competence, but they are never wise. The life of wisdom must be a life of contemplation combined with action. In the past in American culture, contemplation has not been held in high regard. In the 1950s people labeled Adlai Stevenson an "egghead" and believed he would not make a good President precisely because he was a contemplative man, given to deep thinking and self-doubts. I have heard parents tell their adolescent children in all seriousness, "You think too much." What an absurdity this is, given the fact that it is our frontal lobes, our capacity to think and to examine ourselves that most makes us human. Fortunately, such attitudes seem to be changing, and we are beginning to realize that the sources of danger to the world lie more within us than outside, and that the process of constant self-examination and contemplation is essential for ultimate survival. Still, I am talking of relatively small numbers of people who are changing their attitudes. Examination of the world without is never as personally painful as examination of the world within, and it is certainly because of the pain involved in a life of genuine self-examination that the majority steer away from it. Yet when one is dedicated to the truth this pain seems relatively unimportant—and less and less important (and therefore less and less painful) the farther one proceeds on the path of self-examination.

A life of total dedication to the truth also means a life of willingness to be personally challenged. The only way that we can be certain that our map of reality is valid is to expose it to the criticism and challenge of other map-makers. Otherwise we live in a closed system—within a bell jar, to use Sylvia Plath's analogy, rebreathing only our own fetid air, more and more subject to delusion. Yet, because of the pain inherent in the process of revising our map of reality, we mostly seek to avoid or ward off any challenges to its validity. To our children we say, "Don't talk back to me, I'm your parent." To our spouse we give the message, "Let's live and let live. If you criticize me, I'll be a bitch to live with, and you'll regret it." To their families and the world the elderly give the message, "I am old and fragile. If you challenge me I may die or at least you will bear upon your head the responsibility for making my last days on earth miserable." To our employees we communicate, "If you are bold enough to challenge me at all, you had best do so very circumspectly indeed or else you'll find yourself looking for another job."*

* Not only individuals but also organizations are notorious for protecting themselves against challenge. I was once directed by the Chief of Staff of the Army to prepare an analysis of the psychological causes of the My Lai atrocities and their subsequent cover-up, with recommendations for research that might prevent such behavior in the future. The recommendations were disapproved by the Army general staff on the basis that the research recommended could not be kept secret. "The

The tendency to avoid challenge is so omnipresent in human beings that it can properly be considered a characteristic of human nature. But calling it natural does not mean it is essential or beneficial or unchangeable behavior. It is also natural to defecate in our pants and never brush our teeth. Yet we teach ourselves to do the unnatural until the unnatural becomes itself second nature. Indeed, all self-discipline might be defined as teaching ourselves to do the unnatural. Another characteristic of human nature—perhaps the one that makes us most human—is our capacity to do the unnatural, to transcend and hence transform our own nature.

No act is more unnatural, and hence more human, than the act of entering psychotherapy. For by this act we deliberately lay ourselves open to the deepest challenge from another human being, and even pay the other for the service of scrutiny and discernment. This laying open to challenge is one of the things that lying on the couch in the psychoanalyst's office may symbolize. Entering psychotherapy is an act of the greatest courage. The primary reason people do not undergo psychotherapy is not that they lack the money but that they lack the courage. This even includes many psychiatrists them-

---

existence of such research might open us up to further challenge. The President and the Army don't need more challenges at this time," I was told. Thus an analysis of the reasons for an incident that was covered up was itself covered up. Such behavior is not limited to the military or the White House; to the contrary, it is common to Congress, other federal agencies, corporations, even universities and charitable organizations—in short, all human organizations. Just as it is necessary for individuals to accept and even welcome challenges to their maps of reality and *modi operandi* if they are to grow in wisdom and effectiveness, so it is also necessary for organizations to accept and welcome challenges if they are to be viable and progressive institutions. This fact is being increasingly recognized by such individuals as John Gardner of Common Cause, to whom it is clear that one of the most exciting and essential tasks facing our society in the next few decades is to build into the bureaucratic structure of our organizations an institutionalized openness and responsiveness to challenge which will replace the institutionalized resistance currently typical.

selves, who somehow never quite seem to find it convenient to enter their own therapy despite the fact that they have even more reason than others to submit themselves to the discipline involved. It is because they possess this courage, on the other hand, that many psychoanalytic patients, even at the outset of therapy and contrary to their stereotypical image, are people who are basically much stronger and healthier than average.

While undergoing psychotherapy is an ultimate form of being open to challenge, our more ordinary interactions daily offer us similar opportunities to risk openness: at the water cooler, in conference, on the golf course, at the dinner table, in bed when the lights are out; with our colleagues, our supervisors and employees, with our mates, our friends, our lovers, with our parents and our children. A neatly coiffured woman who had been seeing me for some time began to comb her hair each time she got up from the couch at the end of a session. I commented on this new pattern to her behavior. "Several weeks ago my husband noticed that my hairdo was flattened in the back after I returned from a session," she explained, blushing. "I didn't tell him why. I'm afraid he might tease me if he knows I lie on the couch in here." So we had another issue to work on. The greatest value of psychotherapy derives from the extension of the discipline involved during the "fifty-minute hour" into the patient's daily affairs and relationships. The healing of the spirit has not been completed until openness to challenge becomes a way of life. This woman would not be wholly well until she could be as forthright with her husband as she was with me.

Of all those who come to a psychiatrist or psychotherapist very few are initially looking on a conscious level for challenge or an education in discipline. Most are simply seeking "relief." When they realize they are going to be challenged as well as supported, many flee and others are tempted to flee. Teaching them that the only real relief will come through challenge and discipline is a delicate, often lengthy and frequently unsuccessful task. We speak, therefore, of "seducing" patients into psychotherapy. And we may say of some patients whom we have been seeing for a year or more, "They have not really entered therapy yet."

Openness in psychotherapy is particularly encouraged (or demanded, depending upon your point of view) by the technique of "free association." When this technique is used the patient is told: "Put into words whatever comes into your mind, no matter how seemingly insignificant or embarrassing or painful or meaningless. If there is more than one thing in your mind at the same time, then you are to choose to speak that thing about which you are most reluctant to speak." It's easier said than done. Nonetheless, those who work at it conscientiously usually make swift progress. But some are so resistant to challenge that they simply pretend to free-associate. They talk volubly enough about this or that, but they leave out the crucial details. A woman may speak for an hour about unpleasant childhood experiences but neglect to mention that her husband had confronted her in the morning with the fact that she had overdrawn their bank account by a thousand dollars. Such patients attempt to transform the psychotherapeutic hour into a kind of press conference. At best they are wasting time in their effort to avoid challenge, and usually they are indulging in a subtle form of lying.

For individuals and organizations to be open to challenge, it is necessary that their maps of reality be *truly* open for inspection by the public. More than press conferences are required. The third thing that a life of total dedication to the truth means, therefore, is a life of total honesty. It means a continuous and never-ending process of self-monitoring to assure that our communications—not only the words that we say but also the way we say them—invariably reflect as accurately as humanly possible the truth or reality as we know it.

Such honesty does not come painlessly. The reason people lie is to avoid the pain of challenge and its consequences.

President Nixon's lying about Watergate was no more sophisticated or different in kind from that of a four-year-old who lies to his or her mother about how the lamp happened to fall off the table and get broken. Insofar as the nature of the challenge is legitimate (and it usually is), lying is an attempt to circumvent legitimate suffering and hence is productive of mental illness.

The concept of circumvention raises the issue of "shortcutting." Whenever we attempt to circumvent an obstacle, we are looking for a path to our goal which will be easier and therefore quicker: a shortcut. Believing that the growth of the human spirit is the end of human existence, I am obviously dedicated to the notion of progress. It is right and proper that as human beings we should grow and progress as rapidly as possible. It is therefore right and proper that we should avail ourselves of any legitimate shortcut to personal growth. The key word, however, is "legitimate." Human beings have almost as much of a tendency to ignore legitimate shortcuts as they do to search out illegitimate ones. It is, for instance, a legitimate shortcut to study a synopsis of a book instead of reading the original book in its entirety in preparation for an examination for a degree. If the synopsis is a good one, and the material is absorbed, the essential knowledge can be obtained in a manner that saves considerable time and effort. Cheating, however, is not a legitimate shortcut. It may save even greater amounts of time and, if successfully executed, may gain the cheater a passing mark on the exam and the coveted degree. But the essential knowledge has not been obtained. Therefore the degree is a lie, a misrepresentation. Insofar as the degree becomes a basis for life, the cheater's life becomes a lie and misrepresentation and is often devoted to protecting and preserving the lie.

Genuine psychotherapy is a legitimate shortcut to personal growth which is often ignored. One of the most frequent rationalizations for ignoring it is to question its legitimacy by saying, "I'm afraid that psychotherapy would get to be a crutch. I don't want to become dependent on a crutch." But this is usually a cover-up for more significant fears. The use of psychotherapy is no more a crutch than the use of hammer and nails to build a house. It is possible to build a house without hammer and nails, but the process is generally not efficient or desirable. Few carpenters will despair of their dependency on hammer and nails. Similarly, it is possible to achieve personal growth without employing psychotherapy, but often the task is unnecessarily tedious, lengthy and difficult. It generally makes sense to utilize available tools as a shortcut.

On the other hand, psychotherapy may be sought as an illegitimate shortcut. This most commonly occurs in certain cases of parents seeking psychotherapy for their children. They want their children to change in some way: stop using drugs, stop having temper tantrums, stop getting bad grades, and so on. Some parents have exhausted their own resourcefulness in trying to help their children and come to the psychotherapist with a genuine willingness to work on the problem. Others as often as not come with the overt knowledge of the cause of their child's problem, hoping that the psychiatrist will be able to do some magical something to change the child without having to change the basic cause of the problem. For instance, some parents will openly say, "We know that we have a problem in our marriage, and that this likely has something to do with our son's problem. Nonetheless, we do not want our marriage tampered with; we do not want you to do therapy with us; we want you just to work with our son, if possible, to help him be happier." Others are less open. They will come professing a willingness to do anything that's necessary, but when it is explained to them that their child's symptoms are an expression of his resentment toward their whole life style, which leaves no real room for his nurture, they will say, "It is ridiculous to think that we should turn ourselves inside out for him," and they will depart to look for another psychiatrist, one who might offer them a painless shortcut. Farther down the pike they will likely tell their friends and themselves, "We have done everything possible for our boy; we have even gone to four separate psychiatrists with him, but nothing has helped."

We lie, of course, not only to others but also to ourselves. The challenges to our adjustment—our maps—from our own consciences and our own realistic perceptions may be every bit as legitimate and painful as any challenge from the public. Of the myriad lies that people often tell themselves, two of the most common, potent and destructive are "We really love our children" and "Our parents really loved us." It may be that our parents did love us and we do love our children, but when it is not the case, people often go to extraordinary lengths to avoid the realization. I frequently refer to psychotherapy as the "truth game" or the "honesty game" because its business is among other things to help patients confront such lies. One of the roots of mental illness is invariably an interlocking system of lies we have been told and lies we have told ourselves. These roots can be uncovered and excised only in an atmosphere of utter honesty. To create this atmosphere it is essential for therapists to bring to their relationships with patients a total capacity for openness and truthfulness. How can a patient be expected to endure the pain of confronting reality unless we bear the same pain? We can lead only insofar as we go before.

Withholding Truth

Lying can be divided into two types: white lies and black lies.* A black lie is a statement we make that we know is false. A white lie is a statement we make that is not in itself false but that leaves out a significant part of the truth. The fact that a lie is white does not in itself make it any less of a lie or any more excusable. White lies may be every bit as destructive as black ones. A government that withholds essential information from its people by censorship is no more democratic than one that speaks falsely. The patient who neglected to mention that she had overdrawn the family bank account was impeding her growth in therapy no less than if she had lied directly. Indeed, because it may *seem* less reprehensible, the withholding of essential information is the most common form of lying, and because it may be the more difficult to detect and confront, it is often even more pernicious than black-lying.

White-lying is considered socially acceptable in many of our relationships because "we don't want to hurt peoples' feelings." Yet we may bemoan the fact that our social relationships are generally superficial. For parents to feed their children a pap of white lies is not only considered acceptable but is thought to be loving and beneficent. Even husbands and wives who have been brave enough to be open with each other find it difficult often to be open with their children.

* The C.I.A., which has particular expertise in this area, naturally uses a more elaborate system of classification and will speak of white, gray and black propaganda, gray propaganda being a single black lie and black propaganda a black lie falsely attributed to another source.

They do not tell their children that they smoke marijuana, or that they fought with each other the night before concerning their relationship, or that they resent the grandparents for their manipulativeness, or that the doctor has told one or both that they have psychosomatic disorders, or that they are making a risky financial investment or even how much money they have in the bank. Usually such withholding and lack of openness is rationalized on the basis of a loving desire to protect and shield their children from unnecessary worries. Yet more often than not such "protection" is unsuccessful. The children know anyway that Mommy and Daddy smoke pot, that they had a fight the night before, that the grandparents are resented, that Mommy is nervous and that Daddy is losing money. The result, then, is not protection but deprivation. The children are deprived of the knowledge they might gain about money, illness, drugs, sex, marriage, their parents, their grandparents and people in general. They are also deprived of the reassurance they might receive if these topics were discussed more openly. Finally, they are deprived of role models of openness and honesty, and are provided instead with role models of partial honesty, incomplete openness and limited courage. For some parents the desire to "protect" their children is motivated by genuine albeit misguided love. For others, however, the "loving" desire to protect their children serves more as a cover-up and rationalization of a desire to avoid being challenged by their children, and a desire to maintain their authority over them. Such parents are saying in effect, "Look, kids, you go on being children with childish concerns and leave the adult concerns up to us. See us as strong and loving caretakers. Such an image is good for both of us, so don't challenge it. It allows us to feel strong and you to feel safe, and it will be easier for all of us if we don't look into these things too deeply."

Nonetheless, a real conflict may arise when the desire for total honesty is opposed by the needs of some people for certain kinds of protection. For instance, even parents with excellent marriages may occasionally consider divorce as one of their possible options, but to inform their children of this at a time when they are not at all likely to opt for divorce is to place an unnecessary burden upon the children. The idea of divorce is extremely threatening to a child's sense of security —indeed, so threatening that children do not have the capacity to perceive it with much perspective. They are seriously threatened by the possibility of divorce even when it is remote. If their parents' marriage is definitely on the rocks, then children will be dealing with the threatening possibility of divorce whether or not their parents talk about it. But if the marriage is basically sound, parents would indeed be doing their children a disservice if they said with complete openness, "Mommy and Daddy were talking last night about getting a divorce, but we're not at all serious about it at this time." As another instance, it is frequently necessary for psychotherapists to withhold their own thoughts, opinions and insights from patients in the earlier stages of psychotherapy because the patients are not yet ready to receive or deal with them. During my first year of psychiatric training a patient on his fourth visit to me recounted a dream that obviously expressed a concern with homosexuality. In my desire to appear to be a brilliant therapist and make rapid progress I told him, "Your dream indicates that you are concerned with worries that you might be homosexual." He grew visibly anxious, and he did not keep his next three appointments. Only with a good deal of work and an even greater amount of luck was I able to persuade him to return to therapy. We had another twenty sessions before he had to move from the area because of a business reassignment. These sessions were of considerable benefit to him despite the fact that we never again raised the issue of homosexuality. The fact that his unconscious was concerned with the issue did not mean that he was at all ready to deal with it on a conscious level, and by not withholding my insight from him I did him a grave disservice, almost losing him not only as my patient but as anyone's patient.

The selective withholding of one's opinions must also be practiced from time to time in the world of business or politics if one is to be welcomed into the councils of power. If people were always to speak their minds on issues both great and small, they would be considered insubordinate by the average supervisor, and a threat to an organization by management. They would gain reputations for abrasiveness and would be deemed too untrustworthy ever to be appointed as spokesmen for an organization. There is simply no way around the fact that if one is to be at all effective within an organization, he or she must partially become an "organization person," circumspect in the expression of individual opinions, merging at times personal identity with that of the organization. On the other hand, if one regards one's effectiveness in an organization as the only goal of organizational behavior, permitting only the expression of those opinions that would not make waves, then one has allowed the end to justify the means, and will have lost personal integrity and identity by becoming the *total* organization person. The road that a great executive must travel between the preservation and the loss of his or her identity and integrity is extraordinarily narrow, and very, very few really make the trip successfully. It is an enormous challenge.

So the expression of opinions, feelings, ideas and even knowledge must be suppressed from time to time in these and many other circumstances in the course of human affairs. What rules, then, can one follow if one is dedicated to the truth? First, never speak falsehood. Second, bear in mind that the act of withholding the truth is always potentially a lie, and that in each instance in which the truth is withheld a significant moral decision is required. Third, the decision to withhold the truth should never be based on personal needs, such as a need for power, a need to be liked or a need to protect one's map from challenge. Fourth, and conversely, the decision to withhold the truth must always be based entirely upon the needs of the person or people from whom the truth is being withheld. Fifth, the assessment of another's needs is an act of responsibility which is so complex that it can only be executed wisely when one operates with genuine love for the other. Sixth, the primary factor in the assessment of another's needs is the assessment of that person's capacity to utilize the truth for his or her own spiritual growth. Finally, in assessing the capacity of another to utilize the truth for personal spiritual growth, it should be borne in mind that our tendency is generally to underestimate rather than overestimate this capacity.

All this might seem like an extraordinary task, impossible to ever perfectly complete, a chronic and never-ending burden, a real drag. And it is indeed a never-ending burden of self-discipline, which is why most people opt for a life of very limited honesty and openness and relative closedness, hiding themselves and their maps from the world. It is easier that way. Yet the rewards of the difficult life of honesty and dedication to the truth are more than commensurate with the demands. By virtue of the fact that their maps are continually being challenged, open people are continually growing people. Through their openness they can establish and maintain intimate relationships far more effectively than more closed people. Because they never speak falsely they can be secure and proud in the knowledge that they have done nothing to contribute to the confusion of the world, but have served as sources of illumination and clarification. Finally, they are totally free to be. They are not burdened by any need to hide. They do not have to slink around in the shadows. They do not have to construct new lies to hide old ones. They need waste no effort covering tracks or maintaining disguises. And ultimately they find that the energy required for the self-discipline of honesty is far less than the energy required for secretiveness. The more honest one is, the easier it is to continue being honest, just as the more lies one has told, the more necessary it is to lie again. By their openness, people dedicated to the truth live in the open, and through the exercise of their courage to live in the open, they become free from fear.

Balancing

By this time I hope it is becoming clear that the exercise of discipline is not only a demanding but also a complex task, requiring both flexibility and judgment. Courageous people must continually push themselves to be completely honest, yet must also possess the capacity to withhold the whole truth when appropriate. To be free people we must assume total responsibility for ourselves, but in doing so must possess the capacity to reject responsibility that is not truly ours. To be organized and efficient, to live wisely, we must daily delay gratification and keep an eye on the future; yet to live joyously we must also possess the capacity, when it is not destructive, to live in the present and act spontaneously. In other words, discipline itself must be disciplined. The type of discipline required to discipline discipline is what I call balancing, and it is the fourth and final type that I would like to discuss here.

Balancing is the discipline that gives us flexibility. Extraordinary flexibility is required for successful living in all spheres of activity. To use but one example, let us consider the matter of anger and its expression. Anger is an emotion bred into us (and into less evolved organisms) by countless generations of evolution in order that our survival may be encouraged. We experience anger whenever we perceive another organism attempting to encroach upon our geographical or psychological territory or trying, one way or another, to put us down. It leads us to fight back. Without our anger we would indeed be continually stepped on, until we were totally squashed and exterminated. Only with anger can we survive. Yet, more often than not, when we initially perceive others as attempting to encroach on us, we realize upon closer examination that that is not what they intend to do at all. Or even when we determine that people are truly intending to encroach on us, we may realize that, for one reason or another, it is not in our best interests to respond to that imposition with anger. Thus it is necessary that the higher centers of our brain (judgment) be able to regulate and modulate the lower centers (emotion). To function successfully in our complex world it is necessary for us to possess the capacity not only to express our anger but also not to express it. Moreover, we must possess the capacity to express our anger in different ways. At times, for instance, it is necessary to express it only after much deliberation and self-evaluation. At other times it is more to our benefit to express it immediately and spontaneously. Sometimes it is best to express it coldly and calmly; at other times loudly and hotly. We therefore not only need to know how to deal with our anger in different ways at different times but also how most appropriately to match the right time with the right style of expression. To handle our anger with full adequacy and competence, an elaborate, flexible response system is required. It is no wonder, then, that to learn to handle our anger is a complex task which usually cannot be completed before adulthood, or even mid-life, and which often is never completed.

To a greater or lesser degree, all people suffer from inadequacies of their flexible response systems. Much of the work of psychotherapy consists of attempting to help our patients allow or make their response systems become more flexible. Generally, the more crippled by anxiety, guilt and insecurity our patients are, the more difficult and rudimentary this work is. For example, I worked with a brave thirty-two-year-old schizophrenic woman to whom it was a veritable revelation to learn that there are some men she should not let in her front door, some she should let into her living room but not her bedroom, and some she could let into her bedroom. Previously she had operated with a response system by which she either had to let everyone into her bedroom or, when this response did not seem to be working, not let anyone in her front door. Thus she bounced between degrading promiscuity and arid isolation. With the same woman it was necessary for us to spend several sessions focusing on the matter of thank-you notes. She felt compelled to send a lengthy, elaborate, hand-written, phrase- and word-perfect letter in response to each and every gift or invitation she received. Inevitably she could not continually carry such a burden, with the result that she would either write no notes at all or would reject all gifts and invitations. Again, she was astounded to learn that there were some gifts that did not require thank-you notes, and that when these were required, short notes sometimes sufficed.

Mature mental health demands, then, an extraordinary capacity to flexibly strike and continually restrike a delicate balance between conflicting needs, goals, duties, responsibilities, directions, et cetera. The essence of this discipline of balancing is "giving up." I remember first being taught this one summer morning in my ninth year. I had recently learned to ride a bike and was joyously exploring the dimensions of my new skill. About a mile from our house the road went down a steep hill and turned sharply at the bottom. Coasting down the hill on my bike that morning I felt my gathering speed to be ecstatic. To give up this ecstasy by the application of brakes seemed an absurd self-punishment. So I resolved to simultaneously retain my speed and negotiate the corner at the bottom. My ecstasy ended seconds later when I was propelled a dozen feet off the road into the woods. I was badly scratched and bleeding and the front wheel of my new bike was twisted beyond use from its impact against a tree. I had lost my balance.

Balancing is a discipline precisely because the act of giving something up is painful. In this instance I had been unwilling to suffer the pain of giving up my ecstatic speed in the interest of maintaining my balance around the corner. I learned, however, that the loss of balance is ultimately more painful than the giving up required to maintain balance. In one way or another it is a lesson I have continually had to relearn throughout my life. As must everyone, for as we negotiate the curves and corners of our lives, we must continually give up parts of ourselves. The only alternative to this giving up is not to travel at all on the journey of life.

It may seem strange, but most people choose this alternative and elect not to continue with their life journeys—to stop short by some distance—in order to avoid the pain of giving up parts of themselves. If it does seem strange, it is because you do not understand the depth of the pain that may be involved. In its major forms, giving up is the most painful of human experiences. Thus far I have been talking about minor forms of giving up—giving up speed or the luxury of spontaneous anger or the safety of withheld anger or the neatness of a thank-you note. Let me turn now to the giving up of personality traits, well-established patterns of behavior, ideologies, and even whole life styles. These are major forms of giving up that are required if one is to travel very far on the journey of life.

One night recently I decided to spend some free time building a happier and closer relationship with my fourteen-year-old daughter. For several weeks she had been urging me to play chess with her, so I suggested a game. She eagerly accepted and we settled down to a most even and challenging match. It was a school night, however, and at nine o'clock my daughter asked if I could hurry my moves, because she needed to get to bed; she had to get up at six in the morning. I knew her to be rigidly disciplined in her sleeping habits, and it seemed to me that she ought to be able to give up some of this rigidity. I told her, "Come on, you can go to bed a little later for once. You shouldn't start games that you can't finish. We're having fun." We played on for another fifteen minutes, during which time she became visibly discomfited. Finally she pleaded, "Please, Daddy, please hurry your moves." "No goddammit," I replied. "Chess is a serious game. If you're going to play it well, you're going to play it slowly. If you don't want to play it seriously, you might as well not play it at all." And so, with her feeling miserable, we continued for another ten minutes, until suddenly my daughter burst into tears, yelled that she conceded the stupid game, and ran weeping up the stairs.

Immediately I felt as if I were nine years old again, lying bleeding in the bushes by the side of the road, next to my bike. Clearly I had made a mistake. Clearly I had failed to negotiate a turn in the road. I had started the evening wanting to have a happy time with my daughter. Ninety minutes later she was in tears and so angry at me she could hardly speak. What had gone wrong? The answer was obvious. But I did not want to see the answer, so it took me two hours to wade through the pain of accepting the fact that I had botched the evening by allowing my desire to win a chess game become more important than my desire to build a relationship with my daughter. I was depressed in earnest then. How had I gotten so out of balance? Gradually it dawned on me that my desire to win was too great and that I needed to give up some of this desire. Yet even this little giving up seemed impossible. All my life my desire to win had served me in good stead, for I had won many things. How was it possible to play chess without wanting to win? I had never been comfortable doing things unenthusiastically. How could I conceivably play chess enthusiastically but not seriously? Yet somehow I had to change, for I knew that my enthusiasm, my competitiveness and my seriousness were part of a behavior pattern that was working and would continue to work toward alienating my children from me, and that if I were not able to modify this pattern, there would be other times of unnecessary tears and bitterness. My depression continued.

My depression is over now. I have given up part of my desire to win at games. That part of me is gone now. It died. It had to die. I killed it. I killed it with my desire to win at parenting. When I was a child my desire to win at games served me well. As a parent, I recognized that it got in my way. So it had to go. The times have changed. To move with them I had to give it up. I do not miss it. I thought I would, but I don't.

The Healthiness of Depression

The foregoing is a minor example of what those people with the courage to call themselves patients must go through in more major ways, and often many times, in the process of psychotherapy. The period of intensive psychotherapy is a period of intensive growth, during which the patient may undergo more changes than some people experience in a lifetime. For this growth spurt to occur, a proportionate amount of "the old self" must be given up. It is an inevitable part of successful psychotherapy. In fact, this process of giving up usually begins before the patient has his first appointment with the psychotherapist. Frequently, for instance, the act of deciding to seek psychiatric attention in itself represents a giving up of the self-image "I'm OK." This giving up may be particularly difficult for males in our culture for whom "I'm not OK and I need assistance to understand why I'm not OK and how to become OK" is frequently and sadly equated with "I'm weak, unmasculine and inadequate." Actually, the giving-up process often begins even before the patient has arrived at the decision to seek psychiatric attention. I mentioned that during the process of giving up my desire to always win I was depressed. This is because the feeling associated with giving up something loved—or at least something that is a part of ourselves and familiar—is depression. Since mentally healthy human beings must grow, and since giving up or loss of the old self is an integral part of the process of mental and spiritual growth, depression is a normal and basically healthy phenom-enon. It becomes abnormal or unhealthy only when some-thing interferes with the giving-up process, with the result that the depression is prolonged and cannot be resolved by completion of the process.*

A leading reason for people to think about seeking psychi-atric attention is depression. In other words, patients are fre-quently already involved in a giving-up, or growth, process before considering psychotherapy, and it is the symptoms of this growth process that impel them toward the therapist's office. The therapist's job, therefore, is to help the patient complete a growth process that he or she has already begun. This is not to say that patients are often aware of what is happening to them. To the contrary, they frequently desire only relief from the symptoms of their depression "so that things can be as they used to be." They do not know that things can no longer be "the way they used to be." But the unconscious knows. It is precisely because the unconscious in its wisdom knows that "the way things used to be" is no longer tenable or constructive that the process of growing and giving up is begun on an unconscious level and depression is experienced. As likely as not the patient will report, "I have no idea why I'm depressed" or will ascribe the depression to

* There are many factors that can interfere with the giving-up pro-cess and, therefore, prolong a normal, healthy depression into a chronic pathologic depression. Of all the possible factors, one of the most com-mon and potent is a pattern of experiences in childhood wherein parents or fate, unresponsive to the needs of the child, took away "things" from the child before he or she was psychologically ready to give them up or strong enough to truly accept their loss. Such a pattern of experience in childhood sensitizes the child to the experience of loss and creates a tendency far stronger than that found in more fortunate individuals to cling to "things" and seek to avoid the pain of loss or giving up. For this reason, although all pathologic depressions involve some blockage in the giving-up process, I believe there is a type of chronic neurotic depres-sion that has as its central root a traumatic injury to the individual's basic capacity to give up anything, and to this subtype of depression I would apply the name "giving-up neurosis."

irrelevant factors. Since patients are not yet consciously willing or ready to recognize that the "old self" and "the way things used to be" are outdated, they are not aware that their depression is signaling that major change is required for successful and evolutionary adaptation. The fact that the unconscious is one step ahead of the conscious may seem strange to lay readers; it is, however, a fact that applies not only in this specific instance but so generally that it is a basic principal of mental functioning. It will be discussed in greater depth in the concluding section of this work.

Recently we have been hearing of the "mid-life crisis." Actually, this is but one of many "crises," or critical stages of development, in life, as Erik Erikson taught us thirty years ago. (Erikson delineated eight crises; perhaps there are more.) What makes crises of these transition periods in the life cycle —that is, problematic and painful—is that in successfully working our way through them we must give up cherished notions and old ways of doing and looking at things. Many people are either unwilling or unable to suffer the pain of giving up the outgrown which needs to be forsaken. Consequently they cling, often forever, to their old patterns of thinking and behaving, thus failing to negotiate any crisis, to truly grow up, and to experience the joyful sense of rebirth that accompanies the successful transition into greater maturity. Although an entire book could be written about each one, let me simply list, roughly in order of their occurrence, some of the major conditions, desires and attitudes that must be given up in the course of a wholly successful evolving lifetime:

> The state of infancy, in which no external demands need be responded to
> The fantasy of omnipotence
> The desire for total (including sexual) possession of one's parent(s)
> The dependency of childhood
> Distorted images of one's parents

The omnipotentiality of adolescence
The "freedom" of uncommitment
The agility of youth
The sexual attractiveness and/or potency of youth
The fantasy of immortality
Authority over one's children
Various forms of temporal power
The independence of physical health
And, ultimately, the self and life itself.

Renunciation and Rebirth

In regard to the last of the above, it may seem to many that the ultimate requirement—to give up one's self and one's life —represents a kind of cruelty on the part of God or fate, which makes our existence a sort of bad joke and which can never be completely accepted. This attitude is particularly true in present-day Western culture, in which the self is held sacred and death is considered an unspeakable insult. Yet the exact opposite is the reality. It is in the giving up of self that human beings can find the most ecstatic and lasting, solid, durable joy of life. And it is death that provides life with all its meaning. This "secret" is the central wisdom of religion.

The process of giving up the self (which is related to the phenomenon of love, as will be discussed in the next section of this book) is for most of us a gradual process which we get into by a series of fits and starts. One form of temporary giving up of the self deserves special mention because its practice is an absolute requirement for significant learning during adulthood, and therefore for significant growth of the human spirit. I am referring to a subtype of the discipline of balancing which I call "bracketing." Bracketing is essentially the act of balancing the need for stability and assertion of the self with the need for new knowledge and greater understanding by temporarily giving up one's self—putting one's self aside, so to speak—so as to make room for the incorporation of new material into the self. This discipline has been well described by the theologian Sam Keen in *To a Dancing God:*

> The second step requires that I go beyond the idiosyncratic and egocentric perception of immediate experience. Mature awareness is possible only when I have digested and compensated for the biases and prejudices that are the residue of my personal history. Awareness of what presents itself to me involves a double movement of attention: silencing the familiar and welcoming the strange. Each time I approach a strange object, person, or event, I have a tendency to let my present needs, past experience, or expectations for the future determine what I will see. If I am to appreciate the uniqueness of any datum, I must be sufficiently aware of my preconceived ideas and characteristic emotional distortions to bracket them long enough to welcome strangeness and novelty into my perceptual world. This discipline of bracketing, compensating, or silencing requires sophisticated self-knowledge and courageous honesty. Yet, without this discipline each present moment is only the repetition of something already seen or experienced. In order for genuine novelty to emerge, for the unique presence of things, persons, or events to take root in me, I must undergo a decentralization of the ego.*

The discipline of bracketing illustrates the most consequential fact of giving up and of discipline in general: namely, that for all that is given up even more is gained. Self-discipline is a self-enlarging process. The pain of giving up is the pain of death, but death of the old is birth of the new. The pain of death is the pain of birth, and the pain of birth is the pain of death. For us to develop a new and better idea, concept,

---

* New York: Harper & Row, 1970, p. 28.

theory or understanding means that an old idea, concept, theory or understanding must die. Thus, in the conclusion of his poem "Journey of the Magi," T. S. Eliot describes the Three Wise Men as suffering the giving up of their previous world view when they embraced Christianity.

> *All this was a long time ago, I remember,*
> *And I would do it again, but set down*
> *This set down*
> *This: were we led all that way for*
> *Birth or Death? This was a Birth, certainly,*
> *We had evidence and no doubt. I had seen birth and*
> *   death,*
> *But had thought they were different; this Birth was*
> *Hard and bitter agony for us, like Death, our death.*
> *We returned to our places, these Kingdoms,*
> *But no longer at ease here, in the old dispensation,*
> *With an alien people clutching their gods.*
> *I should be glad of another death.* *

Since birth and death seem to be but different sides of the same coin, it is really not at all unreasonable to pay closer heed than we usually do in the West to the concept of reincarnation. But whether or not we are willing to entertain seriously the possibility of some kind of rebirth occurring simultaneously with our physical death, it is abundantly clear that *this* lifetime is a series of simultaneous deaths and births. "Throughout the whole of life one must continue to learn to live," said Seneca two millennia ago, "and what will amaze you even more, throughout life one must learn to die."† It is also clear that the farther one travels on the journey of life, the more births one will experience, and therefore the more deaths—the more joy and the more pain.

* *The Complete Poems and Plays, 1909–1950* (New York: Harcourt Brace, 1952), p. 69.

† Quoted in Erich Fromm, *The Sane Society* (New York: Rinehart, 1955).

This raises the question of whether it is ever possible to become free from emotional pain in this life. Or, putting it more mildly, is it possible to spiritually evolve to a level of consciousness at which the pain of living is at least diminished? The answer is yes and no. The answer is yes, because once suffering is completely accepted, it ceases in a sense to be suffering. It is also yes because the unceasing practice of discipline leads to mastery, and the spiritually evolved person is masterful in the same sense that the adult is masterful in relation to the child. Matters that present great problems for the child and cause it great pain may be of no consequence to the adult at all. Finally, the answer is yes because the spiritually evolved individual is, as will be elaborated in the next section, an extraordinarily loving individual, and with his or her extraordinary love comes extraordinary joy.

The answer is no, however, because there is a vacuum of competence in the world which must be filled. In a world crying out in desperate need for competence, an extraordinarily competent and loving person can no more withhold his or her competence than such a person could deny food to a hungry infant. Spiritually evolved people, by virtue of their discipline, mastery and love, are people of extraordinary competence, and in their competence they are called on to serve the world, and in their love they answer the call. They are inevitably, therefore, people of great power, although the world may generally behold them as quite ordinary people, since more often than not they will exercise their power in quiet or even hidden ways. Nonetheless, exercise power they do, and in this exercise they suffer greatly, even dreadfully. For to exercise power is to make decisions, and the process of making decisions with total awareness is often infinitely more painful than making decisions with limited or blunted awareness (which is the way most decisions are made and why they are ultimately proved wrong). Imagine two generals, each having to decide whether or not to commit a division of ten thousand men to battle. To one the division is but a thing, a unit of personnel, an instrument of strategy and nothing more. To the other it is these things, but he is also aware of each and every one of the ten thousand lives and the lives of the families of each of the ten thousand. For whom is the decision easier? It is easier for the general who has blunted his awareness precisely because he cannot tolerate the pain of a more nearly complete awareness. It may be tempting to say, "Ah, but a spiritually evolved man would never become a general in the first place." But the same issue is involved in being a corporation president, a physician, a teacher, a parent. Decisions affecting the lives of others must always be made. The best decision-makers are those who are willing to suffer the most over their decisions but still retain their ability to be decisive. One measure—and perhaps the best measure—of a person's greatness is the capacity for suffering. Yet the great are also joyful. This, then, is the paradox. Buddhists tend to ignore the Buddha's suffering and Christians forget Christ's joy. Buddha and Christ were not different men. The suffering of Christ letting go on the cross and the joy of Buddha letting go under the bo tree are one.

So if your goal is to avoid pain and escape suffering, I would not advise you to seek higher levels of consciousness or spiritual evolution. First, you cannot achieve them without suffering, and second, insofar as you do achieve them, you are likely to be called on to serve in ways more painful to you, or at least demanding of you, than you can now imagine. Then why desire to evolve at all, you may ask. If you ask this question, perhaps you do not know enough of joy. Perhaps you may find an answer in the remainder of this book; perhaps you will not.

A final word on the discipline of balancing and its essence of giving up: you must have something in order to give it up. You cannot give up anything you have not already gotten. If you give up winning without ever having won, you are where you were at the beginning: a loser. You must forge for yourself an identity before you can give it up. You must develop an ego before you can lose it. This may seem incredibly elementary, but I think it is necessary to say it, since there are many people I know who possess a vision of evolution yet seem to lack the will for it. They want, and believe it is possible, to skip over the discipline, to find an easy short-cut to sainthood. Often they attempt to attain it by simply imitating the superficialities of saints, retiring to the desert or taking up carpentry. Some even believe that by such imitation they have really become saints and prophets, and are unable to acknowledge that they are still children and face the painful fact that they must start at the beginning and go through the middle.

Discipline has been defined as a system of techniques of dealing constructively with the pain of problem-solving—instead of avoiding that pain—in such a way that all of life's problems can be solved. Four basic techniques have been distinguished and elaborated: delaying gratification, assumption of responsibility, dedication to the truth or reality, and balancing. Discipline is a *system* of techniques, because these techniques are very much interrelated. In a single act one may utilize two, three or even all of the techniques at the same time and in such a way that they may be distinguishable from each other. The strength, energy and willingness to use these techniques are provided by love, as will be elaborated in the next section. This analysis of discipline has not been intended to be exhaustive, and it is possible that I have neglected one or more additional basic techniques, although I suspect not. It is also reasonable to ask whether such processes as biofeedback, meditation, yoga, and psychotherapy itself are not techniques of discipline, but to this I would reply that, to my way of thinking, they are technical aids rather than basic techniques. As such they may be very useful but are not essential. On the other hand, the basic techniques herein described, if practiced unceasingly and genuinely, are alone sufficient to enable the practitioner of discipline, or "disciple," to evolve to spiritually higher levels.

SECTION II

Love

Love Defined

Discipline, it has been suggested, is the means of human spiritual evolution. This section will examine what lies in back of discipline—what provides the motive, the energy for discipline. This force I believe to be love. I am very conscious of the fact that in attempting to examine love we will be beginning to toy with mystery. In a very real sense we will be attempting to examine the unexaminable and to know the unknowable. Love is too large, too deep ever to be truly understood or measured or limited within the framework of words. I would not write this if I did not believe the attempt to have value, but no matter how valuable, I begin with the certain knowledge that the attempt will be in some ways inadequate.

One result of the mysterious nature of love is that no one has ever, to my knowledge, arrived at a truly satisfactory definition of love. In an effort to explain it, therefore, love has been divided into various categories: eros, philia, agape; perfect love and imperfect love, and so on. I am presuming, however, to give a single definition of love, again with the awareness that it is likely to be in some way or ways inadequate. I define love thus: The will to extend one's self for the purpose of nurturing one's own or another's spiritual growth.

At the outset I would like to comment briefly on this definition before proceeding to a more thorough elaboration. First, it may be noticed that it is a teleological definition; the behavior is defined in terms of the goal or purpose it seems to serve—in this case, spiritual growth. Scientists tend to hold teleological definitions suspect, and perhaps they will this one. I did not arrive at it, however, through a clearly teleological process of thinking. Instead I arrived at it through observation in my clinical practice of psychiatry (which includes self-observation), in which the definition of love is a matter of considerable import. This is because patients are generally very confused as to the nature of love. For instance, a timid young man reported to me: "My mother loved me so much she wouldn't let me take the school bus to school until my senior year in high school. Even then I had to beg her to let me go. I guess she was afraid that I would get hurt, so she drove me to and from school every day, which was very hard on her. She really loved me." In the treatment of this individual's timidity it was necessary, as it is in many other cases, to teach him that his mother might have been motivated by something other than love, and that what seems to be love is often not love at all. It has been out of such experience that I accumulated a body of examples of what seemed to be acts of love and what seemed not to be love. One of the major distinguishing features between the two seemed to be the conscious or unconscious purpose in the mind of the lover or nonlover.

Second, it may be noticed that, as defined, love is a strangely circular process. For the process of extending one's self is an evolutionary process. When one has successfully extended one's limits, one has then grown into a larger state of being. Thus the act of loving is an act of self-evolution even when the purpose of the act is someone else's growth. It is through reaching toward evolution that we evolve.

Third, this unitary definition of love includes self-love with love for the other. Since I am human and you are human, to love humans means to love myself as well as you. To be dedicated to human spiritual development is to be dedicated to the race of which we are a part, and this therefore means dedication to our own development as well as "theirs." Indeed, as has been pointed out, we are incapable of loving another unless we love ourselves, just as we are incapable of teaching our children self-discipline unless we ourselves are self-disciplined. It is actually impossible to forsake our own spiritual development in favor of someone else's. We cannot forsake self-discipline and at the same time be disciplined in our care for another. We cannot be a source of strength unless we nurture our own strength. As we proceed in our exploration of the nature of love, I believe it will become clear that not only do self-love and love of others go hand in hand but that ultimately they are indistinguishable.

Fourth, the act of extending one's limits implies effort. One extends one's limits only by exceeding them, and exceeding limits requires effort. When we love someone our love becomes demonstrable or real only through our exertion—through the fact that for that someone (or for ourself) we take an extra step or walk an extra mile. Love is not effortless. To the contrary, love is effortful.

Finally, by use of the word "will" I have attempted to transcend the distinction between desire and action. Desire is not necessarily translated into action. Will is desire of sufficient intensity that it *is* translated into action. The difference between the two is equal to the difference between saying "I would like to go swimming tonight" and "I will go swimming tonight." Everyone in our culture desires to some extent to be loving, yet many are not in fact loving. I therefore conclude that the desire to love is not itself love. Love is as love does. Love is an act of will—namely, both an intention and an action. Will also implies choice. We do not have to love. We choose to love. No matter how much we may think we are loving, if we are in fact not loving, it is because we have chosen not to love and therefore do not love despite our good intentions. On the other hand, whenever we do actually exert ourselves in the cause of spiritual growth, it is because we have chosen to do so. The choice to love has been made.

As I indicated, patients who come to psychotherapy are invariably found to be more or less confused about the nature of love. This is because in the face of the mystery of love misconceptions about it abound. While this book will not

remove from love its mystery, I hope it will clarify matters
sufficiently to help do away with these misconceptions, which
cause suffering not only to patients but to all people as they
attempt to make sense out of their own experiences. Some of
this suffering seems to me unnecessary, since these popular
misconceptions could be made less popular through the teaching of a more precise definition of love. I have therefore chosen to begin exploring the nature of love by examining what
love is not.

Falling in "Love"

Of all the misconceptions about love the most powerful and
pervasive is the belief that "falling in love" is love or at least
one of the manifestations of love. It is a potent misconception,
because falling in love is subjectively experienced in a very
powerful fashion as an experience of love. When a person falls
in love what he or she certainly feels is "I love him" or "I love
her." But two problems are immediately apparent. The first
is that the experience of falling in love is specifically a sex-
linked erotic experience. We do not fall in love with our children even though we may love them very deeply. We do not
fall in love with our friends of the same sex—unless we are
homosexually oriented—even though we may care for them
greatly. We fall in love only when we are consciously or unconsciously sexually motivated. The second problem is that
the experience of falling in love is invariably temporary. No
matter whom we fall in love with, we sooner or later fall out
of love if the relationship continues long enough. This is not
to say that we invariably cease loving the person with whom
we fell in love. But it is to say that the feeling of ecstatic

lovingness that characterizes the experience of falling in love always passes. The honeymoon always ends. The bloom of romance always fades.

To understand the nature of the phenomenon of falling in love and the inevitability of its ending, it is necessary to examine the nature of what psychiatrists call ego boundaries. From what we can ascertain by indirect evidence, it appears that the newborn infant during the first few months of its life does not distinguish between itself and the rest of the universe. When it moves its arms and legs, the world is moving. When it is hungry, the world is hungry. When it sees its mother move, it is as if it is moving. When its mother sings, the baby does not know that it is itself not making the sound. It cannot distinguish itself from the crib, the room and its parents. The animate and the inanimate are the same. There is no distinction yet between I and thou. It and the world are one. There are no boundaries, no separations. There is no identity.

But with experience the child begins to experience itself— namely, as an entity separate from the rest of the world. When it is hungry, mother doesn't always appear to feed it. When it is playful, mother doesn't always want to play. The child then has the experience of its wishes not being its mother's command. Its will is experienced as something separate from its mother's behavior. A sense of the "me" begins to develop. This interaction between the infant and the mother is believed to be the ground out of which the child's sense of identity begins to grow. It has been observed that when the interaction between the infant and its mother is grossly disturbed—for example, when there is no mother, no satisfactory mother substitute or when because of her own mental illness the mother is totally uncaring or uninterested—then the infant grows into a child or adult whose sense of identity is grossly defective in the most basic ways.

As the infant recognizes its will to be its own and not that of the universe, it begins to make other distinctions between itself and the world. When it wills movement, its arm waves before its eyes, but neither the crib nor the ceiling move. Thus the child learns that its arm and its will are connected, and therefore that its arm is *its* and not something or someone else's. In this manner, during the first year of life, we learn the fundamentals of who we are and who we are not, what we are and what we are not. By the end of our first year we know that this is my arm, my foot, my head, my tongue, my eyes and even my viewpoint, my voice, my thoughts, my stomachache, and my feelings. We know our size and our physical limits. These limits are our boundaries. The knowledge of these limits inside our minds is what is meant by ego boundaries.

The development of ego boundaries is a process that continues through childhood into adolescence and even into adulthood, but the boundaries established later are more psychic than physical. For instance, the age between two and three is typically a time when the child comes to terms with the limits of its power. While before this time the child has learned that its wish is not necessarily its mother's command, it still clings to the possibility that its wish might be its mother's command and the feeling that its wish should be her command. It is because of this hope and feeling that the two-year-old usually attempts to act like a tyrant and autocrat, trying to give orders to its parents, siblings and family pets as if they were menials in its own private army, and responds with regal fury when they won't be dictated to. Thus parents speak of this age as "the terrible twos." By the age of three the child has usually become more tractable and mellow as a result of an acceptance of the reality of its own relative powerlessness. Still, the possibility of omnipotence is such a sweet, sweet dream that it cannot be completely given up even after several years of very painful confrontation with one's own impotence. Although the child of three has come to accept the reality of the boundaries of its power, it will continue to escape occasionally for some years to come into a world of fantasy in which the possibility of omnipotence (particularly its own) still exists. This is the world of Superman and Captain Marvel. Yet gradually even the superheroes are given up, and by the time of mid-adolescence, young people know that they are individuals, confined to the boundaries of their flesh and the limits of their power, each one a relatively frail and impotent organism, existing only by cooperation within a group of fellow organisms called society. Within this group they are not particularly distinguished, yet they are isolated from others by their individual identities, boundaries and limits.

It is lonely behind these boundaries. Some people—particularly those whom psychiatrists call schizoid—because of unpleasant, traumatizing experiences in childhood, perceive the world outside of themselves as unredeemably dangerous, hostile, confusing and unnurturing. Such people feel their boundaries to be protecting and comforting and find a sense of safety in their loneliness. But most of us feel our loneliness to be painful and yearn to escape from behind the walls of our individual identities to a condition in which we can be more unified with the world outside of ourselves. The experience of falling in love allows us this escape—temporarily. The essence of the phenomenon of falling in love is a sudden collapse of a section of an individual's ego boundaries, permitting one to merge his or her identity with that of another person. The sudden release of oneself from oneself, the explosive pouring out of oneself into the beloved, and the dramatic surcease of loneliness accompanying this collapse of ego boundaries is experienced by most of us as ecstatic. We and our beloved are one! Loneliness is no more!

In some respects (but certainly not in all) the act of falling in love is an act of regression. The experience of merging with the loved one has in it echoes from the time when we were merged with our mothers in infancy. Along with the merging we also reexperience the sense of omnipotence which we had to give up in our journey out of childhood. All things seem possible! United with our beloved we feel we can conquer all obstacles. We believe that the strength of our love will cause the forces of opposition to bow down in submission and melt away into the darkness. All problems will be overcome. The future will be all light. The unreality of these feelings when we have fallen in love is essentially the same as the unreality of the two-year-old who feels itself to be king of the family and the world with power unlimited.

Just as reality intrudes upon the two-year-old's fantasy of omnipotence so does reality intrude upon the fantastic unity of the couple who have fallen in love. Sooner or later, in response to the problems of daily living, individual will reasserts itself. He wants to have sex; she doesn't. She wants to go to the movies; he doesn't. He wants to put money in the bank; she wants a dishwasher. She wants to talk about her job; he wants to talk about his. She doesn't like his friends; he doesn't like hers. So both of them, in the privacy of their hearts, begin to come to the sickening realization that they are not one with the beloved, that the beloved has and will continue to have his or her own desires, tastes, prejudices and timing different from the other's. One by one, gradually or suddenly, the ego boundaries snap back into place; gradually or suddenly, they fall out of love. Once again they are two separate individuals. At this point they begin either to dissolve the ties of their relationship or to initiate the work of real loving.

By my use of the word "real" I am implying that the perception that we are loving when we fall in love is a false perception—that our subjective sense of lovingness is an illusion. Full elaboration of real love will be deferred until later in this section. However, by stating that it is when a couple falls out of love they may begin to really love I am also implying that real love does not have its roots in a feeling of love. To the contrary, real love often occurs in a context in which the feeling of love is lacking, when we act lovingly despite the fact that we don't feel loving. Assuming the reality of the definition of love with which we started, the experience of "falling in love" is not real love for the several reasons that follow.

Falling in love is not an act of will. It is not a conscious choice. No matter how open to or eager for it we may be, the

experience may still elude us. Contrarily, the experience may
capture us at times when we are definitely not seeking it,
when it is inconvenient and undesirable. We are as likely to
fall in love with someone with whom we are obviously ill
matched as with someone more suitable. Indeed, we may not
even like or admire the object of our passion, yet, try as we
might, we may not be able to fall in love with a person whom
we deeply respect and with whom a deep relationship would
be in all ways desirable. This is not to say that the experience
of falling in love is immune to discipline. Psychiatrists, for
instance, frequently fall in love with their patients, just as
their patients fall in love with them, yet out of duty to the
patient and their role they are usually able to abort the collapse of their ego boundaries and give up the patient as a
romantic object. The struggle and suffering of the discipline
involved may be enormous. But discipline and will can only
control the experience; they cannot create it. We can choose
how to respond to the experience of falling in love, but we
cannot choose the experience itself.

Falling in love is not an extension of one's limits or boundaries; it is a partial and temporary collapse of them. The extension of one's limits requires effort; falling in love is
effortless. Lazy and undisciplined individuals are as likely to
fall in love as energetic and dedicated ones. Once the precious
moment of falling in love has passed and the boundaries have
snapped back into place, the individual may be disillusioned,
but is usually none the larger for the experience. When limits
are extended or stretched, however, they tend to stay
stretched. Real love is a permanently self-enlarging experience. Falling in love is not.

Falling in love has little to do with purposively nurturing
one's spiritual development. If we have any purpose in mind
when we fall in love it is to terminate our own loneliness and
perhaps insure this result through marriage. Certainly we are
not thinking of spiritual development. Indeed, after we have
fallen in love and before we have fallen out of love again we
feel that we have arrived, that the heights have been attained,

that there is both no need and no possibility of going higher. We do not feel ourselves to be in any need of development; we are totally content to be where we are. Our spirit is at peace. Nor do we perceive our beloved as being in need of spiritual development. To the contrary, we perceive him or her as perfect, as having been perfected. If we see any faults in our beloved, we perceive them as insignificant—little quirks or darling eccentricities that only add color and charm.

If falling in love is not love, then what is it other than a temporary and partial collapse of ego boundaries? I do not know. But the sexual specificity of the phenomenon leads me to suspect that it is a genetically determined instinctual component of mating behavior. In other words, the temporary collapse of ego boundaries that constitutes falling in love is a stereotypic response of human beings to a configuration of internal sexual drives and external sexual stimuli, which serves to increase the probability of sexual pairing and bonding so as to enhance the survival of the species. Or to put it in another, rather crass way, falling in love is a trick that our genes pull on our otherwise perceptive mind to hoodwink or trap us into marriage. Frequently the trick goes awry one way or another, as when the sexual drives and stimuli are homosexual or when other forces—parental interference, mental illness, conflicting responsibilities or mature self-discipline—supervene to prevent the bonding. On the other hand, without this trick, this illusory and inevitably temporary (it would not be practical were it not temporary) regression to infantile merging and omnipotence, many of us who are happily or unhappily married today would have retreated in wholehearted terror from the realism of the marriage vows.

The Myth of Romantic Love

To serve as effectively as it does to trap us into marriage, the experience of falling in love probably must have as one of its characteristics the illusion that the experience will last forever. This illusion is fostered in our culture by the commonly held myth of romantic love, which has its origins in our favorite childhood fairy tales, wherein the prince and princess, once united, live happily forever after. The myth of romantic love tells us, in effect, that for every young man in the world there is a young woman who was "meant for him," and vice versa. Moreover, the myth implies that there is only one man meant for a woman and only one woman for a man and this has been predetermined "in the stars." When we meet the person for whom we are intended, recognition comes through the fact that we fall in love. We have met the person for whom all the heavens intended us, and since the match is perfect, we will then be able to satisfy all of each other's needs forever and ever, and therefore live happily forever after in perfect union and harmony. Should it come to pass, however, that we do not satisfy or meet all of each other's needs and friction arises and we fall out of love, then it is clear that a dreadful mistake was made, we misread the stars, we did not hook up with our one and only perfect match, what we thought was love was not real or "true" love, and nothing can be done about the situation except to live unhappily ever after or get divorced.

While I generally find that great myths are great precisely because they represent and embody great universal truths (and will explore several such myths later in this book), the

myth of romantic love is a dreadful lie. Perhaps it is a necessary lie in that it ensures the survival of the species by its
encouragement and seeming validation of the falling-in-love
experience that traps us into marriage. But as a psychiatrist I
weep in my heart almost daily for the ghastly confusion and
suffering that this myth fosters. Millions of people waste vast
amounts of energy desperately and futilely attempting to
make the reality of their lives conform to the unreality of the
myth. Mrs. A. subjugates herself absurdly to her husband
out of a feeling of guilt. "I didn't really love my husband when
we married," she says. "I pretended I did. I guess I tricked
him into it, so I have no right to complain about him, and I
owe it to him to do whatever he wants." Mr. B. laments: "I
regret I didn't marry Miss C. I think we could have had a
good marriage. But I didn't feel head over heels in love with
her, so I assumed she couldn't be the right person for me."
Mrs. D., married for two years, becomes severely depressed
without apparent cause, and enters therapy stating: "I don't
know what's wrong. I've got everything I need, including a
perfect marriage." Only months later can she accept the fact
that she has fallen out of love with her husband but that this
does not mean that she made a horrible mistake. Mr. E., also
married two years, begins to suffer intense headaches in the
evenings and can't believe they are psychosomatic. "My home
life is fine. I love my wife as much as the day I married her.
She's everything I ever wanted," he says. But his headaches
don't leave him until a year later, when he is able to admit,
"She bugs the hell out of me the way she is always wanting,
wanting, wanting things without regard to my salary," and
then is able to confront her with her extravagance. Mr. and
Mrs. F. acknowledge to each other that they have fallen out
of love and then proceed to make each other miserable by
mutual rampant infidelity as they each search for the one
"true love," not realizing that their very acknowledgment
could mark the beginning of the work of their marriage instead of its end. Even when couples have acknowledged that
the honeymoon is over, that they are no longer romantically

in love with each other and are able still to be committed to their relationship, they still cling to the myth and attempt to conform their lives to it. "Even though we have fallen out of love, if we act by sheer will power as if we still were in love, then maybe romantic love will return to our lives," their thinking goes. These couples prize togetherness. When they enter couples group therapy (which is the setting in which my wife and I and our close colleagues conduct most serious marriage counseling), they sit together, speak for each other, defend each other's faults and seek to present to the rest of the group a united front, believing this unity to be a sign of the relative health of their marriage and a prerequisite for its improvement. Sooner or later, and usually sooner, we must tell most couples that they are too much married, too closely coupled, and that they need to establish some psychological distance from each other before they can even begin to work constructively on their problems. Sometimes it is actually necessary to physically separate them, directing them to sit apart from each other in the group circle. It is always necessary to ask them to refrain from speaking for each other or defending each other against the group. Over and over again we must say, "Let Mary speak for herself, John," and "John can defend himself, Mary, he's strong enough." Ultimately, if they stay in therapy, all couples learn that a true acceptance of their own and each other's individuality and separateness is the only foundation upon which a mature marriage can be based and real love can grow.*

* Those who have read the O'Neils' book *Open Marriage* will recognize this to be a basic tenet of the open as opposed to the closed marriage. The O'Neils were actually remarkably gentle and restrained in their proselytizing for open marriage. My work with couples has led me to the stark conclusion that open marriage is the only kind of mature marriage that is healthy and not seriously destructive to the spiritual health and growth of the individual partners.

More About Ego Boundaries

Having proclaimed that the experience of "falling in love" is a sort of illusion which in no way constitutes real love, let me conclude by shifting into reverse and pointing out that falling in love is in fact very, very close to real love. Indeed, the misconception that falling in love is a type of love is so potent precisely because it contains a grain of truth.

The experience of real love also has to do with ego boundaries, since it involves an extension of one's limits. One's limits are one's ego boundaries. When we extend our limits through love, we do so by reaching out, so to speak, toward the beloved, whose growth we wish to nurture. For us to be able to do this, the beloved object must first become beloved to us; in other words, we must be attracted toward, invested in and committed to an object outside of ourselves, beyond the boundaries of self. Psychiatrists call this process of attraction, investment and commitment "cathexis" and say that we "cathect" the beloved object. But when we cathect an object outside of ourselves we also psychologically incorporate a representation of that object into ourselves. For example, let us consider a man who gardens for a hobby. It is a satisfying and consuming hobby. He "loves" gardening. His garden means a lot to him. This man has cathected his garden. He finds it attractive, he has invested himself in it, he is committed to it —so much so that he may jump out of bed early Sunday morning to get back to it, he may refuse to travel away from it, and he may even neglect his wife for it. In the process of his cathexis and in order to nurture his flowers and shrubs he learns a great deal. He comes to know much about gardening

—about soils and fertilizers, rooting and pruning. And he knows his particular garden—its history, the types of flowers and plants in it, its layout, its problems and even its future. Despite the fact that the garden exists outside of him, through his cathexis it has also come to exist within him. His knowledge of it and the meaning it has for him are part of him, part of his identity, part of his history, part of his wisdom. By loving and cathecting his garden he has in quite a real way incorporated the garden within him, and by this incorporation his self has become enlarged and his ego boundaries extended.

What transpires then in the course of many years of loving, of extending our limits for our cathexes, is a gradual but progressive enlargement of the self, an incorporation within of the world without, and a growth, a stretching and a thinning of our ego boundaries. In this way the more and longer we extend ourselves, the more we love, the more blurred becomes the distinction between the self and the world. We become identified with the world. And as our ego boundaries become blurred and thinned, we begin more and more to experience the same sort of feeling of ecstasy that we have when our ego boundaries partially collapse and we "fall in love." Only, instead of having merged temporarily and unrealistically with a single beloved object, we have merged realistically and more permanently with much of the world. A "mystical union" with the entire world may be established. The feeling of ecstasy or bliss associated with this union, while perhaps more gentle and less dramatic than that associated with falling in love, is nonetheless much more stable and lasting and ultimately satisfying. It is the difference between the peak experience, typified by falling in love, and what Abraham Maslow has referred to as the "plateau experience."* The heights are not suddenly glimpsed and lost again; they are attained forever.

It is obvious and generally understood that sexual activity

---

* *Religions, Values, and Peak-Experiences* (New York: Viking, 1970), preface.

and love, while they may occur simultaneously, often are disassociated, because they are basically separate phenomena. In itself, making love is not an act of love. Nonetheless the experience of sexual intercourse, and particularly of orgasm (even in masturbation), is an experience also associated with a greater or lesser degree of collapse of ego boundaries and attendant ecstasy. It is because of this collapse of ego boundaries that we may shout at the moment of climax "I love you" or "Oh, God." to a prostitute for whom moments later, after the ego boundaries have snapped back into place, we may feel no shred of affection, liking or investment. This is not to say that the ecstasy of the orgasmic experience cannot be heightened by sharing it with one who is beloved; it can. But even without a beloved partner or any partner the collapse of ego boundaries occurring in conjunction with orgasm may be total; for a second we may totally forget who we are, lose track of self, be lost in time and space, be outside of ourself, be transported. We may become one with the universe. But only for a second.

In describing the prolonged "oneness with the universe" associated with real love as compared to the momentary oneness of orgasm, I used the words "mystical union." Mysticism is essentially a belief that reality is oneness. The most literal of mystics believe that our common perception of the universe as containing multitudes of discrete objects—stars, planets, trees, birds, houses, ourselves—all separated from one another by boundaries is a misperception, an illusion. To this consensual misperception, this world of illusion that most of us mistakenly believe to be real, Hindus and Buddhists apply the word "Maya." They and other mystics hold that true reality can be known only by experiencing the oneness through a giving up of ego boundaries. It is impossible to really see the unity of the universe as long as one continues to see oneself as a discrete object, separate and distinguishable from the rest of the universe in any way, shape or form. Hindus and Buddhists frequently hold, therefore, that the infant before the development of ego boundaries knows reality, while adults do not. Some even suggest that the path toward enlightenment or knowledge of the oneness of reality requires that we regress or make ourselves like infants. This can be a dangerously tempting doctrine for certain adolescents and young adults who are not prepared to assume adult responsibilities, which seem frightening and overwhelming and demanding beyond their capacities. "I do not have to go through all this," such a person may think. "I can give up trying to be an adult and retreat from adult demands into sainthood." Schizophrenia, however, rather than sainthood, is achieved by acting on this supposition.

Most mystics understand the truth that was elaborated at the end of the discussion of discipline: namely, that we must possess or achieve something before we can give it up and still maintain our competence and viability. The infant without its ego boundaries may be in closer touch with reality than its parents, but it is incapable of surviving without the care of these parents and incapable of communicating its wisdom. The path to sainthood goes through adulthood. There are no quick and easy shortcuts. Ego boundaries must be hardened before they can be softened. An identity must be established before it can be transcended. One must find one's self before one can lose it. The temporary release from ego boundaries associated with falling in love, sexual intercourse or the use of certain psychoactive drugs may provide us with a glimpse of Nirvana, but not with Nirvana itself. It is a thesis of this book that Nirvana or lasting enlightenment or true spiritual growth can be achieved only through the persistent exercise of real love.

In summary, then, the temporary loss of ego boundaries involved in falling in love and in sexual intercourse not only leads us to make commitments to other people from which real love may begin but also gives us a foretaste of (and therefore an incentive for) the more lasting mystical ecstasy that can be ours after a lifetime of love. As such, therefore, while falling in love is not itself love, it is a part of the great and mysterious scheme of love.

Dependency

The second most common misconception about love is the idea that dependency is love. This is a misconception with which psychotherapists must deal on a daily basis. Its effect is seen most dramatically in an individual who makes an attempt or gesture or threat to commit suicide or who becomes incapacitatingly depressed in response to a rejection or separation from spouse or lover. Such a person says, "I do not want to live, I cannot live without my husband [wife, girl friend, boyfriend], I love him [or her] so much." And when I respond, as I frequently do, "You are mistaken; you do not love your husband [wife, girl friend, boyfriend]." "What do you mean?" is the angry question. "I just told you I can't live without him [or her]." I try to explain. "What you describe is parasitism, not love. When you require another individual for your survival, you are a parasite on that individual. There is no choice, no freedom involved in your relationship. It is a matter of necessity rather than love. Love is the free exercise of choice. Two people love each other only when they are quite capable of living without each other but *choose* to live with each other."

I define dependency as the inability to experience wholeness or to function adequately without the certainty that one is being actively cared for by another. Dependency in physical healthy adults is pathological—it is sick, always a manifestation of a mental illness or defect. It is to be distinguished from what are commonly referred to as dependency needs or feelings. We all—each and every one of us—even if we try to pretend to others and to ourselves that we don't—have dependency needs and feelings. All of us have desires to be babied, to be nurtured without effort on our parts, to be cared for by persons stronger than us who have our interests truly at heart. No matter how strong we are, no matter how caring and responsible and adult, if we look clearly into ourselves we will find the wish to be taken care of for a change. Each one of us, no matter how old and mature, looks for and would like to have in his or her life a satisfying mother figure and father figure. But for most of us these desires or feelings do not rule our lives; they are not the predominant theme of our existence. When they do rule our lives and dictate the quality of our existence, then we have something more than just dependency needs or feelings; we are dependent. Specifically, one whose life is ruled and dictated by dependency needs suffers from a psychiatric disorder to which we ascribe the diagnostic name "passive dependent personality disorder." It is perhaps the most common of all psychiatric disorders.

People with this disorder, passive dependent people, are so busy seeking to be loved that they have no energy left to love. They are like starving people, scrounging wherever they can for food, and with no food of their own to give to others. It is as if within them they have an inner emptiness, a bottomless pit crying out to be filled but which can never be completely filled. They never feel "full-filled" or have a sense of completeness. They always feel "a part of me is missing." They tolerate loneliness very poorly. Because of their lack of wholeness they have no real sense of identity, and they define themselves solely by their relationships. A thirty-year-old punch press operator, extremely depressed, came to see me three days after his wife had left him, taking their two children. She had threatened to leave him three times before, complaining of his total lack of attention to her and the children. Each time he had pleaded with her to remain and had promised to change, but his change had never lasted more than a day, and this time she had carried out her threat. He had not slept for two nights, was trembling with anxiety, had tears streaming down his face and was seriously contemplating suicide. "I can't live without my family," he said, weeping, "I love them so."

"I'm puzzled," I said to him. "You've told me that your wife's complaints were valid, that you never did anything for her, that you came home only when you pleased, that you weren't interested in her sexually or emotionally, that you wouldn't even talk to the children for months on end, that you never played with them or took them anywhere. You have no relationship with any of your family, so I don't understand why you're so depressed over the loss of a relationship that never existed."

"Don't you see?" he replied. "I'm nothing now. Nothing. I have no wife. I have no children. I don't know who I am. I may not care for them, but I must love them. I am nothing without them."

Because he was so seriously depressed—having lost the identity that his family gave him—I made an appointment to see him again two days later. I expected little improvement. But when he returned he bounced into the office grinning cheerfully and announced, "Everything's OK now."

"Did you get back together with your family?" I asked.

"Oh, no," he replied happily, "I haven't heard from them since I saw you. But I did meet a girl last night down at my bar. She said she really likes me. She's separated, just like me. We've got a date again tonight. I feel like I'm human once more. I guess I don't have to see you again."

This rapid changeability is characteristic of passive dependent individuals. It is as if it does not matter whom they are dependent upon as long as there is just someone. It does not matter what their identity is as long as there is someone to give it to them. Consequently their relationships, although seemingly dramatic in their intensity, are actually extremely shallow. Because of the strength of their sense of inner emptiness and the hunger to fill it, passive dependent people will brook no delay in gratifying their need for others. A beautiful, brilliant and in some ways very healthy young woman had, from the age of seventeen to twenty-one, an almost endless series of sexual relationships with men invariably beneath her in terms of intelligence and capability. She went from one loser to the next. The problem as it emerged was that she was unable to wait long enough to seek out a man suited to her or even to choose from among the many men almost immediately available to her. Within twenty-four hours after the ending of a relationship she would pick up the first man she met in a bar and would come into her next therapy session singing his praises. "I know he's unemployed and drinks too much, but basically he's very talented, and he really cares for me. I know this relationship will work."

But it never did work, not only because she had not chosen well but also because she would then begin a pattern of clinging to the man, demanding more and more evidence of his affection, seeking to be with him constantly, refusing to be left alone. "It is because I love you so much that I cannot bear to be separated from you," she would tell him, but sooner or later he would feel totally stifled and trapped, without room to move, by her "love." A violent blow-up would occur, the relationship would be terminated and the cycle would begin all over again the next day. The woman was able to break the cycle only after three years of therapy, during which she came to appreciate her own intelligence and assets, to identify her emptiness and hunger and distinguish it from genuine love, to realize how her hunger was driving her to initiate and cling to relationships that were detrimental to her, and to accept the necessity for the strictest kind of discipline over her hunger if she was to capitalize on her assets.

In the diagnosis the word "passive" is used in conjunction with the word "dependent" because these individuals concern themselves with what others can do for them to the exclusion of what they themselves can do. Once, working with a group of five single patients, all passive dependent people, I asked them to speak of their goals in terms of what life situations they wanted to find themselves in five years hence. In one way or another each of them replied, "I want to be married to

someone who really cares for me." Not one mentioned holding down a challenging job, creating a work of art, making a
contribution to the community, being in a position where he
or she could love or even have children. The notion of effort
was not involved in their daydreams; they envisioned only an
effortless passive state of receiving care. I told them, as I tell
many others: "If being loved is your goal, you will fail to
achieve it. The only way to be assured of being loved is to be
a person worthy of love, and you cannot be a person worthy
of love when your primary goal in life is to passively be
loved." This is not to say that passive dependent people never
do things for others, but their motive in doing things is to
cement the attachment of the others to them so as to assure
their own care. And when the possibility of care from another
is not directly involved, they do have great difficulty in "doing
things." All the members of the aforementioned group found
it agonizingly difficult to buy a house, separate from their
parents, locate a job, leave a totally unsatisfactory old job or
even invest themselves in a hobby.

In marriage there is normally a differentiation of the roles
of the two spouses, a normally efficient division of labor between them. The woman usually does the cooking, housecleaning and shopping and cares for the children; the man
usually maintains employment, handles the finances, mows
the lawn and makes repairs. Healthy couples instinctively will
switch roles from time to time. The man may cook a meal
now and then, spend one day a week with the children, clean
the house to surprise his wife; the woman may get a part-time
job, mow the lawn on her husband's birthday, or take over
the checking account and bill-paying for a year. The couple
may often think of this role switching as a kind of play that
adds spice and variety to their marriage. It is this, but perhaps
more important (even if it is done unconsciously), it is a process that diminishes their mutual dependency. In a sense,
each spouse is training himself or herself for survival in the
event of the loss of the other. But for passive dependent people the loss of the other is such a frightening prospect that

they cannot face preparing for it or tolerating a process that would diminish the dependency or increase the freedom of the other. Consequently it is one of the behavioral hallmarks of passive dependent people in marriage that their role differentiation is rigid, and they seek to increase rather than diminish mutual dependency so as to make marriage more rather than less of a trap. By so doing, in the name of what they call love but what is really dependency, they diminish their own and each other's freedom and stature. Occasionally, as part of this process, passive dependent people when married will actually forsake skills that they had gained before marriage. An example of this is the not uncommon syndrome of the wife who "can't" drive a car. Half the time in such situations she may never have learned, but in the remaining cases, sometimes allegedly because of a minor accident, she develops a "phobia" about driving at some point after marriage and stops. The effect of this "phobia" in rural and suburban areas, where most people live, is to render her almost totally dependent on her husband and chain her husband to her by her helplessness. Now he must do all the shopping for the family himself or he must chauffeur her on all shopping expeditions. Because this behavior usually gratifies the dependency needs of both spouses, it is almost never seen as sick or even as a problem to be solved by most couples. When I suggested to an otherwise extremely intelligent banker that his wife, who suddenly stopped driving at age forty-six because of a "phobia," might have a problem deserving of psychiatric attention, he said "Oh, no, the doctor told her it was because of menopause, and you can't do anything about that." She was secure in the knowledge that he would not have an affair and leave her because he was so busy after work taking her shopping and driving the children around. He was secure in the knowledge that she would not have an affair and leave him because she did not have the mobility to meet people when he was away from her. Through such behavior, passive dependent marriages may be made lasting and secure, but they cannot be considered either healthy or genuinely loving, because the security is purchased at the price of freedom and the relationship serves to retard or destroy the growth of the individual partners. Again and again we tell our couples that "a good marriage can exist only between two strong and independent people."

Passive dependency has its genesis in lack of love. The inner feeling of emptiness from which passive dependent people suffer is the direct result of their parents' failure to fulfill their needs for affection, attention and care during their childhood. It was mentioned in the first section that children who are loved and cared for with relative consistency throughout childhood enter adulthood with a deepseated feeling that they are lovable and valuable and therefore will be loved and cared for as long as they remain true to themselves. Children growing up in an atmosphere in which love and care are lacking or given with gross inconsistency enter adulthood with no such sense of inner security. Rather, they have an inner sense of insecurity, a feeling of "I don't have enough" and a sense that the world is unpredictable and ungiving, as well as a sense of themselves as being questionably lovable and valuable. It is no wonder, then, that they feel the need to scramble for love, care and attention wherever they can find it, and once having found it, cling to it with a desperation that leads them to unloving, manipulative, Machiavellian behavior that destroys the very relationships they seek to preserve. As also indicated in the previous section, love and discipline go hand in hand, so that unloving, uncaring parents are people lacking in discipline, and when they fail to provide their children with a sense of being loved, they also fail to provide them with the capacity for self-discipline. Thus the excessive dependency of the passive dependent individuals is only the principal manifestation of their personality disorder. Passive dependent people lack self-discipline. They are unwilling or unable to delay gratification of their hunger for attention. In their desperation to form and preserve attachments they throw honesty to the winds. They cling to outworn relationships when they should give them up. Most important, they lack a sense of responsibility for themselves. They passively look to others, frequently even their own children, as the source of their happiness and full-fillment, and therefore when they are not happy or fulfilled they basically feel that others are responsible. Consequently they are endlessly angry, because they endlessly feel let down by others who can never in reality fulfill all their needs or "make" them happy. I have a colleague who often tells people, "Look, allowing yourself to be dependent on another person is the worst possible thing you can do to yourself. You would be better off being dependent on heroin. As long as you have a supply of it, heroin will never let you down; if it's there, it will always make you happy. But if you expect another person to make you happy, you'll be endlessly disappointed." As a matter of fact, it is no accident that the most common disturbance that passive dependent people manifest beyond their relationships to others is dependency on drugs and alcohol. Theirs is the "addictive personality." They are addicted to people, sucking on them and gobbling them up, and when people are not available to be sucked and gobbled, they often turn to the bottle or the needle or the pill as a people-substitute.

In summary, dependency may appear to be love because it is a force that causes people to fiercely attach themselves to one another. But in actuality it is not love; it is a form of antilove. It has its genesis in a parental failure to love and it perpetuates the failure. It seeks to receive rather than to give. It nourishes infantilism rather than growth. It works to trap and constrict rather than to liberate. Ultimately it destroys rather than builds relationships, and it destroys rather than builds people.

Cathexis Without Love

One of the aspects of dependency is that it is unconcerned with spiritual growth. Dependent people are interested in their own nourishment, but no more; they desire filling, they desire to be happy; they don't desire to grow, nor are they willing to tolerate the unhappiness, the loneliness and suffering involved in growth. Neither do dependent people care about the spiritual growth of the other, the object of their dependency; they care only that the other is there to satisfy them. Dependency is but one of the forms of behavior to which we incorrectly apply the word "love" when concern for spiritual evolution is absent. We will now consider other such forms, and we hope to demonstrate again that love is never nurturance or cathexis without regard to spiritual growth.

We frequently speak of people loving inanimate objects or activities. Thus we say, "He loves money" or "He loves power" or "He loves to garden" or "He loves to play golf." Certainly an individual may extend himself or herself much beyond ordinary personal limits, working sixty, seventy, eighty hours a week to amass wealth or power. Yet despite the extent of one's fortune or influence, all this work and accumulation may not be self-enlarging at all. Indeed, we may often say about a self-made tycoon, "He's a small person, mean and petty." While we may talk about how much this person loves money or power, we frequently do not perceive him as a loving person. Why is this so? It is because wealth or power have become for such people ends in themselves rather than means to a spiritual goal. The only true end of love is spiritual growth or human evolution.

Hobbies are self-nurturing activities. In loving ourselves— that is, nurturing ourselves for the purpose of spiritual growth —we need to provide ourselves with all kinds of things that are not directly spiritual. To nourish the spirit the body must also be nourished. We need food and shelter. No matter how dedicated we are to spiritual development, we also need rest and relaxation, exercise and distraction. Saints must sleep and even prophets must play. Thus hobbies may be a means through which we love ourselves. But if a hobby becomes an end in itself, then it becomes a substitute for rather than a means to self-development. Sometimes it is precisely because they are substitutes for self-development that hobbies are so popular. On golf courses, for instance, one may find some aging men and women whose chief remaining goal in life is to knock a few more strokes off their game. This dedicated effort to improve their skill serves to give them a sense of progress in life and thereby assists them in ignoring the reality that they have actually stopped progressing, having given up the effort to improve themselves as human beings. If they loved themselves more they would not allow themselves to passionately settle for such a shallow goal and narrow future.

On the other hand, power and money may be means to a loving goal. A person may, for instance, suffer a career in politics for the primary purpose of utilizing political power for the betterment of the human race. Or some people may yearn for riches, not for money's sake but in order to send their children to college or provide themselves with the freedom and time for study and reflection which are necessary for their own spiritual growth. It is not power or money that such people love; it is humanity.

Among the things that I am saying here and throughout this section of the book is that our use of the word "love" is so generalized and unspecific as to severely interfere with our understanding of love. I have no great expectation that the language will change in this respect. Yet as long as we continue to use the word "love" to describe our relationship with anything that is important to us, anything we cathect, with-

out regard for the quality of that relationship, we will continue to have difficulty discerning the difference between the
wise and the foolish, the good and the bad, the noble and the
ignoble.

Using our more specific definition, it is clear, for instance,
that we can love only human beings. For, as we generally
conceive of things, it is only human beings who possess a
spirit capable of substantial growth.* Consider the matter of
pets. We "love" the family dog. We feed it and bathe it, pet it
and cuddle it, discipline it and play with it. When it is sick
we may drop everything and rush it to the veterinarian. When
it runs away or dies we may be grief-stricken. Indeed, for
some lonely people without children, their pets may become
the sole reason for their existence. If this is not love, then
what is? But let us examine the differences between our relationship with a pet and that with another human being. First
of all, the extent of our communication with our pets is extremely limited in comparison with the extent to which we
may communicate with other humans if we work at it. We do
not know what our pets are thinking. This lack of knowledge
allows us to project onto our pets our own thoughts and feelings, and thereby to feel an emotional closeness with them
which may not correspond to reality at all. Second, we find
our pets satisfactory only insofar as their wills coincide with
ours. This is the basis on which we generally select our pets,
and if their wills begin to diverge significantly from our own,
we get rid of them. We don't keep pets around very long when
they protest or fight back against us. The only school to which

* I recognize the possibility that this conception may be a false one;
that all matter, animate and inanimate, may possess spirit. The distinction of ourselves as humans being different from "lower" animals and
plants and from inanimate earth and rocks, is a manifestation of maya,
or illusion, in the mystical frame of reference. There are levels of understanding. In this book I am dealing with love at a certain level.
Unfortunately my skills of communicating are inadequate to encompass
more than one level at a time or to do more than provide an occasional
glimpse of a level other than the one on which I am communicating.

we send our pets for the development of their minds or spirits is obedience school. Yet it is possible for us to desire that other humans develop a "will of their own"; indeed, it is this desire for the differentiation of the other that is one of the characteristics of genuine love. Finally, in our relationship with pets we seek to foster their dependency. We do not want them to grow up and leave home. We want them to stay put, to lie dependably near the hearth. It is their attachment to us rather than their independence from us that we value in our pets.

This matter of the "love" of pets is of immense import because many, many people are capable of "loving" *only* pets and incapable of genuinely loving other human beings. Large numbers of American soldiers had idyllic marriages to German, Italian or Japanese "war brides" with whom they could not verbally communicate. But when their brides learned English, the marriages began to fall apart. The servicemen could then no longer project upon their wives their own thoughts, feelings, desires and goals and feel the same sense of closeness one feels with a pet. Instead, as their wives learned English, the men began to realize that these women had ideas, opinions and aims different from their own. As this happened, love began to grow for some; for most, perhaps, it ceased. The liberated woman is right to beware of the man who affectionately calls her his "pet." He may indeed be an individual whose affection is dependent upon her being a pet, who lacks the capacity to respect her strength, independence and individuality. Probably the most saddening example of this phenomenon is the very large number of women who are capable of "loving" their children only as infants. Such women can be found everywhere. They may be ideal mothers until their children reach the age of two—infinitely tender, joyously breast-feeding, cuddling and playing with their babies, consistently affectionate, totally dedicated to their nurture, and blissfully happy in their motherhood. Then, almost overnight, the picture changes. As soon as a child begins to assert its own will—to disobey, to whine, to refuse to play, to oc-

casionally reject being cuddled, to attach itself to other people, to move out into the world a little bit on its own—the
mother's love ceases. She loses interest in the child, decathects
it, perceives it only as a nuisance. At the same time she will
often feel an almost overpowering need to be pregnant again,
to have another infant, another pet. Usually she will succeed,
and the cycle is repeated. If not, she may be seen avidly
seeking to baby-sit for the infant children of neighbors while
almost totally ignoring the pleas of her own older child or
children for attention. For her children the "terrible twos" are
not only the end of their infancy, they are also the end of the
experience of being loved by mother. The pain and deprivation they experience are obvious to all except their mother,
busy with her new infant. The effect of this experience is
usually evidenced as the children grow to adulthood in a depressive and/or passive dependent personality pattern.

What this suggests is that the "love" of infants and pets and
even dependently obedient spouses is an instinctual pattern of
behavior to which it is quite appropriate to apply the term
"maternal instinct" or, more generally, "parental instinct."
We can liken this to the instinctual behavior of "falling in
love": it is not a genuine form of love in that it is relatively
effortless, and it is not totally an act of will or choice; it
encourages the survival of the species but is not directed toward its improvement or spiritual growth; it is close to love in
that it is a reaching out for others and serves to initiate interpersonal bonds from which real love might begin; but a good
deal more is required to develop a healthy, creative marriage,
raise a healthy, spiritually growing child or contribute to the
evolution of humanity.

The point is that nurturing can be and usually should be
much more than simple feeding, and that nurturing spiritual
growth is an infinitely more complicated process than can be
directed by any instinct. The mother mentioned at the beginning of this section who would not let her son take the bus to
school is a case in point. By driving him to and from school
she was nurturing him in a sense, but it was a nurturing he

did not need and that clearly retarded rather than furthered his spiritual growth. Other examples abound: mothers who push food on their already overweight children; fathers who buy their sons whole roomfuls of toys and their daughters whole closetfuls of clothes; parents who set no limits and deny no desires. Love is not simply giving; it is *judicious* giving and judicious withholding as well. It is judicious praising and judicious criticizing. It is judicious arguing, struggling, confronting, urging, pushing and pulling in addition to comforting. It is leadership. The word "judicious" means requiring judgment, and judgment requires more than instinct; it requires thoughtful and often painful decisionmaking.

"Self-Sacrifice"

The motives behind injudicious giving and destructive nurturing are many, but such cases invariably have a basic feature in common: the "giver," under the guise of love, is responding to and meeting his or her own needs without regard to the spiritual needs of the receiver. A minister reluctantly came to see me because his wife was suffering from a chronic depression and both his sons had dropped out of college and were living at home and receiving psychiatric attention. Despite the fact that his whole family was "ill," he was initially completely unable to comprehend that he might be playing a role in their illnesses. "I do everything in my power to take care of them and their problems," he reported. "I don't have a waking moment when I am not concerned about them." Analysis of the situation revealed that this man was indeed working himself to the bone to meet the demands of his wife and children. He had given both of his sons new cars and paid the insurance on them even though he felt the boys should be putting more effort into being self-supporting. Each week he took his wife to the opera or the theater in the city even though he intensely disliked going to the city, and opera bored him to death. Busy though he was on his job, he spent most of his free time at home picking up after his wife and sons, who had a total disregard for housecleaning. "Don't you get tired of laying yourself out for them all the time?" I asked him. "Of course," he replied, "but what else am I to do? I love them and I have too much compassion not to take care of them. My concern for them is so great that I will never allow myself to stand by as long as they have needs to be filled. I may not be a brilliant man, but at least I have love and concern."

Interestingly, it emerged that his own father had been a brilliant scholar of considerable renown, but also an alcoholic and philanderer who showed a total lack of concern for the family and was grossly neglectful of them. Gradually my patient was helped to see that as a child he had vowed to be as different from his father as possible, to be as compassionate and concerned as his father was heartless and unconcerned. He was even able to understand after a while that he had a tremendous stake in maintaining an image of himself as loving and compassionate, and that much of his behavior, including his career in the ministry, had been devoted to fostering this image. What he did not understand so easily was the degree to which he was infantilizing his family. He continually referred to his wife as "my kitten" and to his fullgrown, strapping sons as "my little ones." "How else can I behave?" he pleaded. "I may be loving in reaction to my father, but that doesn't mean I'm going to become unloving or turn myself into a bastard." What he literally had to be taught was that loving is a complicated rather than a simple activity, requiring the participation of his entire being—his head as well as his heart. Because of his need to be as unlike his father as possible, he had not been able to develop a flexible response system for expressing his love. He had to learn that not giving at the right time was more compassionate than giving at the wrong time, and that fostering independence was more loving than taking care of people who could otherwise take care of themselves. He even had to learn that expressing his own needs, anger, resentments and expectations was every bit as necessary to the mental health of his family as his self-sacrifice, and therefore that love must be manifested in confrontation as much as in beatific acceptance.

Gradually coming to realize how he infantilized his family, he began to make changes. He stopped picking up after everyone and became openly angry when his sons did not adequately participate in the care of the home. He refused to continue paying for the insurance on his sons' cars, telling them that if they wanted to drive they would have to pay for it themselves. He suggested that his wife should go alone to the opera in New York. In making these changes he had to risk appearing to be the "bad guy" and had to give up the omnipotence of his former role as provider for all the needs of the family. But even though his previous behavior had been motivated primarily by a need to maintain an image of himself as a loving person, he had at his core a capacity for genuine love, and because of this capacity he was able to accomplish these alterations in himself. Both his wife and his sons reacted to these changes initially with anger. But soon one son went back to college, and the other found a more demanding job and got an apartment for himself. His wife began to enjoy her new independence and to grow in ways of her own. The man found himself becoming more effective as a minister and at the same time his life became more enjoyable.

The minister's misguided love bordered on the more serious perversion of love that is masochism. Laymen tend to associate sadism and masochism with purely sexual activity, thinking of them as the sexual enjoyment derived from inflicting or receiving physical pain. Actually, true sexual sadomasochism is a relatively uncommon form of psychopathology. Much, much more common, and ultimately more serious, is the phenomenon of social sadomasochism, in which people unconsciously desire to hurt and be hurt by each other through their nonsexual interpersonal relations. Prototypically a woman will seek psychiatric attention for depression in response to desertion by her husband. She will regale the psychiatrist with an endless tale of repeated mistreatment by her husband: he paid her no attention, he had a string of mistresses, he gambled away the food money, he went away for days at a time whenever he pleased, he came home drunk and beat her, and now, finally, he's deserted her and the children on Christmas Eve—Christmas Eve yet! The neophyte therapist tends to respond to this "poor woman" and her tale with instant sympathy, but it does not take long for the sympathy to evaporate in the light of further knowledge. First the therapist discovers that this pattern of mistreatment has existed for twenty years, and that while the poor woman divorced her brute of a husband twice, she also remarried him twice, and that innumerable separations were followed by innumerable reconciliations. Next, after working with her for a month or two to assist her in gaining independence, and when everything seemingly is going well and the woman appears to be enjoying the tranquillity of life apart from her husband, the therapist sees the cycle enacted all over again. The woman happily bounces into the office one day to announce, "Well, Henry's come back. He called up the other night saying he wanted to see me, so I did see him. He pleaded with me to come back, and he really seems changed, so I took him back." When the therapist points out that this seems to be but a repetition of a pattern they had agreed was destructive, the woman says, "But I love him. You can't deny love." If the therapist attempts to examine this "love" with any strenuousness, then the patient terminates therapy.

What is going on here? In trying to understand what has happened, the therapist recalls the obvious relish with which the woman had recounted the long history of her husband's brutality and mistreatment. Suddenly a strange idea begins to dawn; maybe this woman endures her husband's mistreatment, and even seeks it out, for the very pleasure of talking about it. But what would be the nature of such pleasure? The therapist remembers the woman's self-righteousness. Could it be that the most important thing in the woman's life is to have a sense of moral superiority and that in order to maintain this sense she needs to be mistreated? The nature of the pattern now becomes clear. By allowing herself to be treated basely she can feel superior. Ultimately she can even have the sadistic pleasure of seeing her husband beg and plead to return, and momentarily acknowledge her superiority from his humbled position, while she decides whether or not to magnanimously take him back. And in this moment she achieves her revenge. When such women are examined it is generally found that they were particularly humiliated as children. As a result they seek revenge through their sense of moral superiority, which requires repeated humiliation and mistreatment. If the world is treating us well we have no need to avenge ourselves on it. If seeking revenge is our goal in life, we will have to see to it that the world treats us badly in order to justify our goal. Masochists look on their submission to mistreatment as love, whereas in fact it is a necessity in their never-ceasing search for revenge and is basically motivated by hatred.

The issue of masochism highlights still another very major misconception about love—that it is self-sacrifice. By virtue of this belief the prototypical masochist was enabled to see her tolerance of mistreatment as self-sacrifice and hence as love, and therefore did not have to acknowledge her hatred. The minister also saw his self-sacrificial behavior as love, although actually it was motivated not by the needs of his family but by his own need to maintain an image of himself. Early in his treatment he would continually talk about how he "did things for" his wife and his children, leading one to believe that he himself got nothing out of such acts. But he did. Whenever we think of ourselves as doing something *for* someone else, we are in some way denying our own responsibility.

Whatever we do is done because we choose to do it, and we make that choice because it is the one that satisfies us the most. Whatever we do for someone else we do because it fulfills a need we have. Parents who say to their children, "You should be grateful for all that we have done for you" are invariably parents who are lacking in love to a significant degree. Anyone who genuinely loves knows the pleasure of loving. When we genuinely love we do so because we *want* to love. We have children because we want to have children, and if we are loving parents, it is because we want to be loving parents. It is true that love involves a change in the self, but this is an extension of the self rather than a sacrifice of the self. As will be discussed again later, genuine love is a self-replenishing activity. Indeed, it is even more; it enlarges rather than diminishes the self; it fills the self rather than depleting it. In a real sense love is as selfish as nonlove. Here again there is a paradox in that love is both selfish and unselfish at the same time. It is not selfishness or unselfishness that distinguishes love from nonlove; it is the aim of the action. In the case of genuine love the aim is always spiritual growth. In the case of nonlove the aim is always something else.

Love Is Not a Feeling

I have said that love is an action, an activity. This leads to the final major misconception of love which needs to be addressed. Love is not a feeling. Many, many people possessing a feeling of love and even acting in response to that feeling act in all manner of unloving and destructive ways. On the other hand, a genuinely loving individual will often take loving and constructive action toward a person he or she consciously dislikes, actually feeling no love toward the person at the time and perhaps even finding the person repugnant in some way.

The feeling of love is the emotion that accompanies the experience of cathecting. Cathecting, it will be remembered, is the process by which an object becomes important to us. Once cathected, the object, commonly referred to as a "love object," is invested with our energy as if it were a part of ourselves, and this relationship between us and the invested object is called a cathexis. Since we may have many such relationships going on at the same time, we speak of our cathexes. The process of withdrawing our energy from a love object so that it loses its sense of importance for us is known as decathecting. The misconception that love is a feeling exists because we confuse cathecting with loving. This confusion is understandable since they are similar processes, but there are also striking differences. First of all, as has been pointed out, we may cathect any object, animate or inanimate, with or without a spirit. Thus a person may cathect the stock market or a piece of jewelry and may feel love for these things. Second, the fact that we have cathected another human being does not mean that we care a whit for that person's spiritual development. The dependent person, in fact, usually fears the spiritual development of a cathected spouse. The mother who insisted upon driving her adolescent son to and from school clearly cathected the boy; he was important to her— but his spiritual growth was not. Third, the intensity of our cathexes frequently has nothing to do with wisdom or commitment. Two strangers may meet in a bar and cathect each other in such a way that nothing—not previously scheduled appointments, promises made, or family stability—is more important for the moment than their sexual consummation. Finally, our cathexes may be fleeting and momentary. Immediately following their sexual consummation the just-mentioned couple may find each other unattractive and undesirable. We may decathect something almost as soon as we have cathected it.

Genuine love, on the other hand, implies commitment and

the exercise of wisdom. When we are concerned for someone's spiritual growth, we know that a lack of commitment is likely to be harmful and that commitment to that person is probably necessary for us to manifest our concern effectively. It is for this reason that commitment is the cornerstone of the psychotherapeutic relationship. It is almost impossible for a patient to experience significant personality growth without a "therapeutic alliance" with the therapist. In other words, before the patient can risk major change he or she must feel the strength and security that come from believing that the therapist is the patient's constant and stable ally. For this alliance to occur the therapist must demonstrate to the patient, usually over a considerable length of time, the consistent and steadfast caring that can arise only from a capacity for commitment. This does not mean that the therapist always *feels* like listening to the patient. Commitment means that the therapist listens to the patient, like it or not. It is no different in a marriage. In a constructive marriage, just as in constructive therapy, the partners must regularly, routinely and predictably, attend to each other and their relationship no matter how they feel. As has been mentioned, couples sooner or later always fall out of love, and it is at the moment when the mating instinct has run its course that the opportunity for genuine love begins. It is when the spouses no longer feel like being in each other's company always, when they would rather be elsewhere some of the time, that their love begins to be tested and will be found to be present or absent.

This is not to say that the partners in a stable, constructive relationship such as intensive psychotherapy or marriage do not cathect each other and the relationship itself in various ways; they do. What it does say is that genuine love transcends the matter of cathexes. When love exists it does so with or without cathexis and with or without a loving feeling. It is easier—indeed, it is fun—to love with cathexis and the feeling of love. But it is possible to love without cathexis and without loving feelings, and it is in the fulfillment of this possibility that genuine and transcendent love is distinguished from simple cathexis. The key word in this distinction is "will." I have defined love as the *will* to extend oneself for the purpose of nurturing one's own and another's spiritual growth. Genuine love is volitional rather than emotional. The person who truly loves does so because of a decision to love. This person has made a commitment to be loving whether or not the loving feeling is present. If it is, so much the better; but if it isn't, the commitment to love, the will to love, still stands and is still exercised. Conversely, it is not only possible but necessary for a loving person to avoid acting on feelings of love. I may meet a woman who strongly attracts me, whom I feel like loving, but because it would be destructive to my marriage to have an affair at that time, I will say vocally or in the silence of my heart, "I feel like loving you, but I am not going to." Similarly, I may refuse to take on a new patient who is most attractive and likely to succeed in therapy because my time is already committed to other patients, some of whom may be considerably less attractive and more difficult. My feelings of love may be unbounded, but my capacity to be loving is limited. I therefore must choose the person on whom to focus my capacity to love, toward whom to direct my will to love. True love is not a feeling by which we are overwhelmed. It is a committed, thoughtful decision.

The common tendency to confuse love with the feeling of love allows people all manner of self-deception. An alcoholic man, whose wife and children are desperately in need of his attention at that very moment, may be sitting in a bar with tears in his eyes, telling the bartender, "I really love my family." People who neglect their children in the grossest of ways more often than not will consider themselves the most loving of parents. It is clear that there may be a self-serving quality in this tendency to confuse love with the feeling of love; it is easy and not at all unpleasant to find evidence of love in one's feelings. It may be difficult and painful to search for evidence of love in one's actions. But because true love is an act of will that often transcends ephemeral feelings of love or cathexis, it is correct to say, "Love is as love does." Love and nonlove, as good and evil, are objective and not purely subjective phenomena.

The Work of Attention

Having looked at some of the things that love is not, let us now examine some that love is. It was mentioned in the introduction to this section that the definition of love implied effort. When we extend ourselves, when we take an extra step or walk an extra mile, we do so in opposition to the inertia of laziness or the resistance of fear. Extension of ourselves or moving out against the inertia of laziness we call work. Moving out in the face of fear we call courage. Love, then, is a form of work or a form of courage. Specifically, it is work or courage directed toward the nurture of our own or another's spiritual growth. We may work or exert courage in directions other than toward spiritual growth, and for this reason all work and all courage is not love. But since it requires the extension of ourselves, love is always either work or courage. If an act is not one of work or courage, then it is not an act of love. There are no exceptions.

The principal form that the work of love takes is attention. When we love another we give him or her our attention; we attend to that's person's growth. When we love ourselves we attend to our own growth. When we attend to someone we are caring for that person. The act of attending requires that we make the effort to set aside our existing preoccupations (as was described in regard to the discipline of bracketing) and actively shift our consciousness. Attention is an act of will, of work against the inertia of our own minds. As Rollo May says, "When we analyze will with all the tools modern psychoanalysis brings us, we shall find ourselves pushed back to the level of attention or intention as the seat of will. The effort which goes into the exercise of the will is really effort of attention; the strain in willing is the effort to keep the consciousness clear, i.e., the strain of keeping the attention focused."*

By far the most common and important way in which we can exercise our attention is by listening. We spend an enormous amount of time listening, most of which we waste, because on the whole most of us listen very poorly. An industrial psychologist once pointed out to me that the amount of time we devote to teaching certain subjects to our children in school is inversely proportional to the frequency with which the children will make use of the subject when they grow up. Thus a business executive will spend roughly an hour of his day reading, two hours talking and eight hours listening. Yet in school we spend a large amount of time teaching children how to read, a very small amount of time teaching them how to speak, and usually no time at all teaching them how to listen. I do not believe it would be a good thing to make what we teach in school exactly proportional to what we do after school, but I do think we would be wise to give our children some instruction in the process of listening—not so that listening can be made easy but rather that they will understand how difficult it is to listen well. Listening well is an exercise of attention and by necessity hard work. It is because they do not realize this or because they are not willing to do the work that most people do not listen well.

Not very long ago I attended a lecture by a famous man on an aspect of the relationship between psychology and religion in which I have long been interested. Because of my interest I had a certain amount of expertise in the subject and immediately recognized the lecturer to be a great sage indeed. I also

* *Love and Will* (New York: Delta Books, Dell Pub., 1969), p. 220.

sensed love in the tremendous effort that he was exerting to communicate, with all manner of examples, highly abstract concepts that were difficult for us, his audience, to comprehend. I therefore listened to him with all the intentness of which I was capable. Throughout the hour and a half he talked sweat was literally dripping down my face in the air-conditioned auditorium. By the time he was finished I had a throbbing headache, the muscles in my neck were rigid from my effort at concentration, and I felt completely drained and exhausted. Although I estimated that I had understood no more than 50 percent of what this great man had said to us that afternoon, I was amazed by the large number of brilliant insights he had given me. Following the lecture, which was well attended by culture-seeking individuals, I wandered about through the audience during a coffee break listening to their comments. Generally they were disappointed. Knowing his reputation, they had expected more. They found him hard to follow and his talk confusing. He was not as competent a speaker as they had hoped to hear. One woman proclaimed to nods of agreement, "He really didn't tell us anything."

In contradistinction to the others, I was able to hear much of what this great man said, precisely because I was willing to do the work of listening to him. I was willing to do this work for two reasons: one, because I recognized his greatness and that what he had to say would likely be of great value; second, because of my interest in the field I deeply wanted to absorb what he had to say so as to enhance my own understanding and spiritual growth. My listening to him was an act of love. I loved him because I perceived him to be a person of great value worth attending to, and I loved myself because I was willing to work on behalf of my growth. Since he was the teacher and I the pupil, he the giver and I the receiver, my love was primarily self-directed, motivated by what I could get out of our relationship and not what I could give him. Nonetheless, it is entirely possible that he could sense within his audience the intensity of my concentration, my attention, my love, and he may have been thereby rewarded. Love, as we shall see again and again, is invariably a two-way street, a reciprocal phenomenon whereby the receiver also gives and the giver also receives.

From this example of listening in the receiver role let us proceed to our most common opportunity to listen in the giver role: listening to children. The process of listening to children differs depending upon the age of the child. For the present let us consider a six-year-old first-grader. Given the chance, a first-grader will talk almost incessantly. How can parents deal with this never-ending chatter? Perhaps the easiest way is to forbid it. Believe it or not, there are families in which the children are virtually not allowed to talk, in which the dictum "Children should be seen and not heard" applies twenty-four hours a day. Such children may be seen, never interacting, silently staring at adults from the corners, mute onlookers from the shadows. A second way is to permit the chatter but simply not listen to it, so that your child is not interacting with you but is literally talking to thin air or to him- or herself, creating background noise that may or may not be annoying. A third way is to pretend to listen, proceeding along as best you can with what you are doing or with your train of thought while appearing to give the child your attention and occasionally making "unh huh" or "that's nice" noises at more or less appropriate times in response to the monologue. A fourth way is selective listening, which is a particularly alert form of pretend listening, wherein parents may prick up their ears if the child seems to be saying something of significance, hoping to separate the wheat from the chaff with a minimum of effort. The problem with this way is that the human mind's capacity to filter selectively is not terribly competent or efficient, with the result that a fair amount of chaff is retained and a great deal of the wheat lost. The fifth and final way, of course, is to truly listen to the child, giving him or her your full and complete attention, weighing each word and understanding each sentence.

These five ways of responding to the talking of children have been represented in ascending order of effort, with the fifth way, true listening, requiring from the parent a quantum leap of energy compared to the less effortful ways. The reader may naïvely suppose that I will recommend to parents that they should always follow the fifth way and always truly listen to their children. Hardly! First of all, the six-year-old's propensity to talk is so great that a parent who always truly listened would have negligible time left to accomplish anything else. Second, the effort required to truly listen is so great that the parent would be too exhausted to accomplish anything else. Finally, it would be unbelievably boring, because the fact of the matter is that the chatter of a six-year-old is generally boring. What is required, therefore, is a balance of all five ways. It is necessary at times to tell children simply to shut up—when, for instance, their talk may be distracting in situations that critically require attention elsewhere or when it may represent a rude interruption of others and an attempt to achieve hostile or unrealistic dominance. Frequently six-year-olds will chatter for the pure joy of chattering, and there is nothing to be served by giving them attention when they are not even requesting it and are quite clearly happy talking to themselves. There are other times when children are not content to talk to themselves but desire to interact with parents, and yet their need can be quite adequately met by pretend listening. At these times what children want from interaction is not communication but simply closeness, and pretend listening will suffice to provide them with the sense of "being with" that they want. Furthermore, children themselves often like to drift in and out of communication and will be understanding of their parents' selective listening, since they are only selectively communicating. They understand this to be the rule of the game. So it is only during a relatively small proportion of their total talking time that six-year-old children need or even desire a response of true and total listening. One of the many extremely complex tasks of parenting is to be able to strike a close to ideal balance of styles of listening and not listening, responding with the appropriate style to a child's varying needs.

Such a balance is frequently not struck because, even though the duration need not be long, many parents are unwilling or unable to expend the energy required for true listening. Perhaps most parents. They may think they are truly listening when all they are doing is pretend listening, or at best selective listening, but this is self-deception, designed to hide from themselves their laziness. For true listening, no matter how brief, requires tremendous effort. First of all, it requires total concentration. You cannot truly listen to anyone and do anything else at the same time. If a parent wants to truly listen to a child, the parent must put aside everything else. The time of true listening must be devoted solely to the child; it must be the child's time. If you are not willing to put aside everything, including your own worries and preoccupations for such a time, then you are not willing to truly listen. Second, the effort required for total concentration on the words of a six-year-old child is considerably greater than that required for listening to a great lecturer. The child's speech patterns are uneven—occasional rushes of words interspersed with pauses and repetitions—which makes concentration difficult. Then the child will usually be talking of matters that have no inherent interest for the adult, whereas the great lecturer's audience is specifically interested in the topic of his speech. In other words, it is dull to listen to a six-year-old, which makes it doubly difficult to keep concentration focused. Consequently truly listening to a child of this age is a real labor of love. Without love to motivate the parent it couldn't be done.

But why bother? Why exert all this effort to focus totally on the boring prattlings of a six-year-old? First, your willingness to do so is the best possible concrete evidence of your esteem you can give your child. If you give your child the same esteem you would give a great lecturer, then the child will know him- or herself to be valued and therefore will feel valuable. There is no better and ultimately no other way to teach your children that they are valuable people than by valuing them. Second, the more children feel valuable, the more they will begin to say things of value. They will rise to your expectation of them. Third, the more you listen to your child, the more you will realize that in amongst the pauses, the stutterings, the seemingly innocent chatter, your child does indeed have valuable things to say. The dictum that great wisdom comes from "the mouths of babes" is recognized as an absolute fact by anyone who truly listens to children. Listen to your child enough and you will come to realize that he or she is quite an extraordinary individual. And the more extraordinary you realize your child to be, the more you will be willing to listen. And the more you will learn. Fourth, the more you know about your child, the more you will be able to teach. Know little about your children, and usually you will be teaching things that either they are not ready to learn or they already know and perhaps understand better than you. Finally, the more children know that you value them, that you consider them extraordinary people, the more willing they will be to listen to you and afford you the same esteem. And the more appropriate your teaching, based on your knowledge of them, the more eager your children will be to learn from you. And the more they learn, the more extraordinary they will become. If the reader senses the cyclical character of this process, he or she is quite correct and is appreciating the truth of the reciprocity of love. Instead of a vicious downward cycle, it is a creative upward cycle of evolution and growth. Value creates value. Love begets love. Parents and child together spin forward faster and faster in the *pas de deux* of love.

We have been talking with a six-year-old in mind. With younger or older children the proper balance of listening and nonlistening differs, but the process is basically the same. With younger children the communication is more and more nonverbal but still ideally requires periods of total concentration. You can't play patty-cake very well when your mind is elsewhere. And if you can only play patty-cake halfheartedly, you are running the risk of having a halfhearted child. Adolescent children require less total listening time from their parents than a six-year-old but even more true listening time. They are much less likely to chatter aimlessly, but when they do talk, they want their parents' full attention even more than do the younger children.

The need for one's parents to listen is never outgrown. A thirty-year-old talented professional man in treatment for feelings of anxiety related to low self-esteem could recall numerous instances in which his parents, also professionals, had been unwilling to listen to what he had to say or had regarded what he had to say as being of little worth and consequence. But of all these memories the most vivid and painful was that of his twenty-second year, when he wrote a lengthy provocative thesis that earned his graduation from college with high honors. Being ambitious for him, his parents were absolutely delighted by the honors he had received. Yet despite the fact that for a whole year he left a copy of the thesis around in full view in the family living room and made frequent hints to his parents that "they might like to have a look at it," neither one of them ever took the time to read it. "I daresay they would have read it," he said toward the end of his therapy, "I daresay they would have even complimented me on it had I gone to them and asked them point-blank, 'Look, would you please, please read my thesis? I want you to know and appreciate the kinds of things I am thinking.' But that would have been begging them to listen to me, and I was damned if at twenty-two I was going to go around begging for their attention. Having to beg for it wouldn't have made me feel any more valuable."

True listening, total concentration on the other, is always a manifestation of love. An essential part of true listening is the discipline of bracketing, the temporary giving up or setting aside of one's own prejudices, frames of reference and desires so as to experience as far as possible the speaker's world from the inside, stepping inside his or her shoes. This unification of speaker and listener is actually an extension and enlargement of ourselves, and new knowledge is always gained from this. Moreover, since true listening involves bracketing, a set-

ting aside of the self, it also temporarily involves a total acceptance of the other. Sensing this acceptance, the speaker will
feel less and less vulnerable and more and more inclined to
open up the inner recesses of his or her mind to the listener.
As this happens, speaker and listener begin to appreciate each
other more and more, and the duet dance of love is again
begun. The energy required for the discipline of bracketing
and the focusing of total attention is so great that it can be
accomplished only by love, by the will to extend oneself for
mutual growth. Most of the time we lack this energy. Even
though we may feel in our business dealings or social relationships that we are listening very hard, what we are usually
doing is listening selectively, with a preset agenda in mind,
wondering as we listen how we can achieve certain desired
results and get the conversation over with as quickly as possible or redirected in ways more satisfactory to us.

Since true listening is love in action, nowhere is it more
appropriate than in marriage. Yet most couples never truly
listen to each other. Consequently, when couples come to us
for counseling or therapy, a major task we must accomplish if
the process is to be successful is to teach them how to listen.
Not infrequently we fail, the energy and discipline involved
being more than they are willing to expend or submit themselves to. Couples are often surprised, even horrified, when
we suggest to them that among the things they should do is
talk to each other by appointment. It seems rigid and unro-
mantic and unspontaneous to them. Yet true listening can
occur only when time is set aside for it and conditions are
supportive of it. It cannot occur when people are driving, or
cooking or tired and anxious to sleep or easily interrupted or
in a hurry. Romantic "love" is effortless, and couples are frequently reluctant to shoulder the effort and discipline of true
love and listening. But when and if they finally do, the results
are superbly gratifying. Again and again we have the experience of hearing one spouse say to another with real joy, once
the process of true listening has been started, "We've been

married twenty-nine years and I never knew that about you before." When this occurs we know that growth in the marriage has begun.

While it is true that one's capacity to truly listen may improve gradually with practice, it never becomes an effortless process. Perhaps the primary requisite for a good psychiatrist is a capacity to truly listen, yet half a dozen times during the average "fifty-minute hour" I will catch myself failing to truly listen to what my patient is saying. Sometimes I may lose the thread of my patient's associations entirely, and it is then necessary for me to say, "I'm sorry, but I allowed my mind to wander for a moment and I was not truly listening to you. Could you run over the past few sentences again?" Interestingly, patients are usually not resentful when this occurs. To the contrary, they seem to understand intuitively that a vital element of the capacity to truly listen is being on the alert for those lapses when one is not truly listening, and my acknowledgment that my attention has wandered actually reassures them that most of the time I am truly listening. This knowledge that one is being truly listened to is frequently in and of itself remarkably therapeutic. In approximately a quarter of our cases, whether patients are adults or children, considerable and even dramatic improvement is shown during the first few months of psychotherapy, before any of the roots of problems have been uncovered or significant interpretations have been made. There are several reasons for this phenomenon, but chief among them, I believe, is the patient's sense that he or she is being truly listened to, often for the first time in years, and perhaps for the first time ever.

While listening is by far the most important form of attention, other forms are also necessary in most loving relationships, particularly with children. The variety of such possible forms is great. One is game-playing. With the infant this will be patty-cake and peekaboo; with the six-year-old it will be magic tricks, go fish, or hide-and-seek; with the twelve-year-old it will be badminton and gin rummy; and so on. Reading to young children is attention, as is helping older ones with their homework. Family activities are important: movies, picnics, drives, trips, fairs, carnivals. Some forms of attention are pure service to the child: sitting on the beach attending a four-year-old or the almost endless chauffeuring required by early adolescents. But what all these forms of attention have in common—and they have it in common with listening as well—is that they involve time spent with the child. Basically, to attend is to spend time with, and the quality of the attention is proportional to the intensity of concentration during that time. The time spent with children in these activities, if used well, gives parents countless opportunities to observe their children and come to know them better. Whether children are good losers or bad, how they do their homework and how they learn, what appeals to them and what doesn't, when they are courageous and when they are frightened in such activities—all are vital pieces of information for the loving parent. This time with the child in activity also gives the parents innumerable opportunities for the teaching of skills and the basic principles of discipline. The usefulness of activity for observing and teaching the child is of course the basic principle of play therapy, and experienced child therapists may become extremely adept at using the time spent with their child patients in play for making significant observations and therapeutic interventions.

Keeping one's eye on a four-year-old at the beach, concentrating on an interminable disjointed story told by a six-year-old, teaching an adolescent how to drive, truly listening to the tale of your spouse's day at the office or laundromat, and understanding his or her problems from the inside, attempting to be as consistently patient and bracketing as much as possible—all these are tasks that are often boring, frequently inconvenient and always energy-draining; they mean work. If we were lazier we would not do them at all. If we were less lazy we would do them more often or better. Since love is work, the essence of nonlove is laziness. The subject of laziness is an extremely important one. It is a hidden theme running throughout the first section on discipline and this one on love. We will focus it specifically in the final section, when we should have a clearer perspective.

The Risk of Loss

The act of love—extending oneself—as I have said, requires a moving out against the inertia of laziness (work) or the resistance engendered by fear (courage). Let us turn now from the work of love to the courage of love. When we extend ourselves, our self enters new and unfamiliar territory, so to speak. Our self becomes a new and different self. We do things we are not accustomed to do. We change. The experience of change, of unaccustomed activity, of being on unfamiliar ground, of doing things differently is frightening. It always was and always will be. People handle their fear of change in different ways, but the fear is inescapable if they are in fact to change. Courage is not the absence of fear; it is the making of action in spite of fear, the moving out against the resistance engendered by fear into the unknown and into the future. On some level spiritual growth, and therefore love, always requires courage and involves risk. It is the risking of love that we will now consider.

If you are a regular churchgoer you might notice a woman in her late forties who every Sunday exactly five minutes before the start of the service inconspicuously takes the same seat in a side pew on the aisle at the very back of the church. The moment the service is over she quietly but quickly makes for the door and is gone before any of the other parishioners and before the minister can come out onto the steps to meet with his flock. Should you manage to accost her—which is unlikely—and invite her to the coffee social hour following the service, she would thank you politely, nervously looking away from you, but tell you that she has a pressing engagement, and would then dash away. Were you to follow her toward her pressing engagement you would find that she returns directly to her home, a little apartment where the blinds are always drawn, unlocks her door, enters, immediately locks the door behind her, and is not seen again that Sunday. If you could keep watch over her you might see that she has a job as a low ranking typist in a large office, where she accepts her assignments wordlessly, types them faultlessly, and returns her finished work without comment. She eats her lunch at her desk and has no friends. She walks home, stopping always at the same impersonal supermarket for a few provisions before she vanishes behind her door until she appears again for the next day's work. On Saturday afternoons she goes alone to a local movie theater that has a weekly change of shows. She has a TV set. She has no phone. She almost never receives mail. Were you somehow able to communicate with her and comment that her life seemed lonely, she would tell you that she rather enjoyed her loneliness. If you asked her if she didn't even have any pets, she would tell you that she had had a dog of whom she was very fond but that he had died eight years before and no other dog could take his place.

Who is this woman? We do not know the secrets of her heart. What we do know is that her whole life is devoted to avoiding risks and that in this endeavor, rather than enlarging her self, she has narrowed and diminished it almost to the point of nonexistence. She cathects no other living thing. Now, we have said that simple cathexis is not love, that love transcends cathexis. This is true, but love requires cathexis for a beginning. We can love only that which in one way or another has importance for us. But with cathexis there is always the risk of loss or rejection. If you move out to another human being, there is always the risk that that person will move away from you, leaving you more painfully alone than you were before. Love anything that lives—a person, a pet, a plant—and it will die. Trust anybody and you may be hurt; depend on anyone and that one may let you down. The price of cathexis is pain. If someone is determined not to risk pain, then such a person must do without many things: having children, getting married, the ecstasy of sex, the hope of ambition, friendship—all that makes life alive, meaningful and significant. Move out or grow in any dimension and pain as well as joy will be your reward. A full life will be full of pain. But the only alternative is not to live fully or not to live at all.

The essence of life is change, a panoply of growth and decay. Elect life and growth, and you elect change and the prospect of death. A likely determinant for the isolated, narrow life of the woman described was an experience or series of experiences with death which she found so painful that she was determined never to experience death again, even at the cost of living. In avoiding the experience of death she had to avoid growth and change. She elected a life of sameness free from the new, the unexpected, a living death, without risk or challenge. I have said that the attempt to avoid legitimate suffering lies at the root of all emotional illness. Not surprisingly, most psychotherapy patients (and probably most non-patients, since neurosis is the norm rather than the exception) have a problem, whether they are young or old, in facing the reality of death squarely and clearly. What is surprising is that the psychiatric literature is only beginning to examine the significance of this phenomenon. If we can live with the knowledge that death is our constant companion, traveling on our "left shoulder," then death can become in the words of Don Juan, our "ally," still fearsome but continually a source of wise counsel.* With death's counsel, the constant awareness of the limit of our time to live and love, we can always

---

* See Carlos Casteneda's *The Teachings of Don Juan: A Yaqui Way of Knowledge*, *A Separate Reality*, *Journey to Ixtlan*, and *Tales of Power*. On a major level these are books about the psychotherapeutic process.

be guided to make the best use of our time and live life to the fullest. But if we are unwilling to fully face the fearsome presence of death on our left shoulder, we deprive ourselves of its counsel and cannot possibly live or love with clarity. When we shy away from death, the ever-changing nature of things, we inevitably shy away from life.

The Risk of Independence

Thus all life itself represents a risk, and the more lovingly we live our lives the more risks we take. Of the thousands, maybe even millions, of risks we can take in a lifetime the greatest is the risk of growing up. Growing up is the act of stepping from childhood into adulthood. Actually it is more of a fearful leap than a step, and it is a leap that many people never really take in their lifetimes. Though they may outwardly appear to be adults, even successful adults, perhaps the majority of "grown-ups" remain until their death psychological children who have never truly separated themselves from their parents and the power that their parents have over them. Perhaps because it was so poignantly personal to me, I feel I can best illustrate the essence of growing up and the enormity of the risk involved by describing the giant step I myself took into adulthood at the end of my fifteenth year— fortunately very early in life. Although this step was a conscious decision, let me preface my account of it by saying that I had no awareness whatsoever at the time that what I was doing was growing up. I only knew that I was leaping into the unknown.

At the age of thirteen I went away from home to Phillips

Exeter Academy, a boy's preparatory school of the very highest reputation, to which my brother had gone before me. I knew that I was fortunate to be going there, because attendance at Exeter was part of a well-defined pattern that would lead me to one of the best Ivy League colleges and from there into the highest echelons of the Establishment, whose doors would be wide open to me on account of my educational background. I felt extremely lucky to have been born the child of well-to-do parents who could afford "the best education that money could buy," and I had a great sense of security which came from being a part of what was so obviously a proper pattern. The only problem was that almost immediately after starting Exeter I became miserably unhappy. The reasons for my unhappiness were totally obscure to me then and are still quite profoundly mysterious to me today. I just did not seem to fit. I didn't seem to fit with the faculty, the students, the courses, the architecture, the social life, the total environment. Yet there seemed nothing to do other than to try to make the best of it and try to mold my imperfections so that I could fit more comfortably into this pattern that had been laid out for me and that was so obviously the right pattern. And try I did for two and a half years. Yet daily my life appeared more meaningless and I felt more wretched. The last year I did little but sleep, for only in sleep could I find any comfort. In retrospect I think perhaps in my sleep I was resting and unconsciously preparing myself for the leap I was about to take. I took it when I returned home for spring vacation of my third year and announced that I was not going to return to school. My father said, "But you can't quit—it's the best education money can buy. Don't you realize what you'd be throwing away?"

"I know it's a good school," I replied, "but I'm not going back."

"Why can't you adjust to it, make another go of it?" my parents asked.

"I don't know," I answered, feeling totally inadequate. "I

don't even know why I hate it so. But I hate it and I'm not going back."

"Well, what are you going to do, then? Since you seem to want to play so loose with your future, just what is it you plan to do?"

Again I miserably replied, "I don't know. All I know is I'm not going back there."

My parents were understandably alarmed and took me forthwith to a psychiatrist, who stated that I was depressed and recommended a month's hospitalization, giving me a day to decide whether or not this was what I wanted. That night was the only time I ever considered suicide. Entering a psychiatric hospital seemed quite appropriate to me. I was, as the psychiatrist said, depressed. My brother had adjusted to Exeter; why couldn't I? I knew that my difficulty in adjusting was entirely my fault, and I felt totally inadequate, incompetent and worthless. Worse, I believed that I was probably insane. Had not my father said, "You must be crazy to throw away such a good education"? If I returned to Exeter I would be returning to all that was safe, secure, right, proper, constructive, proven and known. Yet it was not me. In the depths of my being I knew it was not my path. But what was my path? If I did not return, all that lay ahead was unknown, undetermined, unsafe, insecure, unsanctified, unpredictable. Anyone who would take such a path must be mad. I was terrified. But then, at the moment of my greatest despair, from my unconscious there came a sequence of words, like a strange disembodied oracle from a voice that was not mine: "The only real security in life lies in relishing life's insecurity." Even if it meant being crazy and out of step with all that seemed holy, I had decided to be me. I rested. In the morning I went to see the psychiatrist again and told him that I would never return to Exeter but that I was ready to enter his hospital. I had taken the leap into the unknown. I had taken my destiny into my own hands.

The process of growing up usually occurs very gradually,

with multiple little leaps into the unknown, such as when an eight-year-old boy first takes the risk of riding his bike down to the country store all by himself or a fifteen-year-old goes out on his or her first date. If you doubt that these represent real risks, then you cannot remember the anxiety involved. If you observe even the healthiest of children you will see not only an eagerness to risk new and adult activities but also, side by side, a reluctance, a shrinking back, a clinging to the safe and familiar, a holding onto dependency and childhood. Moreover, on more or less subtle levels, you can find this same ambivalence in an adult, including yourself, with the elderly particularly tending to cling to the old, known and familiar. Almost daily at the age of forty I am presented with subtle opportunities to risk doing things differently, opportunities to grow. I am still growing up, and not as fast as I might. Among all the little leaps we might take, there are also some enormous ones, as when by leaving school I was also forsaking a whole pattern of life and values according to which I had been raised. Many never take any of these potential enormous leaps, and consequently many do not ever really grow up at all. Despite their outward appearances they remain psychologically still very much the children of their parents, living by hand-me-down values, motivated primarily by their parents' approval and disapproval (even when their parents are long dead and buried), never having dared to truly take their destiny into their own hands.

While such great leaps are most commonly made during adolescence, they can be made at any age. A thirty-five-year-old mother of three, married to a controlling, stultifying, inflexible, chauvinistic husband, gradually and painfully comes to realize that her dependency on him and their marriage is a living death. He blocks all her attempts to change the nature of their relationship. With incredible bravery she divorces him, sustaining the burden of his recriminations and the criticism of neighbors, and risks an unknown future alone with her children, but free for the first time in her life to be her own person. Depressed following a heart attack, a fifty-two-year-old businessman looks back on a life of frantic ambition to constantly make more money and rise ever higher in the corporate hierarchy and finds it meaningless. After long reflection he realizes that he has been driven by a need for approval from a domineering, constantly critical mother; he has almost worked himself to death so as to be finally successful in her eyes. Risking and transcending her disapproval for the first time in his life, as well as braving the ire of his high-living wife and children, who are reluctant to give up their expensive life style, he moves to the country and opens up a little shop where he restores antique furniture. Such major changes, such leaps into independence and self-determination, are enormously painful at any age and require supreme courage, yet they are not infrequent results of psychotherapy. Indeed, because of the enormity of the risks involved, they often require psychotherapy for their accomplishment, not because therapy diminishes the risk but because it supports and teaches courage.

But what has this business of growing up to do with love, apart from the fact that the extension of the self involved in loving is an enlargement of the self into new dimensions? First of all, the examples of the changes described and all other such major changes are acts of self-love. It is precisely because I valued myself that I was unwilling to remain miserable in a school and whole social environment that did not fit my needs. It is because the housewife had regard for herself that she refused to tolerate any longer a marriage that so totally limited her freedom and repressed her personality. It is because the businessman cared for himself that he was no longer willing to nearly kill himself in order to meet the expectations of his mother. Second, not only does love for oneself provide the motive for such major changes; it also is the basis for the courage to risk them. It is only because my parents had clearly loved and valued me as a young child that I felt sufficiently secure in myself to defy their expectations and radically depart from the pattern they had laid out for me. Although I felt inadequate and worthless and possibly crazy in doing what I did, I was able to tolerate these feelings only because at the same time, on an even deeper level, I sensed myself to be a good person no matter how different I might be. In daring to be different, even if it meant to be crazy, I was responding to earlier loving messages from my parents, hundreds of them, which said, "You are a beautiful and beloved individual. It is good to be you. We will love you no matter what you do, as long as you are you." Without that security of my parents' love reflected in my own self-love, I would have chosen the known instead of the unknown and continued to follow my parents' preferred pattern at the extreme cost of my self's basic uniqueness. Finally, it is only when one has taken the leap into the unknown of total selfhood, psychological independence and unique individuality that one is free to proceed along still higher paths of spiritual growth and free to manifest love in its greatest dimensions. As long as one marries, enters a career or has children to satisfy one's parents or the expectations of anyone else, including society as a whole, the commitment by its very nature will be a shallow one. As long as one loves one's children primarily because one is expected to behave in a loving manner toward them, then the parent will be insensitive to the more subtle needs of the children and unable to express love in the more subtle, yet often most important ways. The highest forms of love are inevitably totally free choices and not acts of conformity.

The Risk of Commitment

Whether it be shallow or not, commitment is the foundation, the bedrock of any genuinely loving relationship. Deep commitment does not guarantee the success of the relationship but does help more than any other factor to assure it. Initially shallow commitments may grow deep with time; if not, the relationship will likely crumble or else be inevitably sickly or chronically frail. Frequently we are not consciously aware of the immensity of the risk involved in making a deep commitment. I have already suggested that one of the functions served by the instinctual phenomenon of falling in love is to provide the participants with a magic cloak of omnipotence which blissfully blinds them to the riskiness of what they are doing when they undertake marriage. For my own part, I was reasonably calm until the very moment that my wife joined me before the altar, when my whole body began to tremble. I then became so frightened that I can remember almost nothing of the ceremony or the reception following. In any case, it is our sense of commitment after the wedding which makes possible the transition from falling in love to genuine love. And it is our commitment after conception which transforms us from biological into psychological parents.* Commitment is inherent in any genuinely loving relationship. Anyone who is truly concerned for the spiritual growth of another knows, consciously or instinctively, that he or she can significantly

* The importance of the distinction between biological and psychological parenting is elegantly elaborated and concretized in Goldstein, Freud and Solnit, *Beyond the Best Interests of the Child* (Macmillan, 1973).

foster that growth only through a relationship of constancy. Children cannot grow to psychological maturity in an atmosphere of unpredictability, haunted by the specter of abandonment. Couples cannot resolve in any healthy way the universal issues of marriage—dependency and independency, dominance and submission, freedom and fidelity, for example —without the security of knowing that the act of struggling over these issues will not itself destroy the relationship.

Problems of commitment are a major, inherent part of most psychiatric disorders, and issues of commitment are crucial in the course of psychotherapy. Character-disordered individuals tend to form only shallow commitments, and when their disorders are severe these individuals seem to lack totally the capacity to form commitments at all. It is not so much that they fear the risk of committing themselves as that they basically do not understand what commitment is all about. Because their parents failed to commit themselves to them as children in any meaningful way, they grew up without experience of commitment. Commitment for them represents an abstract beyond their ken, a phenomenon of which they cannot fully conceive. Neurotics, on the other hand, are generally aware of the nature of commitment but are frequently paralyzed by the fear of it. Usually their experience of early childhood was one in which their parents were sufficiently committed to them for them to form a commitment to their parents in return. Subsequently, however, a cessation of parental love through death, abandonment or chronic rejection, has the effect of making the child's unrequited commitment an experience of intolerable pain. New commitments, then, are naturally dreaded. Such injuries can be healed only if it is possible for the person to have a basic and more satisfying experience with commitment at a later date. It is for this reason, among others, that commitment is the cornerstone of the psychotherapeutic relationship. There are times when I shudder at the enormity of what I am doing when I accept another patient for long-term therapy. For basic healing to take place it is necessary for the psychotherapist to bring to his or her relationship with a new patient the same high sense and degree of commitment that genuinely loving parents bring to their children. The therapist's sense of commitment and constancy of concern will usually be tested and inevitably made manifest to the patient in myriad ways over the course of months or years of therapy.

Rachel, a cold and distantly proper young woman of twenty-seven, came to see me at the end of a brief marriage. Her husband, Mark, had left her because of her frigidity. "I know I'm frigid," Rachel acknowledged. "I thought I would warm up to Mark in time, but it never happened. I don't think it's just Mark. I've never enjoyed sex with anyone. And, to tell you the truth, I'm not sure I want to. One part of me wants to, because I'd like to have a happy marriage someday, and I'd like to be normal—normal people seem to find something wonderful in sex. But another part of me is quite content to stay the way I am. Mark always said, 'Relax and let go.' Well, maybe I don't want to relax and let go even if I could."

In the third month of our work together I pointed out to Rachel that she always said "Thank you" to me at least twice before she even sat down to begin a session—first when I met her in the waiting room and again as she passed through the door into my office. "What's wrong with being polite?" she asked.

"Nothing *per se*," I replied. "But in this particular case it seems so unnecessary. You are acting as if you were a guest in here and not even sure of your welcome."

"But I am a guest in here. It's your house."

"True," I said. "But it's also true that you're paying me forty dollars an hour for your time in here. You have purchased this time and this office space, and because you've purchased it, you have a right to it. You're not a guest. This office, this waiting room, and our time together are your right. It's yours. You've paid me for this right, so why thank me for what is yours?"

"I can't believe you really feel that way," Rachel exclaimed.

"Then you must believe that I can kick you out of here any time I want to," I countered. "You must feel that it's possible for you to come in here some morning and have me tell you, 'Rachel, working with you has become a bore. I've decided not to see you again. Goodbye and good luck.' "

"That's exactly the way I feel," Rachel agreed. "I've never thought of anything being my right before, at least not in regard to any person. You mean you couldn't kick me out?"

"Oh, I suppose I could. But I wouldn't. I wouldn't want to. It wouldn't be ethical, among other things. Look, Rachel," I said, "when I take on a case such as yours in long-term therapy I make a commitment to that case, that person. And I've made a commitment to you. I will work with you as long as is necessary, whether it takes one year or five years or ten years or whatever. I don't know whether you will quit our work together when you're ready or before you're ready. But whichever it is, you are the one who will terminate our relationship. Short of my death, my services will be available to you as long as you want them."

It was not difficult for me to understand Rachel's problem. At the beginning of her therapy her ex-husband, Mark, had said to me: "I think Rachel's mother has a lot to do with this. She's a remarkable woman. She'd make a great president of General Motors, but I'm not sure she's a very good mother." Quite so. Rachel had been raised, or rather ruled, with the feeling that she might be fired at any moment if she didn't toe the line. Rather than giving Rachel the sense that her place in the home as a child was secure—a sense that can come solely from committed parents—Rachel's mother had instead consistently communicated the opposite: like that of an employee, Rachel's position was guaranteed only insofar as she produced what was required and behaved according to expectations. Since her place in the home was not secure as a child, how could she feel that her place with me was secure?

Such injuries caused by a parental failure of commitment are not healed by a few words, a few superficial reassurances. On successively deeper levels they must be worked through again and again. One such working-through, for instance, occurred more than a year later. We had been focusing on the fact that Rachel never cried in my presence—another way in which she could not allow herself to "let go." One day as she was talking of the terrible loneliness that came from having to constantly be on guard, I sensed that she was on the brink of weeping but that some slight push was needed from me, so I did something out of the ordinary: I reached over to where she was lying on the couch and gently stroked her head, murmuring, "Poor Rachel. Poor Rachel." The gesture failed. Rachel immediately stiffened and sat up, dry-eyed. "I cannot do it," she said. "I cannot let myself go." This was toward the end of the session. At her next session Rachel came in and sat on the couch instead of lying down. "Well, now it's your time to talk," she announced.

"What do you mean?" I asked.

"You're going to tell me all the things that are wrong with me."

I was puzzled. "I still don't understand what you mean, Rachel."

"This is our last session. You're going to sum up all the things wrong with me, all the reasons why you can't treat me any more."

"I don't have the foggiest idea what's going on," I said.

It was Rachel's turn to be puzzled. "Well," she said, "last session you wanted me to cry. You've wanted me to cry for a long time. Last session you did everything you could to help me to cry and I still wouldn't do it, so you're going to give up on me. I can't do what you want me to do. That's why today will be our last session."

"You really believe I'm going to fire you, don't you, Rachel?"

"Yes. Anyone would."

"No, Rachel, not anyone. Your mother might have. But I'm not your mother. Not everyone in this world is like your mother. You're not my employee. You're not here to do what I want you to do. You're here to do what you want to do, when you want to do it. I may push you, but I have no power over you. I will never fire you. You're here for as long as you want to be."

One of the problems that people commonly have in their adult relationships if they have never received a firm commitment from their parents is the "I'll desert you before you desert me" syndrome. This syndrome will take many forms or disguises. One form was Rachel's frigidity. Although it was never on a conscious level, what Rachel's frigidity was expressing to her husband and previous boyfriends was, "I'm not going to give myself to you when I know damn well that you're going to dump me one of these days." For Rachel, "letting go," sexually or otherwise, represented a commitment of herself, and she was unwilling to make a commitment when the map of her past experience made it seem certain she would not receive any commitment in return.

The "I'll desert you before you desert me" syndrome becomes more and more powerful the closer such a person as Rachel comes to another. After a year of therapy on a twice-a-week basis Rachel announced to me that she could no longer afford eighty dollars a week. Since her divorce, she said, she was having a difficult time making ends meet, and she would simply have to stop seeing me or cut back to once a week. On a realistic level this was ridiculous. I knew that Rachel had an inheritance of fifty thousand dollars in addition to the modest salary she earned at her job, and in the community she was known to be a member of an old and wealthy family. Ordinarily I would have confronted her vigorously with the fact that she could afford my services more easily than many patients and was clearly using the issue of money spuriously to flee from an increasing closeness to me. On the other hand, I also knew that her inheritance represented something more for Rachel than just money; it was hers, something that would not desert her, a bulwark of security in an uncommitted world. Although it was quite reasonable for me to ask her to dip into her inheritance to pay my standard fee, I guessed that

that was a risk she was not yet ready to make and that if I insisted she would indeed flee. She had said she thought that on her income she could afford to pay fifty dollars a week, and she offered me that amount for just one session. I told her I would reduce my fee to twenty-five dollars a session and continue to see her twice weekly. She looked at me with a mixture of fear, disbelief and joy. "You'd really do that?" she asked. I nodded. A long period of silence followed. Finally, closer to tears than she had ever yet been, Rachel said, "Because I came from a wealthy family, the merchants in town have always charged me the highest the traffic would bear. You are offering me a break. No one ever offered me a break before."

Actually, Rachel quit therapy several times during the following year in the struggle over whether she could permit our mutual commitment to grow. Each time, through a combination of letters and phone calls over a week or two, I was able to persuade her to return. Finally, by the end of the second year of therapy we were able to deal more directly with the issues involved. I'd learned that Rachel wrote poetry and I asked her to show it to me. First she refused. Then she agreed, but week after week she would "forget" to bring it to me. I pointed out that withholding her poetry from me had the same significance as withholding her sexuality from Mark and other men. Why did she feel that the offering of her poems to me represented a total commitment of herself? Why did she feel that the sharing of her sexuality was a similar total commitment? Even if I were not responsive to her poetry, would that mean a total rejection of her? Would I terminate our friendship because she was not a great poet? Perhaps the sharing of her poetry would deepen our relationship. Why was she fearful of such deepening? Et cetera. Et cetera. Et cetera.

Finally coming to accept the fact that she did have a commitment from me, in the third year of her therapy Rachel began to "let go." She finally took the risk of letting me see her poetry. Then she was able to giggle and laugh and tease. Our relationship, which had previously been stiff and formal, became warm, spontaneous and often light-hearted and joyful. "I never knew what it was like to be relaxed with another person before," she said. "This is the first place in my life I've ever felt secure." From the security of my office and our time together she was rapidly able to venture forth into other relationships. She realized that sex was not a matter of commitment but one of self-expression and play and exploration and learning and joyful abandonment. Knowing that I would always be available to her if she became bruised, like the good mother she had never had, she was free to allow her sexuality to burst forth. Her frigidity melted. By the time she terminated therapy in the fourth year, Rachel had become a vivacious and openly passionate person who was busily enjoying all that human relationships have to offer.

I was fortunately able to offer Rachel a sufficient degree of commitment to overcome the ill effects of the lack of commitment that she had never experienced during her childhood. I have often been not so fortunate. The computer technician I described in the first section as an example of transference was a case in point. His need for commitment from me was so total that I was not able, or willing, to meet it. If the therapist's commitment is insufficient to survive the vicissitudes of the relationship, basic healing will not occur. However, if the therapist's commitment is sufficient, then usually—although not inevitably—the patient will respond sooner or later with a developing commitment of his or her own, a commitment to the therapist and to therapy itself. The point at which the patient begins to demonstrate this commitment is the turning point of therapy. For Rachel, I think this point came when she finally offered me her poetry. Strangely, some patients may come to therapy faithfully two or three hours a week for years and yet never reach this point. Others may reach it within the first few months. But reach it they must if they are to be healed. For the therapist it is a wonderful moment of relief and joy when this point is reached, for then he or she knows that the patient has assumed the risk of commitment to getting well and that therefore therapy will succeed.

The risk of commitment to therapy is not only the risk of commitment itself but also the risk of self-confrontation and change. In the previous section, in the discussion of the discipline of dedication to the truth, I elaborated on the difficulties of changing one's map of reality, world views and transferences. Yet changed they must be if one is to lead a life of loving involving frequent extensions of oneself into new dimensions and territories of involvement. There come many points on one's journey of spiritual growth, whether one is alone or has a psychotherapist as guide, when one must take new and unfamiliar actions in consonance with one's new world view. The taking of such new action—behaving differently from the way one has always behaved before—may represent an extraordinary personal risk. The passively homosexual young man for the first time summons the initiative to ask a girl for a date; the person who has never trusted anyone lies down for the first time on the analyst's couch allowing the analyst to be hidden from his view; the previously dependent housewife announces to her controlling husband that she is obtaining a job whether he likes it or not, that she has her own life to live; the fifty-year-old mama's boy tells his mother to stop addressing him by his infantile nickname; the emotionally distant, seemingly self-sufficient "strong" man first allows himself to weep in public; or Rachel "lets go" and cries for the first time in my office: these actions, and many more, involve a risk more personal and therefore frequently more fearsome and frightening than that of any soldier entering battle. The soldier cannot run because the gun is pointed at his back as well as his front. But the individual trying to grow can always retreat into the easy and familiar patterns of a more limited past.

It has been said that the successful psychotherapist must bring to the psychotherapeutic relationship the same courage and the same sense of commitment as the patient. The therapist must also risk change. Of all the good and useful rules of psychotherapy that I have been taught, there are very few that I have not chosen to break at one time or another, not out of laziness and lack of discipline but rather in fear and trembling, because my patient's therapy seemed to require that, one way or another, I should step out of the safety of the prescribed analyst's role, be different and risk the unconventional. As I look back on every successful case I have had I can see that at some point or points in each case I had to lay myself on the line. The willingness of the therapist to suffer at such moments is perhaps the essence of therapy, and when perceived by the patient, as it usually is, it is always therapeutic. It is also through this willingness to extend themselves and suffer with and over their patients that therapists grow and change. Again as I look back on my successful cases, there is not one that did not result in some very meaningful, often radical, change in my attitudes and perspectives. It has to be this way. It is impossible to truly understand another without making room for that person within yourself. This making room, which once again is the discipline of bracketing, requires an extension of and therefore a changing of the self.

So it is in good parenting as well as in good psychotherapy. The same bracketing and extension of ourselves is involved in listening to our children. To respond to their healthy needs we must change ourselves. Only when we are willing to undergo the suffering of such changing can we become the parents our children need us to be. And since children are constantly growing and their needs are changing, we are obliged to change and grow with them. Everyone is familiar with parents, for instance, who can deal effectively with their children until the time of adolescence, but who then become totally ineffective as parents because they are unable to change and adjust their attitudes toward their now older and different children. And, as in all other instances of love, it would be incorrect to view the suffering and changing involved in good parenting as some kind of self-sacrifice or martyrdom; to the contrary, parents have more to gain from the process than their children. Parents who are unwilling to risk the suffering of changing and growing and learning from their children are choosing a path of senility—whether they know it or not—and their children and the world will leave them far behind. Learning from their children is the best opportunity most people have to assure themselves of a meaningful old age. Sadly, most do not take this opportunity.

The Risk of Confrontation

The final and possibly the greatest risk of love is the risk of exercising power with humility. The most common example of this is the act of loving confrontation. Whenever we confront someone we are in essence saying to that person, "You are wrong; I am right." When a parent confronts a child, saying, "You are being sneaky," the parent is saying in effect, "Your sneakiness is wrong. I have the right to criticize it because I am not sneaky myself and I am right." When a husband confronts a wife with her frigidity, he is saying, "You are frigid, because it is wrong for you not to respond to me sexually with greater fervor, since I am sexually adequate and in other ways all right. You have a sexual problem; I do not." When a wife confronts a husband with her opinion that he does not spend enough time with her and the children, she is saying, "Your investment in your work is excessive and wrong. Despite the fact that I do not have your job, I can see things more clearly than you, and I rightly know that it would be more proper for you to invest yourself differently." The capacity to confront, to say "I'm right, you're wrong, you should be different," is one that many people have no difficulty exercising. Parents, spouses and people in various other roles do this routinely and casually, leveling criticism left and right, shooting from the hip. Most such criticism and confrontation, usually made impulsively in anger or annoyance, does more to increase the amount of confusion in the world than the amount of enlightenment.

For the truly loving person the act of criticism or confrontation does not come easily; to such a person it is evident that the act has great potential for arrogance. To confront one's beloved is to assume a position of moral or intellectual superiority over the loved one, at least so far as the issue at hand is concerned. Yet genuine love recognizes and respects the unique individuality and separate identity of the other person. (I will say more about this later.) The truly loving person, valuing the uniqueness and differentness of his or her beloved, will be reluctant indeed to assume, "I am right, you are wrong; I know better than you what is good for you." But the reality of life is such that at times one person does know better than the other what is good for the other, and in actuality is in a position of superior knowledge or wisdom in regard to the matter at hand. Under these circumstances the wiser of the two does in fact have an obligation to confront the other with the problem. The loving person, therefore, is frequently in a dilemma, caught between a loving respect for the beloved's own path in life and a responsibility to exercise loving leadership when the beloved appears to need such leadership.

The dilemma can be resolved only by painstaking self-scrutiny, in which the lover examines stringently the worth of his or her "wisdom" and the motives behind this need to assume leadership. "Do I really see things clearly or am I operating on murky assumptions? Do I really understand my beloved? Could it not be that the path my beloved is taking is wise and that my perception of it as unwise is the result of limited vision on my part? Am I being self-serving in believing that my beloved needs redirection?" These are questions that those who truly love must continually ask themselves. This self-scrutiny, as objective as possible, is the essence of humility or meekness. In the words of an anonymous fourteenth-century

British monk and spiritual teacher, "Meekness in itself is nothing else than a true knowing and feeling of a man's self as he is. Any man who truly sees and feels himself as he is must surely be meek indeed."*

There are, then, two ways to confront or criticize another human being: with instinctive and spontaneous certainty that one is right, or with a belief that one is probably right arrived at through scrupulous self-doubting and self-examination. The first is the way of arrogance; it is the most common way of parents, spouses, teachers and people generally in their day-to-day affairs; it is usually unsuccessful, producing more resentment than growth and other effects that were not intended. The second is the way of humility; it is not common, requiring as it does a genuine extension of oneself; it is more likely to be successful, and it is never, in my experience, destructive.

There are a significant number of individuals who for one reason or another have learned to inhibit their instinctive tendency to criticize or confront with spontaneous arrogance but who go no farther, hiding in the moral safety of meekness, never daring to assume power. One such was a minister and father of a middle-aged patient who was suffering from a lifelong depressive neurosis. My patient's mother was an angry, violent woman who dominated the household with her temper tantrums and manipulations and not infrequently beat her husband physically in front of the daughter. The minister never fought back and counseled his daughter also to respond to her mother by turning the other cheek and, in the name of Christian charity, being unendingly submissive and respectful. When she began therapy my patient revered her father for his mildness and "lovingness." It was not very long, however, before she came to realize that his meekness was weakness, and that in his passivity he had deprived her of adequate parenting every bit as much as her mother had with her mean

* *The Cloud of Unknowing*, trans. Ira Progoff (New York: Julian Press, 1969), p. 92.

self-centeredness. She finally saw that he had done nothing to protect her from her mother's evil and nothing, in fact, to confront evil, leaving her no option but to incorporate her mother's bitter manipulativeness along with his pseudohumility as role models. To fail to confront when confrontation is required for the nurture of spiritual growth represents a failure to love equally as does thoughtless criticism or condemnation and other forms of active deprivation of caring. If they love their children parents must, sparingly and carefully perhaps but nonetheless actively, confront and criticize them from time to time, just as they must allow their children to confront and criticize themselves in turn. Similarly, loving spouses must repeatedly confront each other if the marriage relationship is to serve the function of promoting the spiritual growth of the partners. No marriage can be judged truly successful unless husband and wife are each other's best critics. The same holds true for friendship. There is a traditional concept that friendship should be a conflict-free relationship, a "you scratch my back, I'll scratch yours" arrangement, relying solely on a mutual exchange of favors and compliments as prescribed by good manners. Such relationships are superficial and intimacy-avoiding and do not deserve the name of friendship which is so commonly applied to them. Fortunately, there are signs that our concept of friendship is beginning to deepen. Mutual loving confrontation is a significant part of all successful and meaningful human relationships. Without it the relationship is either unsuccessful or shallow.

To confront or criticize is a form of exercising leadership or power. The exercise of power is nothing more and nothing less than an attempt to influence the course of events, human or otherwise, by one's actions in a consciously or unconsciously predetermined manner. When we confront or criticize someone it is because we want to change the course of the person's life. It is obvious that there are many other, often superior, ways to influence the course of events than by confrontation or criticism: by example, suggestion, parable, reward and punishment, questioning, prohibition or permission, creation of experiences, organizing with others, and so on. Volumes can be written about the art of exercising power. For our purposes, however, suffice it to say that loving individuals must concern themselves with this art, for if one desires to nurture another's spiritual growth, then one must concern oneself with the most effective way to accomplish this in any given instance. Loving parents, for example, must first examine themselves and their values stringently before determining accurately that they know what is best for their child. Then, having made this determination, they also have to give greater thought to the child's character and capacities before deciding whether the child would be more likely to respond favorably to confrontation than to praise or increased attention or storytelling or some other form of influence. To confront someone with something he or she cannot handle will at best be a waste of time, and likely will have a deleterious effect. If we want to be heard we must speak in a language the listener can understand and on a level at which the listener is capable of operating. If we are to love we must extend ourselves to adjust our communication to the capacities of our beloved.

It is clear that exercising power with love requires a great deal of work, but what is this about the risk involved? The problem is that the more loving one is, the more humble one is; yet the more humble one is, the more one is awed by the potential for arrogance in exercising power. Who am I to influence the course of human events? By what authority am I entitled to decide what is best for my child, spouse, my country or the human race? Who gives me the right to dare to believe in my own understanding and then to presume to exert my will upon the world? Who am I to play God? *That* is the risk. For whenever we exercise power we are attempting to influence the course of the world, of humanity, and we are thereby playing God. Most parents, teachers, leaders—most of us who exercise power—have no cognizance of this. In the arrogance of exercising power without the total self-awareness demanded by love, we are blissfully but destructively ignorant of the fact that we are playing God. But those who truly love, and therefore work for the wisdom that love requires, know that to act is to play God. Yet they also know that there is no alternative except inaction and impotence. Love compels us to play God with full consciousness of the enormity of the fact that that is just what we are doing. With this consciousness the loving person assumes the responsibility of attempting to be God and not to carelessly play God, to fulfill God's will without mistake. We arrive, then, at yet another paradox: only out of the humility of love can humans dare to be God.

Love Is Disciplined

I have indicated that the energy for the work of self-discipline derives from love, which is a form of will. It follows, then, not only that self-discipline is usually love, translated into action, but also that any genuine lover behaves with self-discipline and any genuinely loving relationship is a disciplined relationship. If I truly love another, I will obviously order my behavior in such a way as to contribute the utmost to his or her spiritual growth. A young, intelligent, artistic and "bohemian" couple with whom I once attempted to work had a four-year marriage marked by almost daily screaming, dish-throwing and face-clawing quarrels, along with weekly casual infidelity and monthly separations. Shortly after we began our work they each correctly perceived that therapy would lead them toward increasing self-discipline, and consequently to a less disorderly relationship. "But you want to take the passion out of our relationship," they said. "Your notions of love and marriage leave no room for passion." Almost immediately thereafter they quit therapy, and it has

been reported to me that three years later, after several bouts
with other therapists, their daily screaming matches and the
chaotic pattern of their marriage continue unchanged, as well
as the unproductivity of their individual lives. There is no
doubt that their union is, in a certain sense, a highly colorful
one. But it is like the primary colors in the paintings of children, splashed on the paper with abandon, occasionally not
without charm, but generally demonstrating the sameness
that characterizes the art of young children. In the muted,
controlled hues of Rembrandt one can find the color, yet infinitely more richness, uniqueness and meaning. Passion is feeling of great depth. The fact that a feeling is uncontrolled is
no indication whatsoever that it is any deeper than a feeling
that is disciplined. To the contrary, psychiatrists know well
the truth of the old proverbs "Shallow brooks are noisy" and
"Still waters run deep." We must not assume that someone
whose feelings are modulated and controlled is not a passionate person.

While one should not be a slave to one's feelings, self-discipline does not mean the squashing of one's feelings into nonexistence. I frequently tell my patients that their feelings are
their slaves and that the art of self-discipline is like the art of
slave-owning. First of all, one's feelings are the source of one's
energy; they provide the horsepower, or slave power, that
makes it possible for us to accomplish the tasks of living. Since
they work for us, we should treat them with respect. There
are two common mistakes that slave-owners can make which
represent opposite and extreme forms of executive leadership.
One type of slave-owner does not discipline his slaves, gives
them no structure, sets them no limits, provides them with
no direction and does not make it clear who is the boss. What
happens, of course, is that in due time his slaves stop working
and begin moving into the mansion, raiding the liquor cabinet
and breaking the furniture, and soon the slave-owner finds
that he is the slave of his slaves, living in the same kind of
chaos as the aforementioned character-disordered "bohemian"
couple.

Yet the opposite style of leadership, which the guilt-ridden neurotic so often exerts over his feelings, is equally self-destructive. In this style the slave-owner is so obsessed with the fear that his slaves (feelings) might get out of control and so determined that they should cause him no trouble that he routinely beats them into submission and punishes them severely at the first sign of any potency. The result of this style is that in relatively short order the slaves become less and less productive as their will is sapped by the harsh treatment they receive. Or else their will turns more and more toward covert rebellion. If the process is carried out long enough, one night the owner's prediction finally comes true and the slaves rise up and burn down the mansion, frequently with the owner inside. Such is the genesis of certain psychoses and overwhelming neuroses. The proper management of one's feelings clearly lies along a complex (and therefore not simple or easy) balanced middle path, requiring constant judgment and continuing adjustment. Here the owner treats his feelings (slaves) with respect, nurturing them with good food, shelter and medical care, listening and responding to their voices, encouraging them, inquiring as to their health, yet also organizing them, limiting them, deciding clearly between them, redirecting them and teaching them, all the while leaving no doubt as to who is the boss. This is the path of healthy self-discipline.

Among the feelings that must be so disciplined is the feeling of love. As I have indicated, this is not in itself genuine love but the feeling associated with cathexis. It is to be very much respected and nurtured for the creative energy it brings, but if it is allowed to run rampant, the result will not be genuine love but confusion and unproductivity. Because genuine love involves an extension of oneself, vast amounts of energy are required and, like it or not, the store of our energy is as limited as the hours of our day. We simply cannot love everyone. True, we may have a feeling of love for mankind, and this feeling may also be useful in providing us with enough energy to manifest genuine love for a few specific individuals. But genuine love for a relatively few individuals is all that is within our power. To attempt to exceed the limits of our energy is to offer more than we can deliver, and there is a point of no return beyond which an attempt to love all comers becomes fraudulent and harmful to the very ones we desire to assist. Consequently if we are fortunate enough to be in a position in which many people ask for our attention, we must choose those among them whom we are actually to love. This choice is not easy; it may be excruciatingly painful, as the assumption of godlike power so often is. But it must be made. Many factors need to be considered, primarily the capacity of a prospective recipient of our love to respond to that love with spiritual growth. People differ in this capacity, a fact to which more examination will later be given. It is, however, unquestionable that there are many whose spirits are so locked in behind impenetrable armor that even the greatest efforts to nurture the growth of those spirits are doomed to almost certain failure. To attempt to love someone who cannot benefit from your love with spiritual growth is to waste your energy, to cast your seed upon arid ground. Genuine love is precious, and those who are capable of genuine love know that their loving must be focused as productively as possible through self-discipline.

The converse of the problem of loving too many people also needs to be examined. It is possible for some people, at least, to love more than one person at the same time, to simultaneously maintain a number of genuinely loving relationships. This itself is a problem for several reasons. One reason is the American or Western myth of romantic love that suggests that certain people are "meant for each other"; thus, by extrapolation, they are not meant for anyone else. The myth, therefore, prescribes exclusivity for loving relationships, most particularly sexual exclusivity. On balance, the myth is probably helpful in contributing to the stability and productivity of human relationships, since the vast majority of human beings are challenged to the limit of their capacities to extend themselves to develop genuinely loving relationships with their spouses and children alone. Indeed, if one can say that one has built genuinely loving relationships with a spouse and children, then one has already succeeded in accomplishing more than most people accomplish in a lifetime. There is frequently something pathetic about the individual who has failed to build his family into a loving unit, yet restlessly searches for loving relationships outside the family. The first obligation of a genuinely loving person will always be to his or her marital and parental relationships. Nonetheless, there are some whose capacity to love is great enough for them to build loving relationships successfully within the family and still have energy left for additional relationships. For these the myth of exclusivity is not only patently false, but also represents an unnecessary limitation upon their capacity to give of themselves to others outside their family. It is possible for this limitation to be overcome, but great self-discipline is required in the extension of oneself in order to avoid "spreading oneself too thin." It was to this extraordinarily complex issue (here touched only in passing) that Joseph Fletcher, the Episcopalian theologian and author of *The New Morality*, was addressing himself when he reportedly said to a friend of mine, "Free love is an ideal. Unfortunately, it is an ideal of which very few of us are capable." What he meant was that very few of us have a capacity for self-discipline great enough to maintain constructive relationships that are genuinely loving both inside and outside the family. Freedom and discipline are indeed handmaidens; without the discipline of genuine love, freedom is invariably nonloving and destructive.

By this time some readers may feel saturated by the concept of discipline and conclude that I am advocating a style of life of Calvinistic dreariness. Constant self-discipline! Constant self-examination! Duty! Responsibility! Neopuritanism, they might call it. Call it what you will, genuine love, with all the discipline that it requires, is the only path in this life to substantial joy. Take another path and you may find rare moments of ecstatic joy, but they will be fleeting and progressively more elusive. When I genuinely love I am extending myself, and when I am extending myself I am growing. The more I love, the longer I love, the larger I become. Genuine love is self-replenishing. The more I nurture the spirtual growth of others, the more my own spiritual growth is nurtured. I am a totally selfish human being. I never do something for somebody else but that I do it for myself. And as I grow through love, so grows my joy, ever more present, ever more constant. Neopuritan perhaps I am. I am also a joy freak. As John Denver sings:

> *Love is everywhere, I see it.*
> *You are all that you can be, go on and be it.*
> *Life is perfect, I believe it.*
> *Come and play the game with me.**

Love Is Separateness

Although the act of nurturing another's spiritual growth has the effect of nurturing one's own, a major characteristic of genuine love is that the distinction between oneself and the other is always maintained and preserved. The genuine lover always perceives the beloved as someone who has a totally separate identity. Moreover, the genuine lover always respects and even encourages this separateness and the unique individuality of the beloved. Failure to perceive and respect this separateness is extremely common, however, and the cause of much mental illness and unnecessary suffering.

* "Love Is Everywhere," by John Denver, Joe Henry, Steve Weisberg and John Martin Sommers, copyright © 1975 Cherry Lane Music Co. Used by permission.

In its most extreme form the failure to perceive the separateness of the other is called narcissism. Frankly narcissistic individuals are actually unable to perceive their children, spouses or friends as being separate from themselves on an emotional level. The first time I began to understand what narcissism is all about was during an interview with the parents of a schizophrenic patient whom I will call Susan X. Susan at the time was thirty-one. Since the age of eighteen she had made a number of serious suicide attempts, and had had to be hospitalized almost continually in a variety of hospitals and sanatoria for the previous thirteen years. However, largely because of superior psychiatric care that she had received from other psychiatrists during these years she was finally beginning to improve. For some months during our work together she had demonstrated an increasing capacity to trust trustworthy people, to distinguish between trustworthy and untrustworthy people, to accept the fact that she had a schizophrenic illness and would need to exert a great deal of self-discipline for the rest of her life to deal with this illness, to respect herself, and to do what was necessary to care for herself without having to rely on others to continually nurture her. Because of this great progress I felt the moment was soon at hand when Susan would be able to leave the hospital and for the first time in her life lead and maintain a successful independent existence. It was at this point that I met with her parents, an attractive, wealthy couple in their mid-fifties. I was very happy to describe to them Susan's enormous progress and explain in detail the reasons for my optimism. But much to my surprise, soon after I began to do this, Susan's mother started to cry silently and continued to cry as I went on with my hopeful message. At first I thought perhaps her tears were tears of joy, but it was clear from her expression that she was indeed feeling sad. Finally I said, "I'm puzzled, Mrs. X. I've been telling you things today that are most hopeful, yet you seem to be feeling sad."

"Of course I'm sad," she replied. "I just can't help crying when I think of all poor Susan has to suffer."

I then went into a lengthy explanation to the effect that while it was quite true Susan had suffered a good deal in the course of her illness, she had also clearly learned a good deal from this suffering, had come out on top of it and, in my estimation, was unlikely to suffer any more in the future than any other adult. Indeed, she might suffer considerably less than any of us because of the wisdom she had gained from her battle with schizophrenia. Mrs. X. continued to weep silently.

"Frankly, I'm still puzzled, Mrs. X.," I said. "Over the past thirteen years you must have participated in at least a dozen conferences like this with Susan's psychiatrists, and from what I know, none of them was as optimistic as this one. Don't you feel gladness as well as sadness?"

"I can only think of how difficult life is for Susan," Mrs. X. replied tearfully.

"Look, Mrs. X.," I said, "is there anything I could say to you about Susan that would make you feel encouraged and happy about her?"

"Poor Susan's life is so full of pain," Mrs. X. whimpered.

Suddenly I realized that Mrs. X. was not crying for Susan but for herself. She was crying for her own pain and suffering. Yet the conference was about Susan, not about her, and she was doing her crying in Susan's name. How could she do this, I wondered. And then I realized that Mrs. X. was actually not able to distinguish between Susan and herself. What she felt, Susan must feel. She was using Susan as a vehicle to express her own needs. She was not doing this consciously or maliciously; on an emotional level she could not, in fact, perceive Susan as having an identity separate from her own. Susan was she. In her mind Susan as a unique, different individual with a unique, different path in life simply did not exist—nor, probably, did anyone else. Intellectually Mrs. X. could recognize other people as being different from herself. But on a more basic level other people did not exist for her. In the depths of her mind the entirety of the world was she, Mrs. X., she alone.

In subsequent experiences I frequently found the mothers of schizophrenic children to be extraordinarily narcissistic individuals like Mrs. X. This is not to say that such mothers are always narcissistic or that narcissistic mothers can't raise nonschizophrenic children. Schizophrenia is an extremely complex disorder, with obvious genetic as well as environmental determinants. But one can imagine the depth of confusion in Susan's childhood produced by her mother's narcissism, and one can objectively see this confusion when actually observing narcissistic mothers interact with their children. On an afternoon when Mrs. X. was feeling sorry for herself Susan might have come home from school bringing some of her paintings the teacher had graded A. If she told her mother proudly how she was progressing in art, Mrs. X. might well respond: "Susan, go take a nap. You shouldn't get yourself so exhausted over your work in school. The school system is no good anymore. They don't care for children anymore." On the other hand, on an afternoon when Mrs. X. was in a very cheerful mood Susan might have come home in tears over the fact that she had been bullied by several boys on the school bus, and Mrs. X. could say: "Isn't it fortunate that Mr. Jones is such a good bus driver? He is so nice and patient with all you children and your roughhousing. I think you should be sure to give him a nice little present at Christmastime." Since they do not perceive others as others but only as extensions of themselves, narcissistic individuals lack the capacity for empathy, which is the capacity to feel what *another* is feeling. Lacking empathy, narcissistic parents usually respond inappropriately to their children on an emotional level and fail to offer any recognition or verification of their children's feelings. It is no wonder, then, that such children grow up with grave difficulties in recognizing, accepting and hence managing their own feelings.

While not usually as narcissistic as Mrs. X., the vast majority of parents fail in some degree to adequately recognize or fully appreciate the unique individuality or "otherness" of their children. Common examples abound. Parents will say of a child, "He's a chip off the old block" or to a child, "You're just like your Uncle Jim," as if their children are some genetic copy of themselves or the family, when the facts of genetic combinations are such that all children genetically are extremely different from either of their parents and all of their forebears. Athletic fathers push their scholarly sons into football and scholarly fathers push their athletic sons into books, causing the sons much unnecessary guilt and turmoil. A general's wife complains about her seventeen-year-old daughter: "When she's home, Sally sits in her room all the time writing sad poetry. It's morbid, Doctor. And she absolutely refuses to have a coming-out party. I'm afraid that she's seriously ill." After interviewing Sally, a charming and vivacious young woman who is on the honor roll at school and has lots of friends, I tell her parents that I think Sally is perfectly healthy and suggest that perhaps they should lessen their pressure on her to be a carbon copy of themselves. They leave to look for another psychiatrist, one who might be willing to pronounce Sally's differences deviancies.

Adolescents frequently complain that they are disciplined not out of genuine concern but because of parental fear that they will give their parents a bad image. "My parents are continually after me to cut my hair," adolescent boys used to say a few years ago. "They can't explain why long hair is bad for me. They just don't want other people to see they've got long-haired kids. They don't really give a shit about me. All they are really caring about is their own image." Such adolescent resentment is usually justified. Their parents generally do in fact fail to appreciate the unique individuality of their children, and instead regard their children as extensions of themselves, in much the same way as their fine clothes and their neatly manicured lawns and their polished cars are extensions of themselves which represent their status to the world. It is to these milder but nontheless destructive common forms of parental narcissism that Kahlil Gibran addresses himself in what are perhaps the finest words ever written about child-raising:

Your children are not your children.
They are the sons and daughters of Life's longing for
itself.
They come through you but not from you,
And though they are with you they belong not to you.

You may give them your love but not your thoughts,
For they have their own thoughts.
You may house their bodies but not their souls,
For their souls dwell in the house of tomorrow, which you
cannot visit, not even in your dreams.
You may strive to be like them, but seek not to make
them like you.
For life goes not backward nor tarries with yesterday.
You are the bow from which your children as living
arrows are sent forth.
The archer sees the mark upon the path of the infinite,
and He bends you with His might that His arrow may
go swift and far.
Let your bending in the archer's hand be for gladness;
For even as He loves the arrow that flies, so He loves also
the bow that is stable. *

The difficulty that humans so generally seem to have in fully appreciating the separateness of those who they are close to interferes not only with their parenting but with all their intimate relationships, including marriage. Not too long ago in a couples group I heard one of the members state that the "purpose and function" of his wife was to keep their house neat and him well fed. I was aghast at what seemed to me his painfully blatant male chauvinism. I thought I might demonstrate this to him by asking the other members of the group to state how they perceived the purpose and function of their spouses. To my horror the six others, male and female alike, gave very similar answers. All of them defined the purpose and function of their husbands or wives in reference to them-

* *The Prophet* (New York: Alfred A. Knopf, 1951), pp. 17–18.

selves; all of them failed to perceive that their own mates might have an existence basically separate from their own or any kind of destiny apart from their marriage. "Good grief," I exclaimed, "it's no wonder that you are all having difficulties in your marriages, and you'll continue to have difficulties until you come to recognize that each of you has your own separate destiny to fulfill." The group felt not only chastised but profoundly confused by my pronouncement. Somewhat belligerently they asked me to define the purpose and function of my wife. "The purpose and function of Lily," I responded, "is to grow to be the most of which she is capable, not for my benefit but for her own and to the glory of God." The concept remained alien to them for some time, however.

The problem of separateness in close relationships has bedeviled mankind through the ages. However, it has received more attention from a political standpoint than from a marital one. Pure communism, for instance, expresses a philosophy not unlike that of the aforementioned couples—namely, that the purpose and function of the individual is to serve the relationship, the group, the collective, the society. Only the destiny of the state is considered; the destiny of the individual is believed to be of no consequence. Pure capitalism, on the other hand, espouses the destiny of the individual even when it is at the expense of the relationship, the group, the collective, the society. Widows and orphans may starve, but this should not prevent the individual entrepreneur from enjoying all the fruits of his or her individual initiative. It should be obvious to any discerning mind that neither of these pure solutions to the problem of separateness within relationships will be successful. The individual's health depends upon the health of the society; the health of the society depends upon the health of its individuals. When dealing with couples my wife and I draw the analogy between marriage and a base camp for mountain climbing. If one wants to climb mountains one must have a good base camp, a place where there are shelters and provisions, where one may receive nurture and rest before one ventures forth again to seek another summit.

Successful mountain climbers know that they must spend at least as much time, if not more, in tending to their base camp as they actually do in climbing mountains, for their survival is dependent upon their seeing to it that their base camp is sturdily constructed and well stocked.

A common and traditionally masculine marital problem is created by the husband who, once he is married, devotes all his energies to climbing mountains and none to tending to his marriage, or base camp, expecting it to be there in perfect order whenever he chooses to return to it for rest and recreation without his assuming any responsibility for its maintenance. Sooner or later this "capitalist" approach to the problem fails and he returns to find his untended base camp a shambles, his neglected wife having been hospitalized for a nervous breakdown, having run off with another man, or in some other way having renounced her job as camp caretaker. An equally common and traditionally feminine marital problem is created by the wife who, once she is married, feels that the goal of her life has been achieved. To her the base camp is the peak. She cannot understand or empathize with her husband's need for achievements and experiences beyond the marriage and reacts to them with jealousy and never-ending demands that he devote increasingly more energy to the home. Like other "communist" resolutions of the problem, this one creates a relationship that is suffocating and stultifying, from which the husband, feeling trapped and limited, may likely flee in a moment of "mid-life crisis." The women's liberation movement has been helpful in pointing the way to what is obviously the only ideal resolution: marriage as a truly cooperative institution, requiring great mutual contributions and care, time and energy, but existing for the primary purpose of nurturing each of the participants for individual journeys toward his or her own individual peaks of spiritual growth. Male and female both must tend the hearth and both must venture forth.

As an adolescent I used to thrill to the words of love the early American poet Ann Bradstreet spoke to her husband:

"If ever two were one, then we." * As I have grown, however, I have come to realize that it is the separateness of the partners that enriches the union. Great marriages cannot be constructed by individuals who are terrified by their basic aloneness, as so commonly is the case, and seek a merging in marriage. Genuine love not only respects the individuality of the other but actually seeks to cultivate it, even at the risk of separation or loss. The ultimate goal of life remains the spiritual growth of the individual, the solitary journey to peaks that can be climbed only alone. Significant journeys cannot be accomplished without the nurture provided by a successful marriage or a successful society. Marriage and society exist for the basic purpose of nurturing such individual journeys. But, as is the case with all genuine love, "sacrifices" on behalf of the growth of the other result in equal or greater growth of the self. It is the return of the individual to the nurturing marriage or society from the peaks he or she has traveled alone which serves to elevate that marriage or that society to new heights. In this way individual growth and societal growth are interdependent, but it is always and inevitably lonely out on the growing edge. It is from the loneliness of his wisdom that once again the prophet of Kahlil Gibran speaks to us concerning marriage:

> *But let there be spaces in your togetherness,*
> *And let the winds of the heavens dance between you*

> *Love one another, but make not a bond of love:*
> *Let it rather be a moving sea between the shores*
> *   of your souls.*
> *Fill each other's cup but drink not from one cup.*
> *Give one another of your bread but eat not from the*
> *   same loaf*

* "To My Dear and Loving Husband," 1678, contained in *The Literature of the United States*, Walter Blair *et al.*, eds. (Glenview, Ill.: Scott, Foresman, 1953), p. 159.

Sing and dance together and be joyous, but let
each one of you be alone,
Even as the strings of a lute are alone though they
quiver with the same music.

Give your hearts, but not into each other's keeping.
For only the hand of Life can contain your hearts.
And stand together yet not too near together:
For the pillars of the temple stand apart,
And the oak tree and the cypress grow not in
*each other's shadow.**

Love and Psychotherapy

It is hard for me to recapture now the motivation and understanding with which I entered the field of psychiatry fifteen years ago. Certainly I wanted to "help" people. The process of helping people in the other branches of medicine involved technology with which I was uncomfortable and which in other ways seemed too mechanical to suit my tastes. I also found talking to people more fun than poking and prodding them, and the quirks of the human mind seemed inherently more interesting to me than the quirks of the body or the germs infesting it. I had no idea how psychiatrists helped people, except for the fantasy that psychiatrists were the possessors of magical words and magical techniques of interacting with patients which would magically unscramble the knots of the psyche. Perhaps I wanted to be a magician. I had very little notion that the work involved would have something to do with the spiritual growth of patients, and certainly I had

* *The Prophet*, pp. 15–16.

no notion whatsoever that it would involve my own spiritual growth.

During my first ten months of training I worked with highly disturbed inpatients who seemed to benefit much more from pills or shock treatments or good nursing care than they did from me, but I learned the traditional magical words and techniques of interaction. After this period I began to see my first neurotic patient for long-term outpatient psychotherapy. Let me call her Marcia. Marcia came to see me three times a week. It was a real struggle. She wouldn't talk about the things I wanted her to talk about, and she wouldn't talk about them in the way I wanted, and sometimes she just wouldn't talk at all. In some ways our values were quite different; in the struggle she came to modify hers somewhat and I came to modify mine somewhat. But the struggle continued despite my storehouse of magical words and techniques and postures, and there was no sign that Marcia was improving. Indeed, shortly after she started to see me she began a pattern of almost outrageous promiscuity, and for months she recounted unabatedly innumerable incidents of "bad behavior." Finally, after a year of this, she asked me in the middle of a session, "Do you think I'm a bit of a shit?"

"You seem to be asking me to tell you what I think of you," I replied, brilliantly stalling for time.

That was exactly what she wanted, she said. But what did I do now? What magical words or techniques or postures could help me? I could say, "Why do you ask that?" or "What are your fantasies about what I think of you?" or "What's important, Marcia, is not what I think of you but what you think of yourself." Yet I had an overpowering feeling that these gambits were cop-outs, and that after a whole year of seeing me three times a week the least Marcia was entitled to was an honest answer from me as to what I thought of her. But for this I had no precedent; telling a person honestly face to face what you think of him or her was not one of the magical words or techniques that any of my professors had taught me. It was an interaction that had never been suggested or recommended in my training; the very fact that it had not been mentioned indicated to me that it was an interaction that was disapproved of, a situation that any reputable psychiatrist would not allow himself to fall into. How to act? With my heart pounding I went out on what seemed to be a very shaky limb indeed. "Marcia," I said, "you have been seeing me now for over a year. During this long period of time things have not gone smoothly for us. Much of the time we have been struggling, and the strugle has often been boring or nerve-wracking or angry for both of us. Yet despite this you have continued to come back to see me at considerable effort and inconvenience to you, session after session, week after week, month after month. You wouldn't have been able to do this unless you were the kind of person who is determined to grow and willing to work very hard at making yourself a better person. I do not think I would feel that someone who works as hard on herself as you do is a bit of a shit. So the answer is, No, I do not think you are a bit of a shit. In fact, I admire you a great deal."

From among her dozens of lovers Marcia immediately picked one and established a meaningful relationship with him which eventually led to a highly successful and satisfying marriage. She was never again promiscuous. She immediately began to speak about the good things in herself. The sense of unproductive struggle between us instantly vanished, and our work became fluent and joyful, with incredibly rapid progress. Strangely, my going out on a limb by revealing my genuinely positive feelings for her—something I felt I was really not supposed to do—rather than seeming to hurt her, apparently was of great therapeutic benefit and clearly represented the turning point in our work together.

What does this mean? Does it mean that all we have to do to practice successful psychotherapy is to tell our patients that we think well of them? Hardly. First of all, it is necessary to be honest in therapy at all times. I honestly did admire and like Marcia. Second, my admiration and liking was of real significance to her precisely because of the length of time I had known her and the depth of our experiences in therapy. In fact, the essence of this turning point did not even have to do with my liking and admiration; it had to do with the nature of our relationship.

A similarly dramatic turning point came in the therapy of a young woman I will call Helen, whom I had been seeing twice weekly for nine months with a noticeable lack of success and for whom I did not yet have much positive feeling. Indeed, after all that time I did not even have much of a feeling of who Helen was at all. I had never before seen a patient for such a length of time without having gained some idea of who the individual was and the nature of the problem to be resolved. I was totally confused by her and had spent the better part of several nights attempting without any success whatsoever to make some sense out of the case. About all that was clear to me was that Helen did not trust me. She was vociferous in her complaints that I did not genuinely care for her in any way, shape or form and was interested only in her money. She was talking in this fashion during one session, after nine months of therapy: "You cannot imagine, Dr. Peck, how frustrating it is for me to attempt to communicate with you when you are so uninterested in me and therefore so oblivious to my feelings."

"Helen," I replied, "it seems to be frustrating for both of us. I don't know how this will make you feel, but you are the single most frustrating case I have ever had in a decade of practicing psychotherapy. I have never met anyone with whom I have made less headway in so long a time. Perhaps you are right in believing that I am not the right person to work with you. I don't know. I don't want to give up, but I sure as hell am puzzled about you, and I wonder until I'm almost crazy as to what the hell is wrong in our work together."

A glowing smile came over Helen's face. "You really do care for me after all," she said.

"Huh?" I asked.

"If you didn't really care for me you wouldn't feel so frustrated," she replied, as if it were all perfectly obvious.

At the very next session Helen began to tell me things that she had previously either withheld or actually lied about, and within a week I had a clear understanding of her basic problem, could make a diagnosis, and knew generally how the therapy should proceed.

Again, my reaction to Helen was meaningful and significant to her precisely because of the depth of my involvement with her and the intensity of our struggle together. We are now able to see the essential ingredient that makes psychotherapy effective and successful. It is not "unconditional positive regard," nor is it magical words, techniques or postures; it is human involvement and struggle. It is the willingness of the therapist to extend himself or herself for the purpose of nurturing the patient's growth—willingness to go out on a limb, to truly involve oneself at an emotional level in the relationship, to actually struggle with the patient and with oneself. In short, the essential ingredient of successful deep and meaningful psychotherapy is love.

It is remarkable, almost incredible, that the voluminous professional literature in the West on the subject of psychotherapy ignores the issue of love. Hindu gurus frequently make no bones about the fact that their love is the source of their power.* But the closest Western literature comes to the issue are those articles that attempt to analyze differences between successful and unsuccessful psychotherapists and usually end up mentioning such characteristics of successful psychotherapists as "warmth" and "empathy." Basically, we seem to be embarrassed by the subject of love. There are a number of reasons for this state of affairs. One is the confusion between genuine love and romantic love which so pervades our culture, as well as the other confusions that have

* See Peter Brent, *The God Men of India* (New York: Quadrangle Books, 1972).

been dealt with in this section. Another is our bias toward the rational, the tangible and the measurable in "scientific medicine," and it is largely out of "scientific medicine" that the profession of psychotherapy evolved. Since love is an intangible, incompletely measurable and suprarational phenomenon, it has not lent itself to scientific analysis.

Another reason is the strength of the psychoanalytic tradition in psychiatry of the aloof and detached analyst, a tradition for which Freud's followers more than Freud himself seem to be responsible. In this same tradition, any feelings of love that the patient has for the therapist are generally labeled "transference" and any feelings of love that the therapist has for the patient "countertransference," with the implication that such feelings are abnormal, a part of the problem rather than its solution, and are to be avoided. This is all quite absurd. Transference, as mentioned in the previous section, refers to *inappropriate* feelings, perceptions and responses. There is nothing inappropriate about patients coming to love a therapist who truly listens to them hour after hour in a nonjudgmental way, who truly accepts them as they probably have never been accepted before, who totally refrains from using them and who has been helpful in alleviating their suffering. Indeed, the essence of the transference in many cases is that which prevents the patient from developing a loving relationship with the therapist, and the cure consists of working through the transference so that the patient can experience a successful love relationship, often for the first time. Similarly, there is nothing at all inappropriate in the feelings of love that a therapist develops for his or her patient when the patient submits to the discipline of psychotherapy, cooperates in the treatment, is willing to learn from the therapist, and successfully begins to grow through the relationship. Intensive psychotherapy in many ways is a process of reparenting. It is no more inappropriate for a psychotherapist to have feelings of love for a patient than it is for a good parent to have feelings of love for a child. To the contrary, it is essential for the therapist to love a patient for the therapy to be successful, and if the therapy does become successful, then the therapeutic relationship will become a mutually loving one. It is inevitable that the therapist will experience loving feelings coincidental with the genuine love he or she has demonstrated toward the patient.

For the most part, mental illness is caused by an absence of or defect in the love that a particular child required from its particular parents for successful maturation and spiritual growth. It is obvious, then, that in order to be healed through psychotherapy the patient must receive from the psychotherapist at least a portion of the genuine love of which the patient was deprived. If the psychotherapist cannot genuinely love a patient, genuine healing will not occur. No matter how well credentialed and trained psychotherapists may be, if they cannot extend themselves through love to their patients, the results of their psychotherapeutic practice will be generally unsuccessful. Conversely, a totally uncredentialed and minimally trained lay therapist who exercises a great capacity to love will achieve psychotherapeutic results that equal those of the very best psychiatrists.

Since love and sex are so closely related and interconnected, it is appropriate to mention here briefly the issue of sexual relationships between psychotherapists and their patients, an issue that is currently receiving a good deal of attention in the press. Because of the necessarily loving and intimate nature of the psychotherapeutic relationship, it is inevitable that both patients and therapists routinely develop strong or extremely strong sexual attractions to each other. The pressures to sexually consummate such attractions may be enormous. I suspect that some of those in the profession of psychotherapy who cast stones at a therapist who has related sexually with a patient may not themselves be loving therapists and may not therefore have any real understanding of the enormity of the pressures involved. Moreover, were I ever to have a case in which I concluded after careful and judicious consideration that my patient's spiritual growth would be substantially furthered by our having sexual relations, I would proceed to have them. In fifteen years of practice, however, I have not yet had such a case, and I find it difficult to imagine that such a case could really exist. First of all, as I have mentioned, the role of the good therapist is primarily that of the good parent, and good parents do not consummate sexual relationships with their children for several very compelling reasons. The job of a parent is to be of use to a child and not to use the child for personal satisfaction. The job of a therapist is to be of use to a patient and not to use the patient to serve the therapist's own needs. The job of a parent is to encourage a child along the path toward independence, and the job of a therapist with a patient is the same. It is difficult to see how a therapist who related sexually with a patient would not be using the patient to satisfy his or her own needs or how the therapist would be encouraging the patient's independence thereby.

Many patients, particularly those likely to be most seductive, have sexualized attachments to their parents which clearly impede their freedom and growth. Both theory and the scant bit of evidence available strongly suggest that a sexual relationship between a therapist and such a patient is far more likely to cement the patient's immature attachments than to loosen them. Even if the relationship is not sexually consummated, it is detrimental for the therapist to "fall in love" with the patient, since, as we have seen, falling in love involves a collapse of ego boundaries and a diminution of the normal sense of separation that exists between individuals.

The therapist who falls in love with a patient cannot possibly be objective about the patient's needs or separate those needs from his or her own. It is out of love for their patients that therapists do not allow themselves the indulgence of falling in love with them. Since genuine love demands respect for the separate identity of the beloved, the genuinely loving therapist will recognize and accept that the patient's path in life is and should be separate from that of the therapist. For some therapists this means that their own and the patient's paths should never cross outside of the therapeutic hour. While I respect this position, for myself I find it unnecessarily rigid.

Although I have had one experience in which my relating to an ex-patient seemed to be definitely detrimental to her, I have had several other experiences in which social relationships with ex-patients seemed clearly beneficial to them as well as to myself. I have also been fortunate enough to successfully analyze several very close friends. Nonetheless, social contact with the patient outside of the therapeutic hour, even after therapy has been formally terminated, is something that should be entered into only with great caution and stringent self-examination as to whether the therapist's needs are being met by the contact to the detriment of the patient's.

We have been examining the fact that psychotherapy should be (must be, if successful) a process of genuine love, a somewhat heretical notion in traditional psychiatric circles. The other side of the same coin is at least equally heretical: if psychotherapy is genuinely loving, should love always be psychotherapeutic? If we genuinely love our spouse, our parents, our children, our friends, if we extend ourselves to nurture their spiritual growth, should we be practicing psychotherapy with them? My answer is: *Certainly*. From time to time at cocktail parties someone will say to me, "It must be difficult for you, Dr. Peck, to separate your social life from your professional life. After all, one can't go around analyzing one's family and friends, can one?" Usually the speaker is ony making idle conversation and is neither interested in nor ready to assimilate a serious reply. Occasionally, however, the situation gives me the opportunity to teach or practice psychotherapy there and then, on the spot, explaining just why I do not even attempt, or would want to attempt to separate my professional and my personal lives. If I perceive my wife or my children or my parents or my friends suffering from an illusion, a falsehood, an ignorance or an unnecessary impediment, I have every bit as much obligation to extend myself to them to correct the situation insofar as possible, as I do to my patients, who pay me for my services. Am I to withhold my services, my wisdom and my love from my family and my friends because they have not specifically contracted and paid me for my attention to their psychological needs? Hardly. How can I be a good friend, father, husband or son unless I take the opportunities that are available to attempt, with whatever artistry I can command, to teach my beloved what I know and give whatever assistance is in my power to give to his or her personal journeys of spiritual growth? Moreover, I expect the same services from my friends and family to the limits of their ability. Although their criticism of me may be unnecessarily blunt at times and their teaching may not be as thoughtful as an adult's, I learn much to help me from my children. My wife guides me as much as I guide her. I would not call my friends friends were they to withhold from me the honesty of their disapproval and their loving concern as to the wisdom and safety of the directions of my own journey. Can I not grow more rapidly with their help than without it? Any genuinely loving relationship is one of mutual psychotherapy.

I have not always seen it this way. In years past I was more appreciative of my wife's admiration than of her criticism, and did as much to foster her dependency as I did her power. My self-image as a husband and father was that of provider; my responsibility ended with bringing home the bacon. Home I wanted to be a place of comfort, not challenge. At that time I would have agreed with the proposition that it would be dangerous and unethical and destructive for a psychotherapist to practice his art upon his friends and family. But my agreement was motivated as much by laziness as it was by fear of misusing my profession. For psychotherapy, like love, is work, and it's easier to work eight hours a day than it is to work sixteen. It's also easier to love a person who seeks out your wisdom, who travels to your territory to obtain it, who pays you for your attention and whose demands upon you are strictly limited to fifty minutes at a time than it is to love someone who regards your attention as a right, whose demands may not be limited, who does not perceive you as an authority figure and who does not solicit your teaching. Conducting psychotherapy at home or with one's friends requires the same intensity of effort and self-discipline as it does in the office but under much less ideal conditions, which is to say that at home it requires even more effort and love. I hope, therefore, that other psychotherapists will not take these words as an exhortation to immediately begin practicing psychotherapy with their mates and children. If one remains on a journey of spiritual growth, one's capacity to love grows and grows. But it is always limited, and one clearly should not attempt psychotherapy beyond one's capacity to love, since psychotherapy without love will be unsuccessful and even harmful. If you can love six hours a day, be content with that for the moment, for your capacity is already far greater than most; the journey is a long one and it requires time for your capacity to grow. To practice psychotherapy with one's friends and family, to love one another full time, is an ideal, a goal to be striven toward but not instantly achieved.

Since, as I have indicated, laymen can practice successful psychotherapy without great training as long as they are genuinely loving human beings, the remarks I have made concerning the practice of psychotherapy on one's friends and family do not apply solely to professional therapists; they apply to everyone. Occasionally when patients ask me when they will be ready to terminate their therapy, I will reply, "When you yourself are able to be a good therapist." This reply is often most usefully made in group therapy, where patients of course do practice psychotherapy on each other and where their failures to successfully assume the role of psychotherapist can be pointed out to them. Many patients do not like this reply, and some will actually say, "That's too much work. To do that means that I would have to think all the time in my relationships with people. I don't want to think that much. I don't want to work that hard. I just want to enjoy myself." Patients often respond similarly when I point out to them that all human interactions are opportunities either to learn or to teach (to give or receive therapy), and when they neither learn nor teach in an interaction they are passing up an opportunity. Most people are quite correct when they say they do not want to achieve such a lofty goal

or work so hard in life. The majority of patients, even in the
hands of the most skilled and loving therapists, will terminate
their therapy at some point far short of completely fulfilling
their potential. They may have traveled a short or even a
goodly distance along the journey of spiritual growth, but the
whole journey is not for them. It is or seems to be too difficult.
They are content to be ordinary men and women and do not
strive to be God.

The Mystery of Love

This discussion began many pages back by noting that love
is a mysterious subject and that until now the mystery has
been ignored. The questions raised here so far have been
answered. But there are other questions, not so easy to answer.

One set of such questions derives rather logically from the
material thus far discussed. It has been made clear, for instance, that self-discipline develops from the foundation of
love. But this leaves unanswered the question of where love
itself comes from. And if we ask that, we must also ask what
are the sources of the absence of love. It has been further
suggested that the absence of love is the major cause of mental
illness and that the presence of love is consequently the essential healing element in psychotherapy. This being so, how is
it that certain individuals, born and raised in an environment
of nonlove, of unremitting neglect and casual brutality, somehow manage to transcend their childhood, sometimes even
without the loving assistance of psychotherapy, and become
mature, healthy and perhaps even saintly people? Conversely,
how is it that some patients, apparently no more ill than oth-

ers, fail partially or totally to respond to psychotherapeutic treatment by even the most wise and loving therapist?

An attempt will be made to answer this set of questions in the final section, on grace. The attempt will not meet with anyone's complete satisfaction, including my own. I hope, however, what I write will bring some enlightenment.

There is another set of questions having to do with matters deliberately omitted or glossed over in the discussion of love. When my beloved first stands before me naked, all open to my sight, there is a feeling throughout the whole of me: awe. Why? If sex is no more than an instinct, why don't I just feel "horny" or hungry? Such simple hunger would be quite sufficient to insure the propagation of the species. Why awe? Why should sex be complicated with reverence? And for that matter, what is it that determines beauty? I have said the object of genuine love must be a person, since only people have spirits capable of growth. But what about the finest creation by a master woodworker? Or the best sculptures of medieval madonnas? Or the bronze statue of the Greek charioteer at Delphi? Were these inanimate objects not loved by their creators and is not their beauty somehow related to their creators' love? What about the beauty of nature—nature, to which we sometimes give the name "creation"? And why in the presence of beauty or joy do we so often have the strange, paradoxical reaction of sadness or tears? How is it that certain bars of music played or sung in certain ways can move us so? And why do I become wet-eyed when my six-year-old son, still ill on his first night home from the hospital after a tonsillectomy, suddenly comes over to where I am lying, tired, on the floor and begins to rub my back gently?

Clearly there are dimensions of love that have not been discussed and are most difficult to understand. I do not think questions about these aspects (and many more) will be answered by sociobiology. Ordinary psychology with its knowledge of ego boundaries may be of a little help—but only a little. The people who know the most about such things are those among the religious who are students of Mystery. It is to them and to the subject of religion that we must turn if we are to obtain even glimmerings of insight into these matters.

The remainder of this book will deal with certain facets of religion. The next section will discuss in a very limited way the relationship between religion and the growth process. The final section will focus on the phenomenon of grace and the role it plays in this process. The concept of grace has been familiar to religion for millennia, but it is foreign to science, including psychology. Nonetheless, I believe that an understanding of the phenomenon of grace is essential to complete understanding of the process of growth in human beings. What follows will, I hope, represent a contribution to the slowly enlarging interface between religion and the science of psychology.

SECTION III

Growth and Religion

World Views and Religion

As human beings grow in discipline and love and life experience, their understanding of the world and their place in it naturally grows apace. Conversely, as people fail to grow in discipline, love and life experience, so does their understanding fail to grow. Consequently, among the members of the human race there exists an extraordinary variability in the breadth and sophistication of our understanding of what life is all about.

This understanding is our religion. Since everyone has some understanding—some world view, no matter how limited or primitive or inaccurate—everyone has a religion. This fact, not widely recognized, is of the utmost importance: everyone has a religion.

We suffer, I believe, from a tendency to define religion too narrowly. We tend to think that religion must include a belief in God or some ritualistic practice or membership in a worshiping group. We are likely to say of someone who does not attend church or believe in a superior being, "He or she is not religious." I have even heard scholars say such things as: "Buddhism is not really a religion" or "Unitarians have excluded religion from their faith" or "Mysticism is more a philosophy than a religion." We tend to view religion as something monolithic, cut out of whole cloth, and then, with this simplistic concept, we are puzzled as to how two very different people can both call themselves Christians. Or Jews. Or how an atheist might have a more highly developed sense of Christian morality than a Catholic who routinely attends mass.

In supervising other psychotherapists I rather routinely find that they pay too little, if any, attention to the ways in which their patients view the world. There are several reasons for this, but among them is the notion that if patients don't consider themselves religious by virtue of their belief in God or their church membership, they are lacking in religion and the matter therefore needs no further scrutiny. But the fact of the matter is that everyone has an explicit or implicit set of ideas and beliefs as to the essential nature of the world. Do patients envision the universe as basically chaotic and without meaning so that it is only sensible for them to grab whatever little pleasure they can whenever it is available? Do they see the world as a dog-eat-dog place where ruthlessness is essential for their survival? Or do they see it as a nurturing sort of place in which something good will always turn up and in which they need not fret much about the future? Or a place that owes them a living no matter how they conduct their lives? Or a universe of rigid law in which they will be struck down and cast away if they step even slightly out of line? Et cetera. There are all manner of different world views that people have. Sooner or later in the course of psychotherapy most therapists will come to recognize how a patient views the world, but if the therapist is specifically on the lookout for it, he or she will come to this recognition sooner rather than later. And it is essential that therapists arrive at this knowledge, for the world view of patients is always an essential part of their problems, and a correction in their world view is necessary for their cure. So I say to those I supervise: "Find out your patients' religions even if they say they don't have any."

Usually a person's religion or world view is at best only incompletely conscious. Patients are often unaware of how they view the world, and sometimes may even think they possess a certain kind of religion when they actually are possessed by a far different kind. Stewart, a successful industrial engineer, became severely depressed in his mid-fifties. Despite his success at work and the fact that he had been an exemplary husband and father, he felt worthless and evil. "The world would be a better place if I were dead," he said. And meant it. Stewart had made two extremely serious suicide attempts. No amount of realistic reassurance could interrupt the unrealism of his worthless self-image. As well as the usual symptoms of a severe depression, such as insomnia and agitation, Stewart also suffered great difficulty in swallowing his food. "It's not just that the food tastes bad," he said. "That too. But it's as if there's a blade of steel stuck straight in my throat and nothing but liquid can get by it." Special X-rays and tests failed to reveal a physical cause for his difficulty. Stewart made no bones about his religion. "I'm an atheist, plain and simple," he stated. "I'm a scientist. The only things I believe in are those things you can see and touch. Maybe I'd be better off if I had some kind of faith in a sweet and loving God, but, frankly, I can't stomach that kind of crap. I had enough of it when I was a child and I'm glad I've gotten away from it." Stewart had grown up in a small Midwestern community, the son of a rigid fundamentalist preacher and his equally rigid and fundamentalist wife, and had left home and church at the first opportunity.

Several months after he entered treatment Stewart recounted the following brief dream: "It was back in my childhood home in Minnesota. It was like I was still living there as a child, yet I also knew I was the same age as I am now. It was nighttime. A man had entered the house. He was going to cut our throats. I had never seen this man before, but strangely I knew who he was: the father of a girl I had dated a couple of times in high school. That was all. There was no conclusion. I just woke up fearful, knowing that this man wanted to cut our throats."

I asked Stewart to tell me everything he could about this man in his dream. "There's really nothing I can tell you," he said. "I never met the man. I only dated his daughter a couple of times—not really dates, just walking her home to her door after church youth group meetings. I did steal a kiss from her in the dark behind some bushes on one of those walks." Here Stewart gave a little nervous laugh and went on, "In my dream I had the sense I'd never seen her father, although I knew who he was. Actually, in real life I did see him—from a distance. He was the stationmaster for our town. Occasionally I would see him when I used to go to the station and watch the trains come in on summer afternoons."

Something clicked in my mind. I too as a child had spent lazy summer afternoons watching the trains go by. The train station was where the action was. And the stationmaster was the Director of the Action. He knew the distant places from which the great trains were coming to touch our little town and the faraway places to which they were going. He knew which trains would stop and which would roar through, shaking the earth as they went. He worked the switches, the signals. He received the mail and sent it off. And when he was not doing these wonderful things he sat in his office doing something more wonderful: tapping on a magical little key in a mysterious rhythmical language, sending messages out to the whole world.

"Stewart," I said, "you have told me that you're an atheist, and I believe you. There is a part of your mind that believes there is no God. But I am beginning to suspect that there is another part of your mind that does believe in God—a dangerous, cutthroat God."

My suspicion was correct. Gradually, as we worked together, reluctantly, striving against resistance, Stewart began to recognize within himself a strange and ugly faith: an assumption, beyond his atheism, that the world was controlled and directed by a malevolent force, a force that not only could cut his throat but that was eager to do so, eager to punish him for transgressions. Slowly also we began to focus on his "transgressions," mostly minor sexual incidents symbolized by his "stealing a kiss" from the stationmaster's daughter. Eventually it became clear that (among other reasons for his depression) Stewart was doing penance and figuratively cutting his own throat in the hope that by so doing he could prevent God from literally cutting it.

Where did Stewart's notion of a vicious God and a malevolent world come from? How do people's religions develop? What determines a person's particular world view? There are whole complexes of determinants, and this book will not explore the question in depth. But the most important factor in the development of the religion of most people is obviously their culture. If we are European we are likely to believe that Christ was a white man, and if we are African that he was a black man. If one is an Indian who was born and raised in Benares or Bombay, one is likely to become a Hindu and possess what has been described as a pessimistic world view. If one is an American born and raised in Indiana, one is more likely to become a Christian than a Hindu and to possess a somewhat more optimistic world view. We tend to believe what the people around us believe, and we tend to accept as truth what these people tell us of the nature of the world as we listen to them during our formative years.

But less obvious (except to psychotherapists) is the fact that the most important part of our culture is our particular family. The most basic culture in which we develop is the culture of our family, and our parents are its "culture leaders." Moreover, the most significant aspect of that culture is not what our parents tell us about God and the nature of things but rather what they do—how they behave toward each other, toward our siblings and, above all, toward us. In other words, what we learn about the nature of the world when we are growing up is determined by the actual nature of our experience in the microcosm of the family. It is not so much what our parents say that determines our world view as it is the unique world they create for us by their behavior. "I agree that I have this notion of a cutthroat God," Stewart said, "but where did it come from? My parents certainly believed in God —they talked about it incessantly—but theirs was a God of Love. Jesus loves us. God loves us. We love God and Jesus. Love, love, love, that's all I ever heard."

"Did you have a happy childhood?" I asked.

Stewart glared at me. "Stop playing dumb," he said. "You know I didn't. You know it was miserable."

"Why was it miserable?"

"You know that too. You know what it was like. I got the shit beaten out of me. Belts, boards, brooms, brushes, anything they could lay their hands on. There wasn't anything I could do that didn't merit a beating. A beating a day keeps the doctor away and makes a good little Christian out of you."

"Did they ever try to strangle you or cut your throat?"

"No, but I'm sure they would have if I hadn't been careful." There was a long moment of silence. Stewart's face became extremely depressed. Finally, heavily, he said, "I'm beginning to understand."

Stewart was not the only person who believed in what I have come to call the "monster-god." I have had a number of patients with similar concepts of God and similarly bleak or terrifying notions as to the nature of existence. What is surprising is that the monster-god is not more common in the minds of humans. In the first section of this book it was noted that when we are children our parents are godlike figures to our child's eye, and the way they do things seems the way they must be done throughout the universe. Our first (and, sadly, often our only) notion of God's nature is a simple extrapolation of our parents' natures, a simple blending of the characters of our mothers and fathers or their substitutes. If we have loving, forgiving parents, we are likely to believe in a loving and forgiving God. And in our adult view the world is likely to seem as nurturing a place as our childhood was. If our parents were harsh and punitive, we are likely to mature with a concept of a harsh and punitive monster-god. And if they failed to care for us, we will likely envision the universe as similarly uncaring.*

The fact that our religion or world view is initially largely determined by our unique childhood experience brings us face to face with a central problem: the relationship between religion and reality. It is the problem of the microcosm and the macrocosm. Stewart's view of the world as a dangerous place where he would get his throat cut if he wasn't very careful was perfectly realistic in terms of the microcosm of his childhood home; he lived under the domination of two vicious adults. But all parents are not vicious and all adults are not vicious. In the larger world, the macrocosm, there are many different kinds of parents and people and societies and cultures.

To develop a religion or world view that is realistic—that is, conforms to the reality of the cosmos and our role in it, as best we can know that reality—we must constantly revise and extend our understanding to include new knowledge of the larger world. We must constantly enlarge our frame of reference. We are dealing here with the issues of map-making and

---

* Frequently (but not always) the essence of a patient's childhood and hence the essence of his or her world view is captured in the "earliest memory." Consequently I will often ask patients, "Tell me the very first thing that you can remember." They may protest that they cannot do this, that they have a number of early memories. But when I force them to make a choice of one, the response will vary in flavor from "Well, I remember my mother picking me up and carrying me outside in her arms to show me a beautiful sunset" to "I remember sitting on the floor of the kitchen. I had wet my pants and my mother was standing over me waving a big spoon in the air and screaming at me." It is probable that these first memories, like the phenomenon of screen memories, which they so often are, are remembered precisely because they accurately symbolize the nature of a person's early childhood. It is not surprising, then, that the flavor of these earliest memories is so frequently the same as that of a patient's deepest feelings about the nature of existence.

transference, which were discussed at some length in the first section. Stewart's map of reality was accurate for the microcosm of his family, but he had transferred that map inappropriately into a larger adult world, where it was grossly incomplete and hence defective. To some extent the religion of most adults is a product of transference.

Most of us operate from a narrower frame of reference than that of which we are capable, failing to transcend the influence of our particular culture, our particular set of parents and our particular childhood experience upon our understanding. It is no wonder, then, that the world of humanity is so full of conflict. We have a situation in which human beings, who must deal with each other, have vastly different views as to the nature of reality, yet each one believes his or her own view to be the correct one since it is based on the microcosm of personal experience. And to make matters worse, most of us are not even fully aware of our own world views, much less the uniqueness of the experience from which they are derived. Bryant Wedge, a psychiatrist specializing in the field of international relations, studied negotiations between the United States and the U.S.S.R. and was able to delineate a number of basic assumptions as to the nature of human beings and society and the world held by Americans which differed dramatically from the assumptions of Russians. These assumptions dictated the negotiating behavior of both sides. Yet neither side was aware of its own assumptions or the fact that the other side was operating on a different set of assumptions. The inevitable result was that the negotiating behavior of the Russians seemed to the Americans to be either crazy or deliberately evil, and of course the Americans seemed to the Russians equally crazy or evil.* We are indeed like the three

* Bryant Wedge and Cyril Muromcew, "Psychological Factors in Soviet Disarmament Negotiation," *Journal of Conflict Resolution*, 9, No. 1 (March 1965), 18–36. (See also Bryant Wedge, "A Note on Soviet-American Negotiation," *Proceedings of the Emergency Conference on Hostil-*

proverbial blind men, each in touch with only his particular piece of the elephant yet each claiming to know the nature of the whole beast. So we squabble over our different microcosmic world views, and all wars are holy wars.

The Religion of Science

Spiritual growth is a journey out of the microcosm into an ever greater macrocosm. In its earlier stages (which is all this book concerns itself with) it is a journey of knowledge and not of faith. In order to escape the microcosm of our previous experience and free ourselves from transferences, it is necessary that we *learn*. We must continually expand our realm of knowledge and our field of vision through the thorough digestion and incorporation of new information.

The process of expansion of knowledge has been a major theme of this book. It will be recalled that in the previous section love was defined as an extension—that is, an expansion—of ourselves, and it was noted that among the risks of love was the risk of moving into the unknown of new experience. And at the end of the first section on discipline it was also noted that the learning of something new requires a giving up of the old self and a death of outworn knowledge. To develop a broader vision we must be willing to forsake, to kill, our narrower vision. In the short run it is more comfortable not to do this—to stay where we are, to keep using the same microcosmic map, to avoid suffering the death of cherished

―――――――――
ity, Aggression, and War, American Association for Social Psychiatry, Nov. 17–18, 1961.)

notions. The road of spiritual growth, however, lies in the opposite direction. We begin by distrusting what we already believe, by actively seeking the threatening and unfamiliar, by deliberately challenging the validity of what we have previously been taught and hold dear. The path to holiness lies through questioning *everything*.

In a very real sense, we begin with science. We begin by replacing the religion of our parents with the religion of science. We must rebel against and reject the religion of our parents, for inevitably their world view will be narrower than that of which we are capable if we take full advantage of our personal experience, including our adult experience and the experience of an additional generation of human history. There is no such thing as a good hand-me-down religion. To be vital, to be the best of which we are capable, our religion must be a wholly personal one, forged entirely through the fire of our questioning and doubting in the crucible of our own experience of reality. As the theologian Alan Jones has said:

> One of our problems is that very few of us have developed any distinctive personal life. Everything about us seems secondhand, even our emotions. In many cases we have to rely on secondhand information in order to function. I accept the word of a physician, a scientist, a farmer, on trust. I do not like to do this. I have to because they possess vital knowledge of living of which I am ignorant. Secondhand information concerning the state of my kidneys, the effects of cholesterol, and the raising of chickens, I can live with. But when it comes to questions of meaning, purpose, and death, secondhand information will not do. I cannot survive on a secondhand faith in a secondhand God. There has to be a personal word, a unique confrontation, if I am to come alive.*

So for mental health and spiritual growth we must develop

* *Journey Into Christ* (New York: Seabury Press, 1977), pp. 91–92.

our own personal religion and not rely on that of our parents. But what is this about a "religion of science"? Science is a religion because it is a world view of considerable complexity with a number of major tenets. Most of these major tenets are as follows: the universe is real, and therefore a valid object for examination; it is of value for human beings to examine the universe; the universe makes sense—that is, it follows certain laws and is predictable; but human beings are poor examiners, subject to superstition, bias, prejudice, and a profound tendency to see what they want to see rather than what is really there; consequently, to examine and hence understand accurately, it is necessary for human beings to subject themselves to the discipline of scientific method. The essence of this discipline is experience, so that we cannot consider ourselves to know something unless we have actually experienced it; while the discipline of scientific method begins with experience, simple experience itself is not to be trusted; to be trusted, experience must be repeatable, usually in the form of an experiment; moreover, the experience must be verifiable, in that other people must have the same experience under the same circumstances.

The key words are "reality," "examination," "knowledge," "distrust," "experience," "discipline." These are words we have been using all along. Science is a religion of skepticism. To escape from the microcosm of our childhood experience, from the microcosm of our culture and its dogmas, from the half truths our parents told us, it is essential that we be skeptical about what we think we have learned to date. It is the scientific attitude that enables us to transform our personal experience of the microcosm into a personal experience of the macrocosm. We must begin by becoming scientists.

Many patients who have already taken this beginning say to me: "I'm not religious. I don't go to church. I no longer believe much of what the church and my parents told me. I don't have my parents' faith. I guess I'm not very spiritual." It often comes as a shock to them when I question the reality of their assumption that they are not spiritual beings. "You have a religion," I may say, "a rather profound one. You worship the truth. You believe in the possibility of your growth and betterment: the possibility of spiritual progress. In the strength of your religion you are willing to suffer the pains of challenge and the agonies of unlearning. You take the risk of therapy, and all this you do for the sake of your religion. I am not at all certain it is realistic to say that you are less spiritual than your parents; to the contrary, I suspect the reality is that you have spiritually evolved beyond your parents, that your spirituality is greater by a quantum leap than theirs, which is insufficient to provide them with even the courage to question."

One thing to suggest that science as a religion represents an improvement, an evolutionary leap, over a number of other world views, is its international character. We speak of the worldwide scientific community. And it is beginning to approach a true community, to come considerably closer than the Catholic Church, which is probably the next closest thing to a true international brotherhood. Scientists of all lands are able, far better than most of the rest of us, to talk to each other. To some extent they have been successful in transcending the microcosm of their culture. To some extent they are becoming wise.

To some extent. While I believe that the skeptical world view of the scientific-minded is a distinct improvement over a world view based upon blind faith, local superstition and unquestioned assumptions, I also believe that most of the scientific-minded have only barely begun the journey of spiritual growth. Specifically, I believe that the outlook of most scientific-minded people toward the reality of God is almost as parochial as the outlook of simple peasants who blindly follow the faith of their fathers. Scientists have grave difficulty dealing with the reality of God.

When we look from our vantage of sophisticated skepticism at the phenomenon of belief in God we are not impressed. We see dogmatism, and proceeding from dogmatism, we see wars and inquisitions and persecutions. We see hypocrisy: people professing the brotherhood of man killing their fellows in the name of faith, lining their pockets at the expense of others, and practicing all manner of brutality. We see a bewildering multiplicity of rituals and images without consensus: this god is a woman with six arms and six legs; that is a man who sits on a throne; this one is an elephant; that one the essence of nothingness; pantheons, household gods, trinities, unities. We see ignorance, superstition, rigidity. The track record for belief in God looks pretty poor. It is tempting to think that humanity might be better off without a belief in God, that God is not only pie in the sky by and by, but a poisoned pie at that. It would seem reasonable to conclude that God is an illusion in the minds of humans—a destructive illusion—and that belief in God is a common form of human psychopathology that should be healed.

So we have a question: Is belief in God a sickness? Is it a manifestation of transference—a concept of our parents, derived from the microcosm, inappropriately projected into the macrocosm? Or, to put it another way, is such belief a form of primitive or childish thinking which we should grow out of as we seek higher levels of awareness and maturity? If we want to be scientific in attempting to answer this question, it is essential that we turn to the reality of actual clinical data. What happens to one's belief in God as one grows through the process of psychotherapy?

The Case of Kathy

Kathy was the most frightened person I have ever seen. When I came into her room that first time she was sitting on the floor in the corner muttering what sounded like a chant.

She looked up at me standing in the the doorway and her eyes grew wide with terror. She wailed and pushed herself back into the corner and kept straining against the walls as if she wished she could push herself through them. I said, "Kathy, I'm a psychiatrist. I'm not going to hurt you." I took a chair, sat down at some distance from her and waited. For another minute she continued to push herself into the corner. Then she began to relax, but only enough to start weeping inconsolably. After a while her weeping stopped and she began to chant to herself again. I asked her what was wrong. "I'm going to die," she blurted out, hardly pausing to interrupt the cadence of her chant. There was nothing more she could tell me. She continued to chant. Every five minutes or so she would stop, seemingly exhausted, whimper for a few moments, and then resume her chanting. To whatever question I asked she would respond only with "I'm going to die," never breaking the rhythm of the chant. It seemed that she felt she might be able to prevent her death by this chanting and could not allow herself to rest or sleep.

From her husband, Howard, a young policeman, I obtained the minimal facts. Kathy was twenty years old. They had been married for two years. There were no problems with the marriage. Kathy was close to her parents. She had never had any psychiatric difficulty before. This was a complete surprise. She had been perfectly fine that morning. She had driven him to work. Two hours later his sister called him. She had gone to visit Kathy and had found her in this condition. They had brought her to the hospital. No, she had not been acting strange lately. Except maybe for one thing. For about four months she had seemed quite fearful of going into public places. To help her Howard had been doing all the shopping in the supermarket while she waited in the car. She also seemed to be afraid of being left alone. She prayed a lot —but, then, she had done that ever since he had known her. Her family was quite religious. Her mother went to mass at least twice a week. Funny thing—Kathy had stopped going to mass as soon as they were married. Which was just fine with him. But she still prayed a lot. Her physical health? Oh, that was excellent. She'd never been hospitalized. Fainted once at a wedding several years ago. Contraception? She took the pill. Wait a minute. About a month ago she told him she was stopping the pill. She'd read about how it was dangerous or something. He hadn't thought much about it.

I gave Kathy massive amounts of tranquilizers and sedatives so that she was able to sleep at night, but during the next two days her behavior remained unchanged: incessant chanting, inability to communicate anything except the conviction of her imminent death, and unremitting terror. Finally, on the fourth day, I gave her an intravenous injection of sodium amytal. "This injection is going to make you sleepy, Kathy," I said, "but you will not fall asleep. Nor will you die. It will make you able to stop chanting. You will feel very relaxed. You will be able to talk with me. I want you to tell me what happened the morning you came to the hospital."

"Nothing happened," Kathy answered.

"You drove your husband to work?"

"Yes. Then I drove home. Then I knew I was going to die."

"You drove home just as you do every morning after you drop your husband at work?"

Kathy began to chant again.

"Stop chanting, Kathy," I ordered. "You're completely safe. You're feeling very relaxed. Something was different about the way you drove home that morning. You are going to tell me what was different."

"I took a different road."

"Why did you do that?"

"I took the road past Bill's house."

"Who's Bill?" I asked.

Kathy started chanting once more.

"Is Bill a boyfriend of yours?"

"He was. Before I got married."

"You miss Bill a lot, don't you?"

Kathy wailed, "Oh, God, I'm going to die."

"Did you see Bill that day?"

"No."

"But you wanted to see him?"

"I'm going to die," Kathy replied.

"Do you feel that God is going to punish you for wanting to see Bill again?"

"Yes."

"That's why you believe you're going to die?"

"Yes." Once more Kathy started chanting.

I let her chant for ten minutes while I collected my thoughts.

Finally I said to her, "Kathy, you believe you are going to die because you believe you know the mind of God. But you are wrong. Because you do not know the mind of God. All you know is what you have been told about God. Much of what you have been told about God is wrong. I do not know everything about God, but I know more than you do and more than the people who have told you about God. For instance, every day I see men and women, like yourself, who want to be unfaithful, and some are, and they are not punished by God. I know, because they keep coming back to see me. And talk with me. And they become happier. Just as you will become happier. Because we are going to work together. And you are going to learn that you're not a bad person. And you're going to learn the truth—about yourself and about God. And you will become happier, about yourself and about life. But now you're going to sleep. And when you awake you will no longer be afraid that you're going to die. And when you see me tomorrow morning again, you will be able to talk with me, and we will talk about God and we will talk about yourself."

In the morning Kathy was improved. She was still frightened and unconvinced that she would not die, but no longer certain that she would. Slowly, on that day and for many, many days thereafter, her story emerged, piece by piece. During her senior year in high school she had had sexual intercourse with Howard. He wanted to marry her and she had agreed. Two weeks later while at the wedding of a friend, the idea suddenly came to her that she did not want to get married. She fainted. Afterward she was confused as to whether she loved Howard. But she felt that she had to go through with the marriage because she knew she had already sinned by having premarital relations with him, and this sin would be magnified if she did not consecrate their relationship in marriage. Still, she did not want children, at least not until she felt more certain that she loved Howard. So she started on the pill—another sin. She could not bear to confess these sins and was relieved to stop going to mass after they were married. She enjoyed sex with Howard. Almost from the day of their wedding, however, he lost interest in her sexually. He remained an ideal provider, buying her gifts, treating her deferentially, working a great deal of overtime, not allowing her to have a job. But she almost had to beg him for sex, and the sex they had every two weeks was about all there was to relieve her unremitting boredom. Divorce was out; *that* was a sin, unthinkable.

Despite herself Kathy began to have fantasies of sexual infidelity. She thought perhaps she might rid herself of these if she prayed more, so she started to pray ritualistically five minutes every hour. Then Howard noticed and teased her about it. So she decided to hide her praying by doing it more in the daytime when Howard was not home, to make up for not doing it in the evening when he was. This meant she had to pray either more frequently or faster. She decided to do both. She prayed now every half hour, and in her five minutes of praying time she doubled her speed. The fantasies of infidelity continued, however, and gradually became even more frequent and insistent. Whenever she went outside she looked at men. That made things worse. She became fearful of going outside with Howard, and even when she was with him, she became frightened of public places where she might see men. She thought perhaps she ought to return to church. But then she realized that if she returned to church she would be sinning if she did not go to confession and confess her fantasies of infidelity to the priest. This she could not do. She again doubled the speed of her praying. To facilitate this she began to develop an elaborate system in which a single chanted syllable stood for an entire particular prayer. This was the genesis of her chanting. In a while, perfecting her system, she was able to chant a thousand prayers in a five-minute period. Initially, while she was so busy perfecting her chanting, the fantasies of infidelity seemed to abate, but once she had the system down pat they returned full force. She began to consider how she might actually carry them out. She thought of calling Bill, her old boyfriend. She thought of bars she might go to in the afternoon. Terrified that she might really do this, she stopped taking the pill, hoping that the fear of getting pregnant would help her in resisting such acts. But the desire kept growing stronger. One afternoon she found herself starting to masturbate. She was horrified. That was perhaps the worst sin of all. She'd heard of cold showers and took one as cold as she could stand. It helped her until Howard came home. But the next day it was all back again.

Finally, that last morning, she gave in. After dropping Howard off at work she drove directly to Bill's house. She parked right in front. She waited. Nothing happened. No one seemed to be home. She got out of the car and stood leaning against it in a seductive pose. "Please," she pleaded silently, "please let Bill see me, please let him notice me." Still nothing happened. "Please let someone see me, anyone. I've got to fuck someone. Oh, God, I'm a whore. I'm the Whore of Babylon. O God, kill me, I've got to die." She jumped in the car and raced back to the apartment. She got a razor blade and went to cut her wrist. She could not do it. But God could. God would. God would give her what she deserved. He would put an end to it, an end to her. Let the vigil begin. "O God, I'm so scared, I'm so scared, please hurry, I'm so scared." She began to chant, waiting. And that was how her sister-in-law found her.

This story was elicited in its entirety only after months of painstaking work. Much of this work centered around the concept of sin. Where did she learn that masturbation is a sin? Who had told her it was a sin? How did her informant know it was a sin? What made masturbation a sin? Why is infidelity a sin? What makes a sin? And so on, and so on. I know of no profession more exciting and more privileged than the practice of psychotherapy, but at times it may be almost tedious as the attitudes of a lifetime are methodically challenged one by one in all their particulars. Often such challenge is at least partly successful even before the whole story emerges. For instance, Kathy was able to tell me about many of these details, such as her fantasies and her temptation to masturbation, only after she herself had begun to question the validity of her guilt and her conception of these acts as sins. In raising these questions it was also necessary that she question the validity of the authority and wisdom of the whole Catholic Church, or at least the church as she had experienced it. One does not take on the Catholic Church easily. She could do so only because she had the strength of an ally in me, because she had gradually come to feel that I was truly on her side, truly had her best interests at heart and would not lead her into evil. This "therapeutic alliance," such as she and I had slowly constructed, is a prerequisite for all successful major psychotherapy.

Much of this work was conducted on an outpatient basis. Kathy had been able to be discharged from the hospital a week following her sodium amytal interview. But it was only after four months of intensive therapy that she was able to say in regard to her notions of sin, "I guess the Catholic Church sold me a bill of goods." At this point a new phase of therapy was begun, for we began to ask the question: How was it that this had happened? Why had she allowed herself to buy this bill of goods, lock, stock and barrel? How was it that she had not been able to think more for herself and had not until now challenged the church in any way? "But Mother told me I should not question the church," Kathy said. And so we began to work on Kathy's relationship with her parents. With her father there was no relationship. There was no one to relate to. Father worked; that was all he did. He worked and he worked, and when he came home it was to sleep in his chair with his beer. Except on Friday nights. Then he went out for his beer. Mother ran the family. Alone, unchallenged, uncontradicted, unopposed, she ran it. She was kind but firm. She was giving but never gave in. Peaceful and implacable. "You mustn't do that, dear. Good girls don't do that." "You don't want to wear those shoes, dear. Girls from nice homes don't wear those kind of shoes." "It isn't a question of whether you want to go to mass, dear. The Lord wants us to go to mass." Gradually Kathy came to see that behind the power of the Catholic Church lay the enormous power of her mother, a person so softly yet so totally domineering that it seemed unthinkable to defy her.

But psychotherapy seldom goes smoothly. Six months after she had left the hospital Howard called one Sunday morning to say that Kathy was locked in the bathroom of their apartment chanting once again. Upon my instructions he persuaded her to return to the hospital, where I met them. Kathy was almost as frightened as the first day I saw her. Once again Howard had no clue as to what had set it off. I took Kathy into her room. "Stop chanting," I ordered, "and tell me what's the matter."

"I can't."

"Yes, you can, Kathy."

Hardly catching her breath in between her chanting, she suggested, "Maybe I can if you give me the truth drug again."

"No, Kathy," I replied. "This time you're strong enough to do it yourself."

She wailed. Then she looked at me and resumed her chanting. But in her look I thought I detected anger, almost fury, at me.

"You're angry at me," I stated.

She shook her head as she chanted.

"Kathy," I said, "I can think of a dozen reasons why you might be angry at me. But I don't know unless you tell me. You can tell me. It will be all right."

"I'm going to die," she moaned.

"No, you're not, Kathy. You're not going to die because you're angry at me. I'm not going to kill you because you're angry at me. It's all right for you to be angry at me."

"My days are not long," Kathy moaned. "My days are not long."

Something about these words sounded strange to me. They were not the words I would have expected. Somehow they seemed unnatural. But I was not sure what to say except to repeat myself one way or another.

"Kathy, I love you," I said. "I love you even if you hate me. That's what love is. How could I punish you for hating me, since I love you, hating and all?"

"It's not you I hate," she sobbed.

Suddenly it clicked. "Your days are not long. Not long on this earth. That's it, isn't it, Kathy? Honor your mother and your father that your days may be long on this earth. The Fifth Commandment. Honor them or die. That's what's happening, isn't it?"

"I hate her," Kathy muttered. Then louder, as if emboldened by the sound of her own voice saying the dreaded words, "I hate her. I hate my mother. I hate her. She never gave me . . . she never gave me . . . she never gave me *me*. She never let me be me. She made me in her image. She made me, made me, made me. She never let any of me be me."

Actually, Kathy's therapy was still in its early stages. The real day-to-day terror still lay ahead, the terror of being truly herself in a thousand little ways. Recognizing the fact that her mother had totally dominated her, Kathy then had to deal with why she had allowed this to happen. Rejecting her mother's domination, she had to face the process of establishing her own values and making her own decisions, and she was very frightened. It was much safer to let her mother make the decisions, much simpler to adopt her mother's values and those of the church. It took much more work to direct her own existence. Later Kathy was to say, "You know, I wouldn't really trade places for anything with the person I used to be, yet sometimes I still long for those days. My life used to be easier then. At least in a way."

Beginning to function more independently, Kathy confronted Howard with his failure as a lover. Howard promised he would change. But nothing happened. Kathy pressed him. He began to get anxiety attacks. On my urging, when he came to me about these, he went to another psychotherapist for treatment. He started to deal with deep-seated homosexual feelings, against which he had defended himself by his marriage to Kathy. Because she was very physically attractive he had regarded her as a "real catch," a prize the winning of which would prove to himself and the world his masculine competence. In a meaningful way he had never loved her. Having come to accept this, he and Kathy most amicably agreed to a divorce. Kathy went to work as a saleswoman in a large clothing store. With me she agonized over the innumerable small but independent decisions she was required to make in connection with her job. Gradually she became more assertive and confident. She dated many men, intending eventual remarriage and motherhood, but for the time being enjoying her career. She became an assistant buyer for the store. After terminating therapy she was promoted to buyer, and most recently I heard from her that she had moved to another, larger firm in the same capacity, and was quite pleased with herself at the age of twenty-seven. She does not go to church and no longer considers herself a Catholic. She doesn't know whether she believes in God or not, but will tell you frankly that the issue of God just doesn't seem a very important one at this point in her life.

I have described Kathy's case at such length precisely because it is so typical of the relationship between religious upbringing and psychopathology. There are millions of Kathys. I used to tell people only somewhat facetiously that the Catholic Church provided me with my living as a psychiatrist. I could equally well have said the Baptist Church, Lutheran Church, Presbyterian Church, or any other. The church was not, of course, the sole cause of Kathy's neurosis. In a sense the church was only a tool used by Kathy's mother to cement and augment her excessive parental authority. One could justifiably say that the mother's domineering nature, abetted by an absentee father, was the more basic cause of the neurosis, and in this respect too Kathy's case was typical. Nonetheless, the church must share the blame. No nun in her parochial school and no priest in her catechism class ever encouraged Kathy to reasonably question religious doctrine or in any way whatever to think for herself. There was never any evidence of concern on the part of the church that its doctrine might be overtaught, unrealistically rigid or subject to misuse and misapplication. One way of analyzing Kathy's problem would be to state that while she believed wholeheartedly in God, the commandments and the concept of sin, her religion and understanding of the world was of the hand-me-down variety and badly suited to her needs. She had failed to question, to challenge, to think for herself. Yet Kathy's church—and this also is typical—made not the slightest effort to assist her in working out a more appropriate and original personal religion. It would appear that churches generally, if anything, favor the hand-me-down variety.

Because Kathy's case is so typical and others like it are so common in their practice, many psychiatrists and psychotherapists perceive religion as the Enemy. They may even think of religion as being itself a neurosis—a collection of inherently irrational ideas that serve to enchain people's minds and oppress their instincts toward mental growth. Freud, a rationalist and scientist par excellence, seemed to see things in roughly this light, and since he is the most influential figure in modern psychiatry (for many good reasons), his attitudes have contributed to the concept of religion as a neurosis. It is indeed tempting for psychiatrists to view themselves as knights of modern science locked in noble combat with the destructive forces of ancient religious superstition and irrational but authoritarian dogma. And the fact of the matter is that psychotherapists must spend enormous amounts of time and effort in the struggle to liberate their patients' minds from

outmoded religious ideas and concepts that are clearly destructive.

The Case of Marcia

But not all cases are like Kathy's by any means. There are
many other patterns, some also quite common. Marcia was
one of the very first of my long-term-therapy cases. She was
a quite wealthy young woman in her mid-twenties who
sought my attention because of a generalized anhedonia.
While she could not put her finger on anything wrong with
her existence, she found it inexplicably joyless. Certainly she
looked joyless. Despite her wealth and her college education
she looked like an impoverished, bedraggled and aged immi-
grant woman. Throughout the first year of therapy she invariably dressed in badly fitting clothes of blue, gray, black
or brown, and carried with her an enormous, filthy and rag-
ged carpetbag of similar hue. She was the only child of intellectual parents, both highly successful university professors,
both socialists of a sort who believed that religion was "pie in
the sky by and by." They had made fun of her when, as a
young adolescent, she had attended church with a girl friend.

By the time she entered therapy, Marcia agreed with her
parents wholeheartedly. At the very beginning she announced, somewhat proudly and stridently, that she was an
atheist—not a namby-pamby atheist but a real one, who believed that the human race would be much better off if it could
escape from the delusion that God existed or even might exist.
Interestingly, Marcia's dreams were chock-full of religious
symbols, such as birds flying into rooms, their beaks holding
scrolls upon which obscure messages were written in an an-

cient language. But I did not confront Marcia with this aspect of her unconscious. Indeed, we did not deal at all with issues of religion at any time throughout the two-year course of her therapy. What we primarily focused on at great length was her relationship with her parents, two most intelligent and rational individuals who had provided well for her economically but were extraordinarily distant from her emotionally in their intellectually austere way. In addition to their emotional distance, both of them were also so highly invested in their own careers that they had little time or energy for her. The result was that while she had a comfortable and intact home, Marcia was the proverbial "poor little rich girl," a psychological orphan. But she was reluctant to look at this. She resented it when I suggested that her parents had significantly deprived her, and she resented it when I pointed out that she dressed like an orphan. It was just the new style, she said, and I had no right to criticize it.

Progress with Marcia in therapy was painfully gradual, but dramatic. The key element was the warmth and closeness of the relationship that we were slowly able to construct with each other, which contrasted with the relationship she had had with her parents. One morning at the beginning of the second year of therapy Marcia came into her session carrying a new bag. It was but a third the size of her old carpetbag and was a riot of bright colors. Thereafter about once each month she would add a new piece of color—bright oranges, yellows, light blues and greens—to her wardrobe, almost like a flower slowly unfolding its petals. In her next-to-last session with me she was musing about how well she felt and said, "You know, it's strange, but not only has the inside of me changed; everything outside of me seems to have changed too. Even though I'm still here, living in the same old house and doing some of the same old things, the whole world looks very different, feels very different. It feels warm and safe and loving and exciting and good. I remember telling you I was an atheist. I'm not sure I am any more. In fact, I don't think I am. Sometimes now when the world feels right, I say to myself,

'You know, I bet there really is a God. I don't think the world could be so right without a God.' It's funny. I don't know how to talk about this sort of thing. I just feel connected, real, like I'm a real part of a very big picture, and even though I can't see much of the picture, I know it's there and I know it's good and I know I'm a part of it."

Through therapy Kathy moved from a place where the notion of God was all-important to a place where it was of no importance. Marcia, on the other hand, moved from a position where she rejected the notion of God to one where it was becoming quite meaningful for her. The same process, the same therapist, yet with seemingly opposite results, both successful. How are we to explain this? Before we attempt to do so, let us consider yet another type of case. In Kathy's case it was necessary for the therapist to actively challenge her religious ideas in order to bring about change in the direction of a dramatically diminished influence of the God-concept in her life. In the case of Marcia the concept of God began to assume an increased influence, but without the therapist ever challenging her religious concepts in any way. Is it ever necessary, we may ask, for a therapist to actively challenge a patient's atheism or agnosticism and deliberately lead the patient in the direction of religiosity?

The Case of Theodore

Ted was thirty when he came to see me, and a hermit. For the preceding seven years he had lived in a small cabin deep in the woods. He had few friends and no one close. For three years he had not dated. Occasionally he performed minor carpentry jobs, but mostly he filled his days by fishing, reading and spending endless time making unimportant decisions, such as what he would cook for dinner and how he might cook it or whether he could or could not afford to purchase an inexpensive tool. Actually, by virtue of an inheritance he was quite wealthy. He was also intellectually brilliant. And, as he said that first session, paralyzed. "I know I should be doing something more constructive and creative with my life," he complained, "but I can't even make the most minor decisions, much less big ones. I ought to have a career. I ought to go to graduate school and learn some kind of occupation, but I can't get enthusiastic about anything. I've thought of everything—teaching, scholarly work, international relations, medicine, agriculture, ecology—but nothing turns me on. I may get interested in it for a day or two, but then every field seems to have insurmountable problems. Life seems to be an insurmountable problem."

His problem began, Ted said, when he was eighteen and entered college. Until then everything had been fine. He had had basically an ordinary childhood in a stable well-to-do home with two older brothers; parents who cared for him even if they didn't care much for each other; good grades and satisfactions in a private boarding school. Then—and perhaps this was crucial—came a passionate love affair with a woman who rejected him the week before he entered college. Dejected, he had spent most of his freshman year drunk. Still, he maintained good grades. Then he had several other love affairs, each one more halfhearted and unsuccessful than the last. His grades began to slip. He could not decide what to write papers about. A close friend, Hank, was killed in an automobile accident in the middle of his junior year, but he'd gotten over it. He even stopped drinking that year. But the problem with decision-making became still worse. He simply could not choose a topic on which to write his senior thesis. He finished his course work. He rented an off-campus room. All he needed to graduate was to submit a short thesis, the

kind of thing one could do in a month. It took him the following three years. Then, nothing. Seven years before, he had
come here to the woods.

Ted felt certain that his problem was rooted in his sexuality. After all, his difficulties had begun, had they not, with
an unsuccessful love affair? Besides, he had read almost everything that Freud had ever written (and much more than I
myself had read). So during the first six months of therapy
we plumbed the depths of his childhood sexuality, getting
nowhere in particular. But in that period several interesting
facets of his personality did emerge. One was his total lack of
enthusiasm. He might wish for good weather, but when it
came he would shrug his shoulders and say, "It doesn't really
make any difference. Basically one day's just like the next."
Fishing in the lake, he caught an enormous pike, "But it was
more than I could eat and I have no friends to share it with,
so I threw it back."

Related to this lack of enthusiasm was a kind of global
snobbishness, as if he found the world and all that was in it
to be in poor taste. His was the critics's eye. I came to suspect
he employed this snobbishness to keep a kind of distance
between himself and things that might otherwise affect him
emotionally. Finally, Ted had an enormous penchant for se-
crecy, which made therapy very slow going indeed. The most
important facts of any incident had to be pried out of
him. He had a dream: "I was in a classroom. There was
an object—I don't know what—which I had placed inside
a box. I had built the box around the object so that no one
could tell what was inside it. I had placed the box inside
a dead tree, and with finely fashioned wooden screws had
replaced the bark over the box. But sitting in the classroom
I suddenly remembered that I had not been certain to
make the screws flush with the bark. I became quite anxious.
So I rushed out to the woods and worked the screws so that
no one could distinguish them from the bark. Then I felt
better and came back to class." As with many people,
class and classroom were symbols for therapy in Ted's

dreams. It was clear he did not want me to find the core of his neurosis.

The first small chink in Ted's armor occurred during one session in the sixth month of therapy. He had spent the evening before at the house of an acquaintance. "It was a dreadful evening," Ted lamented. "He wanted me to listen to this new record he'd bought, Neil Diamond's sound track for the movie of *Jonathan Livingston Seagull.* It was excruciating. I do not understand how educated people can actually enjoy such putrid mucilage or even call it music."

The intensity of his snobbish reaction caused me to pick up my ears. "*Jonathan Livingston Seagull* was a religious book," I commented. "Was the music also religious?"

"I suppose you could call it religious as much as you could call it music."

"Perhaps it was the religion that offended you," I suggested, "and not so much the music."

"Well, I certainly do find that kind of religion offensive," Ted replied.

"What kind of religion is that kind?"

"Sentimental. Mawkish." Ted almost spat the words out.

"What other kind of religion is there?" I asked.

Ted looked puzzled, disconcerted. "Not much, I guess. I guess I generally find religion unappealing."

"Has it always been that way?"

He laughed ruefully. "No, when I was a fuzzy-brained adolescent I was quite into religion. My senior year of boarding school I was even a deacon of the little church we had."

"Then what?"

"Then what what?"

"Well, what happened to your religion?" I asked.

"I just grew out of it, I guess."

"How did you grow out of it?"

"What do you mean, how did I grow out of it?" Ted was clearly becoming irritated now. "How does one grow out of anything? I just did, that's all."

"When did you grow out of it?"

"I don't know. It just happened. I told you. I never went to church in college."

"Never?"

"Never once."

"So your senior year of high school you're a deacon in the church," I commented. "Then that summer you have an unsuccessful love affair. And then you never go to church again. It was an abrupt change. You don't suppose your girl friend's rejection had anything to do with it, do you?"

"I don't suppose anything. The same pattern was true of lots of my classmates. We were coming of age in a time when religion wasn't fashionable anyway. Maybe my girl friend had something to do with it, maybe she didn't. How should I know? All I know is I just became uninterested in religion."

The next break came a month later. We had been focusing on Ted's notable lack of enthusiasm about anything, which he readily acknowledged. "The last time I can distinctly remember being enthusiastic," he said, "was ten years ago, in my junior year. It was over a paper I was writing at the end of a fall semester course in modern British poetry."

"What was the paper about?" I asked.

"I really don't think I can remember, it was so long ago."

"Poppycock," I said. "You can remember if you want to."

"Well, I think it had to do with Gerard Manley Hopkins. He was one of the first of the truly modern poets. 'Pied Beauty' was probably the poem it centered on."

I left the office, went to my library, and came back with a dusty volume of British poetry from my college years. "Pied Beauty" was there on page 819. I read:

> Glory be to God for dappled things—
>   For skies of couple-colour as a brindled cow;
>   For rose-moles all in stipple upon trout that swim;
> Fresh-firecoal chestnut-falls; finches' wings;
>   Landscape plotted and pieced—fold, fallow, and
>   plough;
>   And all trades, their gear and tackle and trim.

All things counter, original, spare, strange;
   Whatever is fickle, freckled (who knows how?)
   With swift, slow; sweet, sour; adazzle, dim;
   He fathers-forth whose beauty is past change;
        Praise him.

Tears came to my eyes. "It is, itself, a poem about enthusiasm," I said.

"Yes."

"It's also a very religious poem."

"Yes."

"You wrote the paper on it at the end of the fall semester. That would have been January?"

"Yes."

"If I calculate correctly, it was in the next month, February, that your friend Hank died."

"Yes."

I could feel an incredible tension growing. I was not sure what was the right thing to do. Hoping, I ploughed ahead. "So you were rejected by your first real girl friend at seventeen and you gave up your enthusiasm for the church. Three years later your best friend died and you gave up your enthusiasm for everything."

"I didn't give it up, it was taken from me." Ted was almost shouting now, more emotional than I had ever seen him.

"God rejected you so you rejected God."

"Well, why shouldn't I ?" he demanded. "It's a shitty world. It's always been a shitty world."

"I thought your childhood was quite happy."

"No, that was shitty too."

And so it was. Underneath its calm exterior Ted's childhood home had been a continual bloody battleground for him. His two older brothers had picked on him with unparalleled viciousness. His parents, too involved in their own affairs and their hatred of each other to concern themselves with the seemingly minor problems of children, had offered him, the smallest and the weakest, no protection. Escape to the countryside for long, solitary walks was his greatest solace, and we were able to establish that his hermitlike pattern had its roots in the years before he was even ten. Boarding school, with its minor cruelties, had been a relief. As he talked of these things, Ted's resentment of the world—or rather his ventilation of that resentment—gathered momentum. In the months that followed he relived not only the pain of his childhood and the pain of Hank's death but also the pain of a thousand smaller deaths and rejections and losses. All of life seemed a maelstrom of death and suffering, danger and savagery.

After fifteen months of therapy there came a turning point. Ted brought into his session a little book. "You're always talking about how secretive I am—and, of course, I am," he said. "Last night I was rummaging through some old stuff and I found this journal that I kept during my sophomore year at college. I haven't even looked at it to censor it. I thought perhaps you might like to read the unexpurgated me of a decade ago."

I said I would, and I did for the next two nights. Actually, it was hardly revelatory except to confirm that his pattern as a loner, isolated by a snobbishness born of hurt, was deeply entrenched even then. But one little vignette caught my eye. He described how he had gone hiking alone on a Sunday in January and had been caught in a heavy snowstorm and had gotten back to his dormitory several hours after dark. "I felt a certain sense of exhilaration," he had written, "upon my return to the safety of my room, not unlike that which I experienced last summer when I came so near to death." The next day in our session I asked him to tell me how he had come near to death.

"Oh, I've told you about that," Ted said.

By this time I knew well that whenever Ted proclaimed he had already told me something, he was trying to hide it. "You're being secretive again," I responded.

"Well, I'm sure I told you. I must have. Anyway, there wasn't all that much to it. You remember I worked in Florida that summer between my freshman and sophomore years.

There was a hurricane. I kind of like storms, you know. At the height of the storm I went out on a pier. A wave washed me off. Then another washed me back on. That was all there was to it. It was over very quickly."

"You went out to the end of a pier at the height of a hurricane?" I asked incredulously.

"I told you. I like storms. I wanted to be close to that elemental fury."

"I can understand that," I said. "We both like storms. But I don't know that I would have put myself in jeopardy like that."

"Well, you know I have a suicidal streak," Ted replied almost impishly. "And I was certainly feeling suicidal that summer. I've analyzed it. Frankly, I can't remember going out on the pier with any conscious suicidal intent. But I certainly didn't care much about life and I acknowledge the possibility that I was being suicidal."

"You were washed off?"

"Yes. I hardly knew what was happening. There was so much spray you really couldn't see much of anything. I guess a particularly big wave came. I felt it slam into me, felt myself swept away, felt myself lost in the water. There was nothing I could do to save myself. I was certain I was going to die. I felt terrified. After about a minute I felt myself tossed backward by the water—it must have been some kind of backwash wave—and a second later I was slammed down against the concrete of the pier. I crawled to the side of the pier, gripped it, and hand over hand I crawled back to the land. I was a bit bruised. That was all."

"How do you feel about the experience?"

"What do you mean, how do I feel about it?" Ted asked in his resisting way.

"Just what I asked. How do you feel about it?"

"You mean about being saved?" he queried.

"Yes."

"Well, I guess I feel I was fortunate."

"Fortunate?" I queried. "Just an unusual coincidence, that backwash wave?"

"Yes, that's all."

"Some might call it miraculous," I commented.

"I guess I was lucky."

"You guess you were lucky," I repeated, goading him.

"Yes, goddammit, I guess I was lucky."

"It's interesting, Ted," I said, "that whenever something significantly painful happens to you, you rail against God, you rail against what a shitty, terrible world it is. But when something good happens to you, you guess you're lucky. A minor tragedy and it's God's fault. A miraculous blessing and it's a bit lucky. What do you make of that?"

Confronted with the inconsistency of his attitude toward good and bad fortune, Ted began to focus more and more on things that were right with the world, on the sweet as well as the sour, the dazzle as well as the dim. Having worked through the pain of Hank's death and the other deaths he had experienced, he began to examine the other side of the coin of life. He came to accept the necessity of suffering and to embrace the paradoxical nature of existence, the "dappled things." This acceptance occurred, of course, in the context of a warm, loving and increasingly pleasurable relationship between us. He began to move out. Very tentatively, he started dating again. He began to express faint enthusiasm. His religious nature blossomed. Everywhere he looked he saw the mystery of life and death, of creation and decay and regeneration. He read theology. He listened to *Jesus Christ, Superstar*, to *Godspell*, and even bought his own copy of *Jonathan Livingston Seagull*.

After two years of therapy Ted announced one morning that the time had come for him to get on with it. "I've been thinking about applying to a graduate school in psychology," he said. "I know you're going to say that I'm just imitating you, but I've looked at that and I don't think that's it."

"Go on," I requested.

"Well, in thinking about this it seemed to me I ought to try to do what is most important. If I am going back to school I want to study the most important things."

"Go on."

"So I decided that the human mind is important. And doing therapy is important."

"The human mind and psychotherapy, that's the *most* important thing?" I queried.

"Well, I suppose God is the most important thing."

"So why don't you study God?" I asked.

"What do you mean?"

"If God is the most important thing, why don't you study God?"

"I'm sorry. I simply don't understand you," Ted said.

"That's because you're blocking yourself from understanding," I replied.

"Really, I don't understand. How can one study God?"

"One studies psychology in a school. One studies God in a school," I answered.

"You mean theology school?"

"Yes."

"You mean, become a minister?"

"Yes."

"Oh, no, I couldn't do that." Ted was aghast.

"Why not?"

Ted became shifty. "There isn't necessarily any difference between a psychotherapist and a minister. I mean, ministers do lots of therapy. And doing psychotherapy, well, it's like a ministry."

"So why couldn't you become a minister?"

"You're pressuring me," Ted fumed. "A career is my personal decision. It's up to me to go into the career I want. Therapists aren't supposed to direct patients. It's not your role to make choices for me. I'll make my own choices."

"Look," I said, "I am not making any choice for you. I am in this instance being purely analytical. I am analyzing the alternatives open to you. You are the one who for some reason does not want to look at one of those alternatives. You are the one who wants to do the most important thing. You are the one who feels that God is the most important thing. Yet when

I drag you to finally look at the alternative of a career in God, you exclude it. You say you couldn't do it. Fine if you can't do it. But it *is* my province to be interested in why you feel you can't do it, why you exclude it as an alternative."

"I just couldn't be a minister," Ted said lamely.

"Why not?"

"Because . . . because to be a minister one is publicly a man of God. I mean, I'd have to go public with my belief in God. I'd have to be publicly enthusiastic about it. I just couldn't do that."

"No, you've got to be secret, don't you?" I said. "That's your neurosis and you've got to keep it. You can't be publicly enthusiastic. You've got to keep your enthusiasm in the closet, don't you?"

"Look," Ted wailed, "you don't know what it's like for me. You don't know what it's like to be me. Every time I opened my mouth to be enthusiastic about something my brothers would tease me for it."

"So I guess you're still ten years old," I remarked, "and your brothers are still around."

Ted was actually crying now with frustration at me. "That's not all," he said, weeping. "That's how my parents punished me. Whenever I did something wrong they took what I loved away from me. 'Let's see, what is it that Ted's most enthusiastic about? Oh, yes, the trip to his aunt's next week. He's really excited about that. So we'll tell him that because he's been bad he can't go see his aunt. That's it. Then there's his bow and arrows. He really loves his bow and arrows. So we'll take that away.' Simple. Simple system. Everything I was enthusiastic about they took away. Everything I loved I lost."

And so we arrived at the deepest core of Ted's neurosis. Gradually, by act of will, continually having to remind himself that he was not still ten, that he was not still under the thumb of his parents or within striking distance of his brothers, bit by bit he forced himself to communicate his enthusiasm, his love of life and his love of God. He did decide to go on to divinity school. A few weeks before he left I received a check from him for the previous month's sessions. Something about it caught my eye. His signature seemed longer. I looked at it closely. Previously he had always signed his name "Ted." Now it was "Theodore." I called his attention to the change.

"I was hoping you would notice it," he said. "I guess in a way I'm still keeping secrets, aren't I? When I was very young my aunt told me that I should be proud of the name Theodore because it means 'lover of God.' I was proud. So I told my brothers about it. Christ, did they make fun of me. They called me a sissy in ten different ways. 'Sissy choir boy. Why don't you go kiss the altar? Why don't you go kiss the choir-master?' " Ted smiled. "You know the whole routine. So I became embarrassed by the name. A few weeks ago it occurred to me that I was no longer embarrassed. So I decided it was all right to use my full name now. After all, I am a lover of God, aren't I?"

The Baby and the Bath Water

The foregoing case histories were offered in response to a question: Is belief in God a form of psychopathology? If we are to rise out of the mire of childhood teaching, local tradition and superstition, it is a question that must be asked. But these case histories indicate that the answer is not a simple one. The answer sometimes is yes. Kathy's unquestioning belief in the God her church and mother taught clearly retarded her growth and poisoned her spirit. Only by questioning and discarding her belief was she able to venture forth into a wider, more satisfying, more productive life. Only then was she free to grow. But the answer also is sometimes no. As Marcia grew out of the cold microcosm of her childhood into a larger, warmer world, a belief in God also grew within her, quietly and naturally. And Ted's forsaken belief in God had to be resurrected as an essential part of the liberation and resurrection of his spirit.

What are we to do with this yes-and-no answer? Scientists are dedicated to asking questions in the search for truth. But they too are human, and like all humans, they would like their answers to be clean and clear and easy. In their desire for simple solutions, scientists are prone to fall into two traps as they question the reality of God. The first is to throw the baby out with the bath water. And the second is tunnel vision.

There is clearly a lot of dirty bath water surrounding the reality of God. Holy wars. Inquisitions. Animal sacrifice. Human sacrifice. Superstition. Stultification. Dogmatism. Ignorance. Hypocrisy. Self-righteousness. Rigidity. Cruelty. Book-burning. Witch-burning. Inhibition. Fear. Conformity. Morbid guilt. Insanity. The list is almost endless. But is all this what God has done to humans or what humans have done to God? It is abundantly evident that belief in God is often destructively dogmatic. Is the problem, then, that humans tend to believe in God, or is the problem that humans tend to be dogmatic? Anyone who has known a died-in-the-wool atheist will know that such an individual can be as dogmatic about unbelief as any believer can be about belief. Is it belief in God we need to get rid of, or is it dogmatism?

Another reason that scientists are so prone to throw the baby out with the bath water is that science itself, as I have suggested, is a religion. The neophyte scientist, recently come or converted to the world view of science, can be every bit as fanatical as a Christian crusader or a soldier of Allah. This is particularly the case when we have come to science from a culture and home in which belief in God is firmly associated with ignorance, superstition, rigidity and hypocrisy. Then we have emotional as well as intellectual motives to smash the idols of primitive faith. A mark of maturity in scientists, however, is their awareness that science may be as subject to dogmatism as any other religion.

I have firmly stated that it is essential to our spiritual growth for us to become scientists who are skeptical of what we have been taught—that is, the common notions and assumptions of our culture. But the notions of science themselves often become cultural idols, and it is necessary that we become skeptical of these as well. It is indeed possible for us to mature out of a belief in God. What I would now like to suggest is that it is also possible to mature into a belief in God. A skeptical atheism or agnosticism is not necessarily the highest state of understanding at which human beings can arrive. To the contrary, there is reason to believe that behind spurious notions and false concepts of God there lies a reality that is God. This is what Paul Tillich meant when he referred to the "god beyond God" and why some sophisticated Christians used to proclaim joyfully, "God is dead. Long live God." Is it possible that the path of spiritual growth leads first out of superstition into agnosticism and then out of agnosticism toward an accurate knowledge of God? It was of this path that the Sufi Aba Said ibn Abi-l-Khair was speaking more than nine hundred years ago when he said:

> *Until college and minaret have crumbled*
> *This holy work of ours will not be done.*
> *Until faith becomes rejection, and rejection becomes belief*
> *There will be no true Muslim.* *

Whether or not the path of spiritual growth necessarily leads from a skeptical atheism or agnosticism toward an accurate belief in God, the fact of the matter is that some intellectually sophisticated and skeptical people, such as Marcia and Ted, do seem to grow in the direction of belief. And it should

* Quoted from Idries Shah, *The Way of the Sufi* (New York: Dutton paperback, 1970), p. 44.

be noted that this belief into which they grew was not at all like that out of which Kathy evolved. The God that comes before skepticism may bear little resemblance to the God that comes after. As I mentioned at the beginning of this section, there is no single, monolithic religion. There are many religions, and perhaps many levels to belief. Some religions may be unhealthy for some people; others may be healthy.

All this is of particular import for those scientists who are psychiatrists or psychotherapists. Dealing so directly with the growth process, they more than anyone else are called upon to make judgments as to the healthiness of an individual's belief system. Because psychotherapists generally belong to a skeptical if not strictly Freudian tradition, there is a tendency for them to consider any passionate belief in God to be pathological. Upon occasion this tendency may go over the line into frank bias and prejudice. Not long ago I met a college senior who was giving serious consideration to the possibility of entering a monastery a few years hence. He had been in psychotherapy for the preceding year and was continuing. "But I have not been able to tell my therapist about the monastery or the depth of my religious belief," he confided. "I don't think he would understand." I did not begin to know this young man well enough to assess the meaning that the monastery held for him or whether his desire to join it was neurotically determined. I very much would have liked to say to him: "You really ought to tell your therapist about it. It is essential for your therapy that you be open about everything, particularly a serious matter such as this. You should trust your therapist to be objective." But I did not. For I was not at all sure that his therapist would be objective, that he would understand, in the true meaning of the word.

Psychiatrists and psychotherapists who have simplistic attitudes toward religion are likely to do a disservice to some of their patients. This will be true if they regard all religion as good or healthy. It will also be true if they throw out the baby with the bath water and regard all religion as sickness or the Enemy. And, finally, it will be true if in the face of the complexity of the matter they withdraw themselves from dealing at all with the religious issues of their patients, hiding behind a cloak of such total objectivity that they do not consider it to be their role to be, themselves, in any way spiritually or religiously involved. For their patients often need their involvement. I do not mean to imply that they should forsake their objectivity, or that balancing their objectivity with their own spirituality is an easy matter. It is not. To the contrary, my plea would be that psychotherapists of all kinds should push themselves to become not less involved but rather more sophisticated in religious matters than they frequently are.

Scientific Tunnel Vision

Occasionally psychiatrists encounter patients with a strange disturbance of vision; these patients are able to see only a very narrow area directly in front of them. They cannot see anything to the left or to the right, above or below their narrow focus. They cannot see two objects adjacent to each other at the same time, they can see only one thing at a time and must turn their heads if they are to see another. They liken this symptom to looking down a tunnel, being able to see only a small circle of light and clarity at the end. No physical disturbance in their visual system can be found to account for the symptom. It is as if for some reason they do not want to see more than immediately meets the eye, more than what they choose to focus their attention upon.

Another major reason that scientists are prone to throw the baby out with the bath water is that they do not see the baby. Many scientists simply do not look at the evidence of the reality of God. They suffer from a kind of tunnel vision, a psychologically self-imposed psychological set of blinders which prevents them from turning their attention to the realm of the spirit.

Among the causes of this scientific tunnel vision I would like to discuss two that result from the nature of scientific tradition. The first of these is an issue of methodology. In its laudable insistence upon experience, accurate observation and verifiability, science has placed great emphasis upon measurement. To measure something is to experience it in a certain dimension, a dimension in which we can make observations of great accuracy which are repeatable by others. The use of measurement has enabled science to make enormous strides in the understanding of the material universe. But by virtue of its success, measurement has become a kind of scientific idol. The result is an attitude on the part of many scientists of not only skepticism but outright rejection of what cannot be measured. It is as if they were to say, "What we cannot measure, we cannot know; there is no point in worrying about what we cannot know; therefore, what cannot be measured is unimportant and unworthy of our observation." Because of this attitude many scientists exclude from their serious consideration all matters that are—or seem to be—intangible. Including, of course, the matter of God.

This strange but remarkably common assumption that things that are not easy to study do not merit study is beginning to be challenged by several relatively recent developments within science itself. One is the development of increasingly sophisticated methods of study. Through the use of hardware such as electron microscopes, spectrophotometers and computers, and software such as statistical techniques we are now able to make measurements of increasingly complex phenomena which a few decades ago were unmeasurable. The range of scientific vision is consequently expanding. As it continues to expand, perhaps we shall soon be able to say: "There is nothing beyond the limits of our vision. If we decide to study something, we can always find the methodology with which to do it."

The other development that is assisting us to escape from scientific tunnel vision is the relatively recent discovery by science of the reality of paradox. A hundred years ago paradox meant error to the scientific mind. But exploring such phenomena as the nature of light, electromagnetism, quantum mechanics and relativity theory, physical science has matured over the past century to the point where it is increasingly recognized that at a certain level reality *is* paradoxical. Thus J. Robert Oppenheimer wrote:

> To what appear to be the simplest questions, we will tend to give either no answer or an answer which will at first sight be reminiscent more of a strange catechism than of the straightforward affirmatives of physical science. If we ask, for instance, whether the position of the electron remains the same, we must say "no"; if we ask whether the electron's position changes with time, we must say "no"; if we ask whether the electron is at rest, we must say "no"; if we ask whether it is in motion, we must say "no." The Buddha has given such answers when interrogated as to the conditions of a man's self after his death; but they are not the familiar answers for the tradition of seventeenth and eighteenth century science.*

Mystics have spoken to us through the ages in terms of paradox. Is it possible that we are beginning to see a meeting ground between science and religion? When we are able to say that "a human is both mortal and eternal at the same time" and "light is both a wave and a particle at the same time," we have begun to speak the same language. Is it possible that the path of spiritual growth that proceeds from religious supersti-

* *Science and the Common Understanding* (New York: Simon and Schuster, 1953), p. 40.

tion to scientific skepticism may indeed ultimately lead us to a genuine religious reality?

This beginning possibility of unification of religion and science is the most significant and exciting happening in our intellectual life today. But it is only just beginning. For the most part both the religious and the scientific remain in self-imposed narrow frames of reference, each still largely blinded by its own particular type of tunnel vision. Examine, for instance, the behavior of both in regard to the question of miracles. Even the idea of a miracle is anathema to most scientists. Over the past four hundred years or so science has elucidated a number of "natural laws," such as "Two objects attract each other in proportion to their mass and in inverse proportion to the distance between them" or "Energy can neither be created nor destroyed." But having been successful in discovering natural laws, scientists in their world view have made an idol out of the concept of natural law, just as they made an idol out of the notion of measurement. The result is that any event that cannot be explained by currently understood natural law is assumed to be unreal by the scientific establishment. In regard to methodology, science has tended to say, "What is very difficult to study doesn't merit study." And in regard to natural law, science tends to say, "What is very difficult to understand doesn't exist."

The church has been a bit more broad-minded. To the religious establishment what cannot be understood in terms of known natural law is a miracle, and miracles do exist. But beyond authenticating their existence, the church has not been anxious to look at miracles very closely. "Miracles need not be scientifically examined" has been the prevailing religious attitude. "They should simply be accepted as acts of God." The religious have not wanted their religion shaken by science, just as the scientific have not wanted their science to be shaken by religion.

Events of miraculous healing, for instance, have been used by the Catholic Church to authenticate its saints, and they are almost standard fare for many Protestant denominations. Yet the churches have never said to physicians, "Would you join with us to study these most fascinating phenomena?" Nor have physicians said, "May we get together with you to examine scientifically these occurrences which should be of such interest to our profession?" Instead the attitude of the medical profession has been that miracle cures are nonexistent, that the disease of which a person was cured did not exist in the first place, either because it was an imaginary disorder, such as a hysterical conversion reaction, or else because it was a misdiagnosis. Fortunately, however, a few serious scientists, physicians and religious truth-seekers are currently in the process of beginning to examine the nature of such phenomena as spontaneous remissions in cancer patients and apparently successful examples of psychic healing.

Fifteen years ago, when I graduated from medical school, I was certain that there were no miracles. Today I am certain that miracles abound. This change in my consciousness has been the result of two factors working hand in hand. One factor is a whole variety of experiences I have had as a psychiatrist which initially seemed quite commonplace but which, when I thought about them more deeply, seemed to indicate that my work with patients toward their growth was being remarkably assisted in ways for which I had no logical explanation—that is, ways that were miraculous. These experiences, some of which I shall be recounting, led me to question my previous assumption that miraculous occurrences were impossible. Once I questioned this assumption I became open to the possible existence of the miraculous. This openness, which was the second factor causing my change in consciousness, then allowed me to begin routinely looking at ordinary existence with an eye for the miraculous. The more I looked, the more I found. If there were but one thing I could hope for from the reader of the remainder of this book, it would be that he or she possesses the capacity to perceive the miraculous. Of this capacity it has recently been written:

Self realization is born and matures in a distinctive kind of awareness, an awareness that has been described in many different ways by many different people. The mystics, for example, have spoken of it as the perception of the divinity and perfection of the world. Richard Bucke referred to it as cosmic consciousness; Buber described it in terms of the I-Thou relationship; and Maslow gave it the label "Being-cognition." We shall use Ouspensky's term and call it the perception of the miraculous. "Miraculous" here refers not only to extraordinary phenomena but also to the common-place, for absolutely anything can evoke this special aware-ness provided that close enough attention is paid to it. Once perception is disengaged from the domination of preconcep-tion and personal interest, it is free to experience the world as it is in itself and to behold its inherent magnificence . . . Perception of the miraculous requires no faith or assump-tions. It is simply a matter of paying full and close attention to the givens of life, i.e., to what is so ever-present that it is usually taken for granted. The true wonder of the world is available everywhere, in the minutest parts of our bodies, in the vast expanses of the cosmos, and in the intimate interconnectedness of these and all things. . . . We are part of a finely balanced ecosystem in which interdependency goes hand-in-hand with individuation. We are all individ-uals, but we are also parts of a greater whole, united in something vast and beautiful beyond description. Percep-tion of the miraculous is the subjective essence of self reali-zation, the root from which man's highest features and experiences grow.*

In thinking about miracles, I believe that our frame of ref-erence has been too dramatic. We have been looking for the burning bush, the parting of the sea, the bellowing voice from heaven. Instead we should be looking at the ordinary day-to-day events in our lives for evidence of the miraculous, main-

* Michael Stark and Michael Washburn, "Beyond the Norm: A Speculative Model of Self-Realization," *Journal of Religion and Health*, Vol. 16, No. 1 (1977), pp. 58-59.

taining at the same time a scientific orientation. This is what I shall be doing in the next section as I examine ordinary occurrences in the practice of psychiatry which have led me to an understanding of the extraordinary phenomenon of grace.

But I would like to conclude on another note of caution. This interface between science and religion can be shaky, dangerous ground. We shall be dealing with extrasensory perception and "psychic" or "paranormal" phenomena as well as other varieties of the miraculous. It is essential that we keep our wits about us. I recently attended a conference on the subject of faith healing at which a number of well-educated speakers presented anecdotal evidence to indicate that they or others were possessors of healing power in such a manner as to suggest their evidence to be rigorous and scientific when it was not. If a healer lays hands on a patient's inflamed joint and the next day the joint is no longer inflamed, this does not mean that the patient has been healed by the healer. Inflamed joints usually become uninflamed sooner or later, slowly or suddenly, no matter what is done unto them. The fact that two events occur together in time does not necessarily mean that they are causally related. Because this whole area is so murky and ambiguous, it is all the more important that we approach it with healthy skepticism lest we mislead ourselves and others. Among the ways that others may be misled, for instance, is by perceiving the lack of skepticism and rigorous reality-testing so often present in those individuals who are public proponents of the reality of psychic phenomena. Such individuals give the field a bad name. Because the field of psychic phenomena attracts so many people with poor reality-testing, it is tempting for more realistic observers to conclude that psychic phenomena themselves are unreal although such is not the case. There are many who attempt to find simple answers to hard questions, marrying popular scientific and religious concepts with high hopes but little thought. The fact that many such marriages fail should not be taken to mean that marriage is either impossible or inadvisable. But just as it is essential that our sight not be crippled by scientific tunnel vision, so also is it essential that our critical faculties and capacity for skepticism not be blinded by the brilliant beauty of the spiritual realm.

SECTION IV

Grace

The Miracle of Health

Amazing grace! How sweet the sound
That saved a wretch like me!
I once was lost, but now am found,
Was blind, but now I see.

'Twas grace that taught my heart to fear,
And grace my fears relieved;
How precious did that grace appear
The hour I first believed!

Through many dangers, toils and snares,
I have already come;
'Tis grace hath brought me safe thus far,
And grace will lead me home.

And when we've been there ten thousand years,
Bright shining as the sun,
We'll have no less days to sing God's praise
Then when we first begun.*

The first word associated with grace in this famous early American evangelical hymn is "amazing." Something amazes us when it is not in the ordinary course of things, when it is not predictable by what we know of "natural law." What follows will demonstrate grace to be a common phenomenon and, to a certain extent, a predictable one. But the reality of

* "Amazing Grace," by John Newton (1725–1807).

grace will remain unexplainable within the conceptual framework of conventional science and "natural law" as we understand it. It will remain miraculous and amazing.

There are a number of aspects of the practice of psychiatry which never cease to amaze me as well as many other psychiatrists. One of these is the fact that our patients are amazingly healthy mentally. It is customary for other medical specialists to accuse psychiatrists of practicing an inexact and unscientific discipline. The fact of the matter, however, is that more is known about the causes of neurosis than is known about the vast majority of other human disorders. Through psychoanalysis it is possible to trace the etiology and development of a neurosis in an individual patient with an exactitude and precision that is seldom matched elsewhere in medicine. It is possible to come to know exactly and precisely how, when, where and why an individual develops a particular neurotic symptom or behavior pattern. It is also possible to know with equal exactitude and precision just how, when, where and why a particular neurosis can be cured or has been healed. What we do not know, however, is why the neurosis is not more severe—why our mildly neurotic patient is not severely neurotic, why our severely neurotic patient is not totally psychotic. Inevitably we find that a patient has suffered a trauma or traumas of a particular quality so as to produce a particular neurosis, but the traumas are of an intensity that *in the ordinary course of things* should have been expected to produce a neurosis more severe than the one the patient has.

A thirty-five-year-old remarkably successful businessman came to see me because of a neurosis that could only be described as mild. He was born illegitimate, and through infancy and early childhood was raised solely by his mother, who was both deaf and dumb, in the slums of Chicago. When he was five years old the state, believing that no such mother could be competent to raise a child, took him away from her without warning or explanation and placed him in a succession of three foster homes, where he was treated to rather routine indignities and with a total absence of affection. At the age of fifteen he became partially paralyzed as the result of a rupture of a congential aneurysm of one of the blood vessels in his brain. At sixteen he left his final set of foster parents and began living by himself. Predictably, at the age of seventeen he was jailed for a particularly vicious and meaningless assault. He received no psychiatric treatment in jail.

Upon his release, after six months of boring confinement, the authorities got him a job as a menial stock-room clerk in a rather ordinary company. No psychiatrist or social worker in the world would have foreseen his future as anything but grim. Within three years, however, he had become the youngest department head in the history of the company. In five years, after marrying another executive, he left the company and eventually succeeded in his own business, becoming a relatively wealthy man. By the time he entered treatment with me he had in addition become a loving and effective father, a self-educated intellectual, a community leader and an accomplished artist. How, when, why, where did this all come about? Within the ordinary concepts of causality, I do not know. Together we were able to trace with exactitude, within the usual framework of cause and effect, the determinants of his mild neurosis and heal him. We were not able in the slightest degree to determine the origins of his unpredictable success.

This case is quoted precisely because the observable traumas were so dramatic and the circumstances of his success so obvious. In the vast majority of cases the traumas of childhood are considerably more subtle (although usually equally devastating) and the evidence of health less simple, but the pattern is basically the same. One seldom sees patients, for instance, who are not basically healthier mentally than their parents. We know very well why people become mentally ill. What we don't understand is why people survive the traumas of their lives as well as they do. We know exactly why certain people commit suicide. We don't know, within the ordinary concepts of causality, why certain others don't commit suicide. All we can say is that there is a force, the mechanics of which we do not fully understand, that seems to operate routinely in most people to protect and to foster their mental health even under the most adverse conditions.

Although the processes involved in mental disorders frequently do not correspond to the processes of physical disorders, in this respect they apparently do. We know a great deal more about the causes of physical disease than we do about the causes of physical health. Ask any physician, for instance, what causes meningococcal meningitis and the instant response will be, "Why, the meningococcus, of course." There is a problem here, however. If this winter I were to make daily cultures of this bacterium from the throats of the inhabitants of the small village in which I make my home, I would discover it living there at some point in approximately nine out of ten people. Yet no one in my little village has suffered from meningococcal meningitis for many years, nor is likely to do so this winter. What is happening here? Meningococcal meningitis is a relatively rare disease, yet the causative agent is extremely common. Physicians use the concept of resistance to explain this phenomenon, postulating that the body possesses a set of defenses that resist invasion of the body cavities by meningococcus as well as a whole host of other ubiquitous disease-producing organisms. There is no question that this is true; we actually know a good deal about these defenses and how they operate. But enormous questions remain. While some of the people in the nation who will die from meningococcal meningitis this winter will be debilitated or otherwise known to have a defective resistance, the majority will be previously healthy individuals with no known defects in their resistance systems. On a certain level, we will be able to say with confidence that meningococcus was the cause of their death, but this level is clearly superficial. On a deeper level, we will not know why they died. The most we will be able to say is that the forces that normally protect our lives somehow failed to operate in them.

Although the concept of resistance is most commonly applied to the infectious diseases, such as meningitis, it can also be applied to all physical disease in one way or another, except that in the instance of noninfectious disease we have almost no knowledge of how resistance works. An individual may suffer a single, relatively mild attack of ulcerative colitis—a disorder generally accepted to be psychosomatic—recover completely, and go on to live through life without ever again experiencing this difficulty. Another may have repeated attacks and become chronically crippled by the disorder. A third may demonstrate a fulminating course and go on to die rapidly from even the first attack. The disease appears to be the same, but the outcome is totally different. Why? We have no idea except to say that individuals with a certain personality pattern seem to have different types of difficulty in resisting the disorder while the vast majority of us have no difficulty whatsoever. How does this happen? We don't know. These kinds of questions can be asked about almost all diseases, including the most common ones, such as heart attacks, strokes, cancer, peptic ulcers, and others. An increasing number of thinkers are beginning to suggest that almost all disorders are psychosomatic—that the psyche is somehow involved in the causation of the various failures that occur in the resistance system. But the amazing thing is not these failures of the resistance system; it is that the resistance system works as well as it does. In the ordinary course of things we should be eaten alive by bacteria, consumed by cancer, clogged up by fats and clots, eroded by acids. It is hardly remarkable that we sicken and die; what is truly remarkable is that we don't usually sicken very often and we don't die very quickly. We can therefore say the same thing about physical disorders that we said about mental disorders: There is a force, the mechanism of which we do not fully understand, that seems to operate routinely in most people to protect and encourage their physical health even under the most adverse conditions.

The matter of accidents raises further interesting questions. Many physicians and most psychiatrists have had the experience of coming face to face with the phenomenon of accident-proneness. Among the many examples in my career the most dramatic was that of a fourteen-year-old boy whom I was asked to see as part of his admission to a residential treatment center for delinquent youths. His mother had died in the month of November of his eighth year. In November of his ninth year he fell from a ladder and fractured his humerus (upper arm). In November of his tenth year he was in a bike accident and sustained a fractured skull and severe concussion. In November of his eleventh year he fell through a skylight, fracturing his hip. In November of his twelfth year he fell from his skateboard and fractured his wrist. In November of his thirteenth year he was hit by a car, sustaining a fractured pelvis. No one would question that this boy was indeed accident-prone, or the reason why. But how did these accidents occur? The boy did not consciously cause himself to be hurt. Neither was he conscious of his grief over his mother's death, blandly telling me he had "forgotten all about her." To begin to understand the question of how these accidents occurred, I think we need to apply the concept of resistance to the phenomenon of accidents as well as to the phenomenon of disease, to think in terms of accident-resistance as well as accident-proneness. It is not simply that certain people at certain times in their lives are accident-prone; it is also that in the ordinary course of things most of us are accident-resistant.

One winter day when I was nine, carrying my books home from school across a snowy street as the light was turning, I slipped and fell. By the time a rapidly approaching car skidded to a stop my head was even with the front fender; my legs and torso were underneath the middle of the car. I pulled myself out from under the car and, in a panic, ran off home unharmed. By itself this incident does not seem so remarkable; one might simply say I was lucky. But put it together with all the other instances: times I just missed being hit by cars while on foot, on a bicycle or driving; times when I was driving a car and almost struck pedestrians or barely missed bike riders in the dark; times when I jammed on the brakes, coming to a stop no more than an inch or two from another vehicle; times when I narrowly missed skiing into trees, almost fell out of windows; times when a swinging golf club brushed through my hair, and so on. What is this? Do I lead a charmed existence? If readers examine their own lives at this point, I suspect the majority will find in their own personal experiences similar patterns of repeated narrowly averted disasters, a number of accidents that almost happened that is many times greater than the number of accidents that actually did happen. Furthermore, I believe readers will acknowledge that their personal patterns of survival, of accident-resistance, are not the result of any process of conscious decision-making. Could it be that most of us do lead "charmed lives"? Could it really be that the line in the song is true: "'Tis grace hath brought me safe thus far"?

Some may think that there is nothing exciting about all this, that all the things we have been talking about are simply manifestations of the survival instinct. But does the naming of something explain it? Does the fact that we have an instinct to survive seem humdrum because we have called it an instinct? Our understanding of the origins and mechanisms of instincts is minuscule at best. Actually, the matter of accidents suggests that our tendency toward survival may be something other than, and even more miraculous than, an instinct, which is a phenomenon miraculous enough in itself. While we understand hardly anything about instincts, we do conceive of them as operating within the boundaries of the individual who possesses them. Resistance to mental disorders or physical disease we can imagine being localized within the unconscious mind or bodily processes of the individual. Accidents, however, involve interactions between individuals or between individuals and inanimate things. Did the wheels of the man's car fail to run over me when I was nine because of my survival instinct or because the driver possessed an instinctual resistance to killing me? Perhaps we have an instinct not only to preserve our own lives but also to preserve the lives of others.

While I have personally not experienced this, I have several friends who have witnessed automobile accidents in which "victims" have crawled virtually intact out of vehicles smashed beyond recognition. Their reaction has been one of pure amazement. "I don't see how anyone could have survived such a wreck at all, much less without serious injury!" is the pronouncement. How do we explain this? Pure chance? These friends, who are not religious people, were amazed precisely because chance did not seem to be involved in these incidents. "No one could have survived," they say. Although not religious, and without even thinking deeply about what they were saying, in attempting to digest these experiences my friends made such remarks as "Well, I guess God loves drunks" or "I guess his number wasn't up yet." The reader may choose to assign the mystery of such incidents to "pure chance," an unexplainable "quirk" or a "twist of fate" and be satisfied thus to close the door on further exploration. If we are to examine such incidents further, however, our concept of an instinct to explain them is not terribly satisfactory. Does the inanimate machinery of a motor vehicle possess an instinct to collapse itself in just such a manner as to preserve the contours of the human body within? Or does the human being possess an instinct at the moment of impact to conform his contours to the pattern of the collapsing machinery? Such questions seem inherently absurd. While I choose to explore further the possibility that such incidents have an explanation, it is clear that our traditional concept of instinct will not be of help. Of more assistance perhaps will be the concept of synchronicity. Before considering the concept of synchronicity, however, it will be helpful to first examine some aspects of the functioning of that part of the human mind which we call the unconscious.

The Miracle of the Unconscious

When beginning to work with a new patient I will frequently draw a large circle. Then at the circumference I will draw a small niche. Pointing to the inside of the niche, I say, "That represents your conscious mind. All the rest of the circle, 95 percent or more, represents your unconscious. If you work long enough and hard enough to understand yourself, you will come to discover that this vast part of your mind, of which you now have little awareness, contains riches beyond imagination."

One of the ways, of course, that we know of the existence of this vast but hidden realm of the mind and the wealth it contains is through our dreams. A man of some prominence came to see me for a depression of many years' duration. He found no joy in his work, but had little idea why. Although his parents were relatively poor and unknown, a number of his father's forebears had been famous men. My patient made little mention of them. His depression was caused by many factors. Only after some months did we begin to consider the matter of his ambition. To the session following the one in which the subject of ambition was first raised he brought a dream from the night before, a fragment of which follows: "We were in an apartment filled with huge, oppressive pieces of furniture. I was much younger than I am now. My father wanted me to sail across the bay to pick up a boat he had for some reason left on an island across the bay. I was eager to make this journey and asked him how I could find the boat. He took me to one side where there was this particularly huge and oppressive piece of furniture, an enormous chest, at least twelve feet long and extending all the way up to the ceiling, with maybe twenty or thirty gigantic drawers in it, and told me I could find the boat if I sighted along the edge of the chest." Initially the meaning of the dream was unclear, so, as is customary, I asked him to associate to this huge chest of drawers. Immediately he said, "For some reason—maybe because the piece seemed so oppressive—it makes me think of a sarcophagus." "What about the drawers," I asked. Suddenly he grinned. "Maybe I wanted to kill off all my ancestors," he said. "It makes me think of a family tomb or vault, each one of the drawers big enough to hold a body." The meaning of the dream was then clear. He had indeed in his youth been given a sighting, a sighting for life, along the tombs of his famous dead paternal ancestors, and had been following this sighting toward fame. But he found it an oppressive force in his life and wished that he could psychologically kill off his ancestors so as to be free from this compulsive force.

Anyone who has worked much with dreams will recognize this one to be typical. I would like to focus on its helpfulness as one of the respects in which it is typical. This man had started to work on a problem. Almost immediately his unconscious produced a drama that elucidated the cause of his problem, a cause of which he had previously been unaware. It did this through use of symbols in a manner as elegant as that of the most accomplished playwright. It is difficult to imagine that any other experience occuring at this point in his therapy could have been as eloquently edifying to him and me as this particular dream. His unconscious clearly seemed to want to assist him and our work together, and did so with consummate skill.

It is precisely because they are so routinely helpful that psychotherapists generally make the analysis of dreams a significant part of their work. I must confess that there are many dreams whose significance completely eludes me, and it is tempting to wish petulantly that the unconscious would often have the decency to speak to us in clearer language. However, on those occasions when we succeed in making the translation, the message always seems to be one designed to nurture our spiritual growth. In my experience, dreams that can be interpreted invariably provide helpful information to the dreamer. This assistance comes in a variety of forms: as warnings of personal pitfalls; as guides to the solution of problems we have been unable to solve; as proper indication that we are wrong when we think we are right, and as correct encouragement that we are right when we think we are probably wrong; as sources of necessary information about ourselves that we are lacking; as direction-finders when we feel lost; and as pointers to the way we need to go when we are floundering.

The unconscious may communicate to us when we are awake with as much elegance and beneficence as when we are asleep, although in a slightly different form. This is the form of "idle thoughts," or even fragments of thoughts. Most of the time, as with dreams, we pay these idle thoughts no attention and cast them aside as if they were without significance. It is for this reason that patients in psychoanalysis are instructed again and again to say *whatever* comes into their minds no matter how silly or insignificant it may initially seem. Whenever a patient says, "It's ridiculous, but this silly thought keeps coming to my mind—it doesn't make any sense, but you've told me I have to say these things," I know that we have hit pay dirt, that the patient has just received an extremely valuable message from the unconscious, a message that will significantly illuminate his or her situation. While these "idle thoughts" usually provide us with insight into ourselves, they may also provide us with dramatic insights into others or into the world outside ourselves. As an example of an "idle thought" message from the unconscious, and one that falls into the latter category, let me describe an experience of my own mind while working with a patient. The patient was a young woman who was suffering since early adolescence from a sensation of dizziness, a sensation that she was about to topple over any moment, for which no physical cause had ever been found. Because of this sensation of dizziness she walked with a straight-legged, wide-based gait, almost a waddle. She was quite intelligent and charming, and initially I had no idea as to what might be causing her dizziness, of which psychotherapy of some years' duration had failed to cure her, but for which she had nonetheless recently come to me for assistance. In the middle of our third session, as she was comfortably seated and talking about this or that, a single word suddenly popped into my mind: "Pinocchio." I was trying to concentrate on what my patient was saying, so I immediately pushed the word out of consciousness. But within a minute, despite myself, the word came back into my mind, almost visible, as if spelled out in the back of my eyes: P i n o c c h i o. Annoyed now, I blinked my eyes and forced my attention back to my patient. Yet, as if it had a will of its own, within another minute the word was back into my awareness, somehow demanding to be recognized. "Wait a second," I finally said to myself, "if this word is so anxious to get into my mind, maybe I'd better damn well pay attention to it, because I know these things can be important, and I know if my unconscious is trying to say something to me I ought to listen." So I did. "Pinocchio! What the hell could Pinocchio mean? You don't suppose it could have anything to do with my patient, do you? You don't suppose she's Pinocchio, is she? Hey, wait a minute; she's cute, like a little doll. She's dressed in red, white and blue. Each time she's been here she's been dressed in red, white and blue. She walks funnily, like a stiff-legged wooden soldier. Hey, that's it! She's a puppet. By God, she is Pinocchio! She's a puppet!" Instantly the essence of the patient was revealed to me: she was not a real person; she was a stiff, wooden little puppet trying to act alive but afraid that at any moment she would topple over and collapse in a tangle of sticks and strings. One by one the supporting facts rapidly emerged: an incredibly domineering mother who pulled strings, who took great pride in having toilet-trained her daughter "overnight"; a will totally devoted to fulfilling the external expectations of others, to being clean, neat, proper, tidy and saying all the right things, frantically trying to juggle the demands upon her; a total lack of self-motivation and ability to make autonomous decisions.

This immensely valuable insight about my patient presented itself to my awareness as an unwelcome intruder. I had not invited it. I did not want it. Its presence seemed alien to me and irrelevant to the business in which I was engaged, a needless distraction. Initially I resisted it, attempting several times to kick it out the door through which it had come. This seemingly alien and unwanted quality is characteristic of unconscious material and its manner of presentation to the conscious mind. It was partly because of this quality and the associated resistance of the conscious mind that Freud and his initial followers tended to perceive the unconscious as a repository of the primitive, the antisocial and the evil within us. It is as if they assumed, from the fact that our consciousness did not want it, that unconscious material was therefore "bad." Along these same lines, they tended to assume that mental illness somehow resided in the unconscious as a demon in the subterranean depths of our mind. To Jung fell the responsibility of initiating a correction in this view, which he did in a variety of ways, including coining the phrase: "The Wisdom of the Unconscious." My own experience has confirmed Jung's views in this regard to the point where I have come to conclude that mental illness is not a product of the unconscious; it is instead a phenomenon of consciousness or a disordered relationship between the conscious and the unconscious. Consider the matter of repression, for instance. Freud discovered in many of his patients sexual desires and hostile feelings of which they were not aware yet which were clearly making them ill. Because these desires and feelings resided in the unconscious, the notion arose that it was the unconscious that "caused" mental illness. But why were these desires and feelings located in the unconscious in the first place? Why were they repressed? The answer is that the conscious mind did not want them. And it is in this not-wanting, this disowning, that the problem lies. The problem is not that human beings have such hostile and sexual feelings, but rather that human beings have a conscious mind that is so often unwilling to face these feelings and tolerate the pain of dealing with them, and that is so willing to sweep them under the rug.

A third way in which the unconscious manifests itself and speaks to us if we care to listen (which we usually don't) is through our behavior. I am referring to slips of the tongue and other "mistakes" in behavior, or "Freudian slips," which Freud, in his *Psychopathology of Everyday Life*, initially demonstrated to be manifestations of the unconscious. Freud's use of the word "psychopathology" to describe these phenomenon is again indicative of his negative orientation toward the unconscious; he perceived it as acting a spiteful role or at least a mischievous devil trying to trip us up rather than seeing it as a kind of good fairy working very hard to make us honest. When a patient makes a slip in psychotherapy, the event is invariably helpful to the process of therapy or healing. At these times the conscious mind of the patient is engaged in trying to combat therapy, intent upon hiding the true nature of the self from the therapist and from self-awareness. It is the unconscious, however, that is allied with the therapist, struggling toward openness, honesty, truth, and reality, fighting to "tell it like it is."

Let me give some examples. A meticulous woman, totally unable to acknowledge in herself the emotion of anger and therefore unable to express anger openly, began a pattern of arriving a few minutes late for her therapy sessions. I suggested to her that this was because she was feeling some resentment toward me or toward therapy or both. She firmly denied that this was a possibility, explaining that her lateness was purely a matter of this or that accidental force in life and proclaiming her wholehearted appreciation of me and motivation for our work together. On the evening following this session she paid her monthly bills, including my own. Her check to me arrived unsigned. At her next session I informed her of this, suggesting that she had not paid me properly because she was angry. She said, "But that's ridiculous! I have never in my life not signed a check. You know how meticulous I am in these matters. It is impossible that I did not sign your check." I showed her the unsigned check. Although she had always been extremely controlled in our sessions, she now suddenly broke into sobs. "What is happening to me?" she wailed. "I'm falling apart. It's like I'm two people." In her agony, and with my acknowledgment that she was indeed like a house divided against itself, she began for the first time to accept the possibility that at least a part of her might harbor the feeling of anger. The first step of progress was made. Another patient with a problem with anger was a man who believed it unconscionable to feel, much less express, anger toward any member of his family. Because his sister was visiting him at the time, he was telling me about her, describing her as a "perfectly delightful person." Later in the session he began telling me about a small dinner party he was hosting that night, which, he said, would include a neighboring couple and "of course, my sister-in-law." I pointed out to him that he had just referred to his sister as sister-in-law. "I suppose you're going to tell me this is one of those Freudian slips," he remarked blithely. "Yes, I am," I replied. "What your unconsciousness is saying is that you don't want your sister to be your sister, that as far as you're concerned, she's your sister-in-law only, and that actually you hate her guts." "I don't hate her guts," he responded, "but she does talk incessantly, and I know that at dinner tonight she will monopolize the whole conversation. I guess maybe I am embarrassed by her sometimes." Again a small beginning was made.

Not all slips express hostility or denied "negative" feelings. They express all denied feelings, negative or positive. They express the truth, the way things really are as opposed to the way we like to think they are. Perhaps the most touching slip of the tongue in my experience was made by a young woman on her initial visit with me. I knew her parents to be distant and insensitive individuals who had raised her with a great deal of propriety but an absence of affection or genuine caring. She presented herself to me as an unusually mature, self-confident, liberated and independent woman of the world who sought treatment from me because, she explained, "I am sort of at loose ends for the moment, with time on my hands, and I thought that a little bit of psychoanalysis might contribute to my intellectual development." Inquiring as to why she was at loose ends at the moment, I learned that she had just dropped out of college because she was five months' pregnant. She did not want to get married. She vaguely thought she might put the baby up for adoption following its delivery and then proceed to Europe for further education. I asked her if she had informed the father of the baby, whom she had not seen for four months, of her pregnancy. "Yes," she said, "I did drop him a little note to let him know that our relationship was the product of a child." Meaning to say that a child was the product of their relationship, she had instead told me that underneath her mask of a woman of the world she was a hungry little girl, starved for affection, who had gotten pregnant in a desperate attempt to obtain mothering by becoming herself a mother. I did not confront her with her slip, because she was not at all ready to accept her dependency needs or experience them as being safe to have. Nonetheless, the slip was helpful to her by helping me be aware that the person really seeing me was a frightened young child who needed to be met with protective gentleness and the simplest, almost physical kind of nurture possible for a long time to come.

These three patients who made slips were not trying to hide themselves from me as much as from themselves. The first really believed that there was no shred of resentment in her. The second was totally convinced that he bore no animosity toward any member of his family. The last thought of herself in no other way than as a woman of the world. Through a complex of factors, our conscious self-concept almost always diverges to a greater or lesser degree from the reality of the person we actually are. We are almost always either less or more competent than we believe ourselves to be. The unconscious, however, knows who we really are. A major and essential task in the process of one's spiritual development is the continuous work of bringing one's conscious self-concept into progressively greater congruence with reality. When a large part of this lifelong task is accomplished with relative rapidity, as it may be through intensive psychotherapy, the individual will often feel "reborn." "I am not the person I was," a patient will say with real joy about the dramatic change in his or her consciousness; "I am a totally new and different person." Such a person has no difficulty in understanding the words of the song: "I once was lost, but now am found, was blind, but now I see."

If we identify our self with our self-concept or self-awareness or consciousness in general, then we must say concerning the unconscious that there is a part of us that is wiser than we are. We have talked about this "wisdom of the unconscious" primarily in terms of self-knowledge and self-revelation. In the example of my patient whom my unconscious revealed to me to be Pinocchio, I attempted to demonstrate that the unconscious is wiser than we are about other people as well as ourselves. The fact of the matter is that our unconscious is wiser than we are about everything. Having arrived after dark on a vacation in Singapore for the first time, my wife and I left our hotel for a stroll. We soon came to a large open space at the far end of which, two or three blocks away, we could just make out in the darkness the vague shape of a sizable building. "I wonder what that building is," my wife said. I immediately answered with casual and total certainty, "Oh, that's the Singapore Cricket Club." The words had popped out of my mouth with utter spontaneity. Almost immediately I regretted them. I had no basis whatever for saying them. I had not only never been in Singapore before, I had never seen a cricket club before—in daylight, much less in darkness. Yet to my amazement, as we walked on and came to the other side of the building, which was its front, there by the entrance was a brass plaque reading *Singapore Cricket Club.*

How did I know this which I did not know? Among the

possible explanations, one is that of Jung's theory of the "collective unconscious," in which we inherit the wisdom of the experience of our ancestors without ourselves having the personal experience. While this kind of knowledge may seem bizarre to the scientific mind, strangely enough its existence is recognized in our common everyday language. Take the word "recognize" itself. When we are reading a book and come across an idea or theory that appeals to us, that "rings a bell" with us, we "recognize" it to be true. Yet this idea or theory may be one of which we have never before consciously thought. The word says we "re-know" the concept, as if we knew it once upon a time, forgot it, but then recognized it as an old friend. It is as if all knowledge and all wisdom were contained in our minds, and when we learn "something new" we are actually only discovering something that existed in our self all along. This concept is similarly reflected in the word "education," which is derived from the Latin *educare*, literally translated as "to bring out of" or "to lead forth." Therefore when we educate people, if we use the word seriously, we do not stuff something new into their minds; rather, we lead this something out of them; we bring it forth from the unconscious into their awareness. They were the possessors of the knowledge all along.

But what is its source, this part of us that is wiser than we are? We do not know. Jung's theory of the collective unconscious suggests that our wisdom is inherited. Recent scientific experiments with genetic material in conjunction with the phenomenon of memory suggest that it is indeed possible to inherit knowledge, which is stored in the form of nucleic acid codes within cells. The concept of chemical storage of information allows us to begin to understand how the information potentially available to the human mind might be stored in a few cubic inches of brain substance. But even this extraordinary sophisticated model, allowing for the storage of inherited as well as experiential knowledge in a small space, leaves unanswered the most mind-boggling questions. When we speculate on the technology of such a model—how it might be constructed, how synchronized, and so on—we are still left standing in total awe before the phenomenon of the human mind. Speculation on these matters is hardly different in quality from speculation about such models of cosmic control as God having at His command armies and choirs of archangels, angels, seraphims and cherubims to assist Him in the task of ordering the universe. The mind, which sometimes presumes to believe that there is no such thing as a miracle, is itself a miracle.

The Miracle of Serendipity

While it is perhaps possible for us to conceive of the extraordinary wisdom of the unconscious, as discussed thus far, as being an ultimately explainable part of a molecular brain operating with miraculous technology, we still have no conceivable explanation for so-called "psychic phenomena," which are clearly related to the operation of the unconscious. In a series of sophisticated experiments Montague Ullman, M.D., and Stanley Krippner, Ph.D., conclusively demonstrated that it is possible for an awake individual to repeatedly and routinely "transmit" images to another individual sleeping many rooms away, and that these images will appear in the dreams of the sleeper.* Such transmission does not occur only in the laboratory. For instance, it is not uncommon for two individuals known to each other to independently have the same or

---

* "An Experimental Approach to Dreams and Telepathy: II Report of Three Studies," *American Journal of Psychiatry* (March 1970), pp. 1282–89. Anyone as yet unconvinced about the reality of ESP or skeptical of its scientific validity is urged to read this article.

incredibly similar dreams. How does this happen? We don't have the faintest idea.

But happen it does. The validity of such happenings is scientifically proven in terms of their probability. I myself had a dream one night that consisted of a series of seven images. I later learned that a friend, while sleeping in my house two nights previously, had awakened from a dream in which the same seven images occurred in the same sequence. He and I could not determine any reason for this happening. We were unable to relate the dreams to any experience we had had, shared or otherwise, nor were we able to interpret the dreams in any meaningful way. Yet we knew that something most significant had happened. My mind has available to it millions of images from which to construct a dream. The probability that by chance alone I would select the same seven as my friend had in the same sequence was astronomically low. The event was so implausible that we knew it could not have occurred by accident.

The fact that highly implausible events, for which no cause can be determined within the framework of known natural law, occur with implausible frequency has come to be known as the principle of synchronicity. My friend and I don't know the cause or reason why we had such implausibly similar dreams, but one aspect of the event was that we had them close in time. Somehow the timing seems the important, perhaps even crucial element in these implausible events. Earlier, in the discussion of accident-proneness and -resistance, it was mentioned that people not infrequently walk unharmed out of vehicles crushed beyond recognition, and it seemed ridiculous to speculate that the machinery instinctively crumpled in a configuration to protect the rider or that the rider crumpled instinctively in a form to fit the machinery. There is no known natural law whereby the configuration of the vehicle (Event A) caused the rider to survive, or the form of the rider (Event B) caused the vehicle to crumple in a certain way. Nonetheless, although one did not cause the other, Event A and Event

B implausibly occurred synchronously—that is, together in time—in such a way that the rider did in fact survive. The principle of synchronicity does not explain why or how this happened; it simply states that such implausible conjunctions of events in time occur more frequently than would be predicted by chance alone. It does not explain miracles. The principle serves only to make it clear that miracles seem to be matters of timing and matters that are amazingly commonplace.

The incident of the similar, almost synchronous dreams is one that qualifies by virtue of its statistical improbability as a genuine psychic or "paranormal" phenomenon even though the meaning of the incident is obscure. Probably the meaning of at least the majority of genuine psychic, paranormal phenomena is similarly obscure. Nonetheless, another characteristic of psychic phenomena, apart from their statistical implausibility, is that a significant number of such occurrences seem to be fortunate—in some way beneficial to one or more of the human participants involved. A mature, highly skeptical and respectable scientist in analysis with me just recently recounted the following incident: "After our last session, it was such a beautiful day, I decided to drive home by the route around the lake. As you know, the road around the lake has a great many blind curves. I was approaching perhaps the tenth of these curves when the thought suddenly occurred to me that a car could be racing around the corner far into my side of the road. Without any more thought than that, I vigorously braked my car and came to a dead stop. No sooner had I done this than a car did indeed come barreling around the curve with its wheels six feet across the yellow line and barely missed me even though I was standing still on my side of the road. Had I not stopped, it is inevitable that we would have collided at the curve. I have no idea what made me decide to stop. I could have stopped at any one of a dozen other curves, but I didn't. I've traveled that road many times before, and while I've had the thought that it was dangerous,

I've never stopped before. It makes me wonder whether there really isn't something to ESP and things like that. I don't have any other explanation."

It is possible that occurrences statistically improbable to a degree to suggest they are examples of synchronicity or the paranormal are as likely to be harmful as they are beneficial. We hear of freak accidents as well as freak nonaccidents. Even though full of methodologic pitfalls, research into this issue clearly needs to be done. At this time I can state only a very firm but "unscientific" impression that the frequency of such statistically improbable occurrences that are clearly beneficial is far greater than that in which the result seems detrimental. The beneficial results of such occurrences need not be life-saving; far more often they are simply life-enhancing or growth-producing. An excellent example of such an occur-rence is the "scarab dream" experience of Carl Jung, re-counted in his article "On Synchronicity" and quoted here in toto: *

My example concerns a young woman patient, who, in spite of efforts made on both sides, proved to be psycholog-ically inaccessible. The difficulty lay in the fact that she always knew better about everything. Her excellent educa-tion had provided her with a weapon ideally suited to this purpose, namely, a highly polished Cartesian rationalism with an impeccably "geometrical" idea of reality. After sev-eral fruitless attempts to sweeten her rationalism with a somewhat more human understanding, I had to confine myself to the hope that something unexpected and irra-tional would turn up, something which would burst the intellectual retort into which she had sealed herself. Well, I was sitting opposite her one day, with my back to the win-dow, listening to her flow of rhetoric. She had had an im-pressive dream the night before, in which someone had given her a golden scarab—a costly piece of jewelry. While

* *The Portable Jung,* Joseph Campbell, ed. (New York: Viking Press, 1971), pp. 511-12.

she was still telling me this dream, I heard something behind me gently tapping on the window. I turned around
and saw that it was a fairly large flying insect that was
knocking against the window pane from the outside in the
obvious effort to get into the dark room. This seemed to me
very strange. I opened the window immediately and caught
the insect in the air as it flew in. It was a scarabaeid beetle,
or common rose-chafer (Cetonia aurata), whose gold-green
color most nearly resembles that of a golden scarab. I
handed the beetle to my patient with the words, "Here is
your scarab." The experience punctured the desired hole in
her rationalism, and broke the ice of her intellectual resistance. The treatment could now be continued with satisfactory results.

What we are talking of here in regard to paranormal events
with beneficial consequences is the phenomenon of serendipity. Webster's Dictionary defines serendipity as "the gift of
finding valuable or agreeable things not sought for." There
are several intriguing features to this definition. One is the
terming of serendipity as a gift, thereby implying that some
people possess it while others don't, that some people are
lucky and others are not. It is a major thesis of this section
that grace, manifested in part by "valuable or agreeable things
not sought for," is available to everyone, but that while some
take advantage of it, others do not. By letting the beetle in,
catching it, and giving it to his patient, Jung was clearly taking
advantage of it. Some of the reasons why and ways that people fail to take advantage of grace will be explored later under
the subject heading of "Resistance to Grace." But for the
moment let me suggest that one of the reasons we fail to take
full advantage of grace is that we are not fully aware of its
presence—that is, we don't find valuable things not sought
for, because we fail to appreciate the value of the gift when it
is given us. In other words, serendipitous events occur to all
of us, but frequently we fail to recognize their serendipitous
nature; we consider such events quite unremarkable, and consequently we fail to take full advantage of them.

Five months ago, having two hours to spend between appointments in a certain town, I asked a colleague who lived there if I could spend them in the library of his house working on the rewriting of the first section of this book. When I got there I was met by my colleague's wife, a distant and reserved woman who had never seemed to care for me very much and had been actually hostile to me on several occasions in an almost arrogant way. We chatted awkwardly for perhaps five minutes. In the course of our superficial conversation she said she'd heard I was writing a book and asked about the subject. I told her it concerned spiritual growth and did not elaborate further. I then sat down in the library to work. Within a half hour I had run into a snag. A portion of what I had written on the subject of responsibility seemed completely unsatisfactory to me. It clearly had to be extensively enlarged in order to make meaningful the concepts I had discussed therein, yet I felt this enlargement would detract from the flow of the work. On the other hand, I was unwilling to delete the section entirely, since I felt that some mention of these concepts was necessary. I wrestled with this delemma for an hour, getting absolutely nowhere, becoming more and more frustrated, feeling more and more helpless to resolve the situation.

At this point my colleague's wife quietly came into the library. Her manner was timid and hesitant, respectful, yet somehow warm and soft, quite unlike that in any encounter I had had with her previously. "Scotty, I hope I'm not intruding," she said. "If I am, tell me." I told her that she wasn't, that I'd hit a snag and was not going to be able to make any more progress for the moment. In her hands she was carrying a little book. "I happened to find this book," she said. "Somehow I thought you might be interested in it. Probably you won't be. But the thought occurred to me that it might be helpful to you. I don't know why." Feeling irritated and pressured, I might ordinarily have told her that I was up to my ears in books—which was true—and there was no way I could get around to reading it in the foreseeable future. But her strange humility evoked a different response. I told her I appreciated her kindness and would try to get to it as soon as possible. I took it home with me, not knowing when "as soon as possible" might be. But that very evening something compelled me to put aside all the other books I was consulting to read hers. It was a slim volume entitled, "How People Change," by Allen Wheelis. Much of it concerned issues of responsibility. One chapter elegantly expressed in depth what I would have tried to say had I enlarged the difficult section in my own book. The next morning I condensed the section of my book to a small concise paragraph, and in a footnote referred the reader to the Wheelis book for an ideal elaboration of the subject. My dilemma was solved.

This was not a stupendous event. There were no trumpets to announce it. I might well have ignored it. I could have survived without it. Nonetheless, I was touched by grace. The event was both extraordinary and ordinary—extraordinary because it was highly unlikely, ordinary because such highly unlikely beneficial events happen to us all the time, quietly, knocking on the door of our awareness no more dramatically than the beetle gently tapping on the windowpane. Similar sorts of events have happened dozens of times in the months since my colleague's wife lent me her book. They have always been happening to me. Some of them I recognize. Some of them I may take advantage of without even being aware of their miraculous nature. There is no way I have of knowing how many I have let slip by.

The Definition of Grace

Thus far in this section I have described a whole variety of phenomena that have the following characteristics in common:

(a) They serve to nurture—support, protect and enhance —human life and spiritual growth.

(b) The mechanism of their action is either incompletely understandable (as in the case of physical resistance and dreams) or totally obscure (as in the case of paranormal phenomena) according to the principles of natural law as interpreted by current scientific thinking.

(c) Their occurrence is frequent, routine, commonplace and essentially universal among humanity.

(d) Although potentially influenced by human consciousness, their origin is outside of the conscious will and beyond the process of conscious decision-making.

Although generally regarded as separate, I have come to believe that their commonality indicates that these phenomena are part of or manifestations of a single phenomenon: a powerful force originating outside of human consciousness which nurtures the spiritual growth of human beings. For hundreds and even thousands of years before the scientific conceptualization of such things as immune globulins, dream states, and the unconscious, this force has been consistently recognized by the religious, who have applied to it the name of grace. And have sung its praise. "Amazing grace, how sweet the sound . . . "

What are we to do—we who are properly skeptical and

scientific-minded—with this "powerful force originating out-side of human consciousness which nurtures the spiritual growth of human beings"? We cannot touch this force. We have no decent way to measure it. Yet it exists. It is real. Are we to operate with tunnel vision and ignore it because it does not fit in easily with traditional scientific concepts of natural law? To do so seems perilous. I do not think we can hope to approach a full understanding of the cosmos, of the place of man within the cosmos, and hence the nature of mankind itself, without incorporating the phenomenon of grace into our conceptual framework.

Yet we cannot even locate this force. We have said only where it is not: residing in human consciousness. Then, where does it reside? Some of the phenomena we have dis-cussed, such as dreams, suggest that grace resides in the un-conscious mind of the individual. Other phenomena, such as synchronicity and serendipity, indicate this force to exist be-yond the boundaries of the single individual. It is not simply because we are scientists that we have difficulty locating grace. The religious, who, of course, ascribe the origins of grace to God, believing it to be literally God's love, have through the ages had the same difficulty locating God. There are within theology two lengthy and opposing traditions in this regard: one, the doctrine of Emanance, which holds that grace emanates down from an external God to men; the other, the doctrine of Immanence, which holds that grace immanates out from the God within the center of man's being.

This problem—and, for that matter, the whole problem of paradox—results from our desire, in the first place, to locate things. Human beings have a profound tendency to concep-tualize in terms of discrete entities. We perceive the world composed of such entities: ships, shoes and sealing wax, and other categories. And we then tend to understand a phenom-enon by placing it in a particular category, saying it is such and such an entity. It is either this or that, but it cannot be both. Ships are ships and not shoes. I am I and you are you.

The I-entity is my identity and the you-entity is your identity, and we tend to be quite discomfited if our identities
become mixed up or confused. As we have previously noted,
Hindu and Buddhist thinkers believe our perception of discrete entities to be illusion, or maya, and modern physicists,
concerned with relativity, wave-particle phenomena, electromagnetism, et cetera, are becoming increasingly aware of the
limitations of our conceptual approach in terms of entities.
But it is hard to escape from. Our tendency to entity-thinking
compels us to want to locate things, even such things as God
or grace and even when we know our tendency is interfering
with our comprehension of these matters.

I attempt not to think of the individual as a true entity at
all, and insofar as my intellectual limitations compel me to
think (or write) in terms of entities, I conceive of the boun-
dries of the individual as being marked by a most permeable
membrane—a fence, if you will, instead of a wall; a fence
through which, under which and over which other "entities"
may climb, crawl or flow. Just as our conscious mind is continually partially permeable to our unconscious, so is our unconscious permeable to the "mind" without, the "mind" that
permeates us yet is not us as entities. More elegantly and
adequately descriptive of the situation than the twentieth-
century scientific language of permeable membranes is the
fourteenth-century (c. 1393) religious language of Dame Julian, an anchoress of Norwich, describing the relationship
between grace and the individual entity: "For as the body is
clad in the cloth, and the flesh in the skin and the bones in the
flesh and the heart in the whole, so are we, soul and body,
clad in the goodness of God and enclosed. Yea, and more
homely; for all these may wear and waste away, but the
Goodness of God is ever whole."*

In any case, regardless of how we ascribe them or where

---

* *Revelations of Divine Love*, Grace Warrack, ed. (New York: British
Book Centre, 1923), Chap. VI

we locate them, the "miracles" described indicate that our growth as human beings is being assisted by a force other than our conscious will. To further understand the nature of this force I believe we can benefit from considering yet another miracle: the growth process of all life itself, to which we have given the name evolution.

The Miracle of Evolution

Although we have not until now focused upon it as a concept, in one way or another we have been concerned with evolution throughout this book. Spiritual growth is the evolution of an individual. An individual's body may undergo the changes of the life cycle, but it does not evolve. New physical patterns are not forged. Decline of physical competence in old age is an inevitability. Within an individual lifetime, however, the human spirit may evolve dramatically. New patterns may be forged. Spiritual competence may increase (although it usually does not) until the moment of death in advanced old age. Our lifetime offers us unlimited opportunities for spiritual growth until the end. While the focus of this book is on spiritual evolution, the process of physical evolution is similar to that of the spirit and provides us with a model for the further understanding of the process of spiritual growth and the meaning of grace.

The most striking feature of the process of physical evolution is that it is a miracle. Given what we understand of the universe, evolution should not occur; the phenomenon should not exist at all. One of the basic natural laws is the second law of thermodynamics, which states that energy naturally flows from a state of greater organization to a state of lesser organization, from a state of higher differentiation to a state of lower differentiation. In other words, the universe is in a process of winding down. The example frequently used to describe this process is that of a stream, which naturally flows downhill. It takes energy or work—pumps, locks, humans carrying buckets, or other means—to reverse this process, to get back to the beginning, to put the water back on top of the hill. And this energy has to come from somewhere else. Some other energy system has to be depleted if this one is to be maintained. Ultimately, according to the second law of thermodynamics, in billions and billions of years, the universe will completely wind down until it reaches the lowest point as an amorphous, totally disorganized, totally undifferentiated "blob" in which nothing happens any more. This state of total disorganization and undifferentiation is termed entropy.

The natural downhill flow of energy toward the state of entropy might be termed the force of entropy. We can now realize that the "flow" of evolution is against the force of entropy. The process of evolution has been a development of organisms from lower to higher and higher states of complexity, differentiation and organization. A virus is an extremely simple organism, little more than a molecule. A bacterium is more complex, more differentiated, possessing a cell wall and different types of molecules and a metabolism. A paramecium has a nucleus, cilia, and a rudimentary digestive system. A sponge not only has cells but begins to have different types of cells interdependent upon each other. Insects and fish have nervous systems with complex methods of locomotion, and even social organizations. And so it goes, up the scale of evolution, a scale of increasing complexity and organization and differentiation, with man, who possesses an enormous cerebral cortex and extraordinarily complex behavior patterns, being, as far as we can tell, at the top. I state that the process of evolution is a miracle, because insofar as it is a process of increasing organization and differentiation, it runs counter to natural law. In the ordinary course of things, we who write and read this book should not exist.*

The process of evolution can be diagrammed by a pyramid, with man, the most complex but least numerous organism, at the apex, and viruses, the most numerous but least complex organisms, at the base:

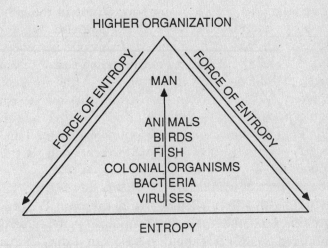

The apex is thrusting out, up, forward against the force of entropy. Inside the pyramid I have placed an arrow to symbolize this thrusting evolutionary force, this "something" that has so successfully and consistently defied "natural law" over millions upon millions of generations and that must itself represent natural law as yet undefined.

* The concept that evolution runs counter to natural law is neither new nor original. I seem to remember someone I studied in my college days stating, "Evolution is an eddy in the second law of thermodynamics," but I have unfortunately not been able to locate the reference. More recently the concept has been articulated by Buckminster Fuller in his book *And It Came to Pass—Not to Stay* (New York: Macmillan, 1976).

The spiritual evolution of humanity can be similarly diagrammed:

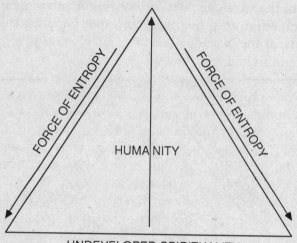

Again and again I have emphasized that the process of spiritual growth is an effortful and difficult one. This is because it
is conducted against a natural resistance, against a natural
inclination to keep things the way they were, to cling to the
old maps and old ways of doing things, to take the easy path.
About this natural resistance, this force of entropy as it operates in our spiritual lives, I will have still more to say shortly.
But as in the case of physical evolution, the miracle is that this
resistance is overcome. We do grow. Despite all that resists
the process, we do become better human beings. Not all of
us. Not easily. But in significant numbers humans somehow
manage to improve themselves and their cultures. There is a
force that somehow pushes us to choose the more difficult
path whereby we can transcend the mire and muck into which
we are so often born.

This diagram of the process of spiritual evolution can apply
to the existence of a single individual. Each of us has his or
her own urge to grow, and each of us, in exercising that urge,
must single-handedly fight against his or her own resistance.

The diagram also applies to humanity as a whole. As we evolve as individuals, so do we cause our society to evolve. The culture that nurtures us in childhood is nurtured by our leadership in adulthood. Those who achieve growth not only enjoy the fruits of growth but give the same fruits to the world. Evolving as individuals, we carry humanity on our backs. And so humanity evolves.

The notion that the plane of mankind's spiritual development is in a process of ascension may hardly seem realistic to a generation disillusioned with the dream of progress. Everywhere is war, corruption and pollution. How could one reasonably suggest that the human race is spiritually progressing? Yet that is exactly what I suggest. Our very sense of disillusionment arises from the fact that we expect more of ourselves than our forebears did of themselves. Human behavior that we find repugnant and outrageous today was accepted as a matter of course yesteryear. A major focus of this book, for instance, has been on the responsibilities of parenthood for the spiritual nurture of children. This is hardly a radical theme today, but several centuries ago it was generally not even a human concern. While I find the average quality of present parenting appallingly poor, I have every reason to believe it far superior to that of just a few generations back. A recent review of an aspect of child care begins, for instance, by noting:

> Roman law gave the father absolute control over his children, whom he could sell or condemn to death with impunity. This concept of absolute right carried over into English law, where it prevailed until the fourteenth century without appreciable change. In the Middle Ages childhood was not seen as the unique phase of life we now consider it to be. It was customary to send children as young as seven into service or apprenticeship, where learning was secondary to the labor a child performed for his or her master. The child and the servant appear to have been indistinguishable in terms of how they were treated; even the language often failed to use separate terms for each. It was not

until the sixteenth century that children began to be looked
on as being of particular interest, having important and
specific developmental tasks to perform, and being worthy
of affection.*

But what is this force that pushes us as individuals and as a
whole species to grow against the natural resistance of our
own lethargy? We have already labeled it. It is love. Love was
defined as "the will to extend one's self for the purpose of
nurturing one's own or another's spiritual growth." When we
grow, it is because we are working at it, and we are working
at it because we love ourselves. It is through love that we
elevate ourselves. And it is through our love for others that
we assist others to elevate themselves. Love, the extension of
the self, is the very act of evolution. It is evolution in progress.
The evolutionary force, present in all of life, manifests itself
in mankind as human love. Among humanity love is the miraculous force that defies the natural law of entropy.

The Alpha and the Omega

We are still left, however, with the question asked at the
end of the section on love: Where does love come from? Only
now it can be enlarged to a perhaps even more basic question:
Whence comes the whole force of evolution? And to this we
can add our puzzlement about the origins of grace. For love is
conscious, but grace is not. Whence comes this "powerful

* André P. Derdeyn, "Child Custody Contests in Historical Perspective," *American Journal of Psychiatry*, Vol. 133, No. 12 (Dec. 1976),
p. 1369.

force originating outside of human consciousness which nurtures the spiritual growth of human beings"?

We cannot answer these questions in the same scientific way we can answer where flour or steel or maggots come from. It is not simply that they are too intangible, but more that they are too basic for our "science" as it currently exists. For these are not the only basic questions that science cannot answer. Do we really know what electricity is, for instance? Or where energy comes from in the first place? Or the universe? Perhaps someday our science of answers will catch up with the most basic questions. Until then, if ever, we can only speculate, theorize, postulate, hypothesize.

To explain the miracles of grace and evolution we hypothesize the existence of a God who wants us to grow—a God who loves us. To many this hypothesis seems too simple, too easy; too much like fantasy; childlike and naïve. But what else do we have? To ignore the data by using tunnel vision is not an answer. We cannot obtain an answer by not asking the questions. Simple though it may be, no one who has observed the data and asked the questions has been able to produce a better hypothesis or even really a hypothesis at all. Until someone does, we are stuck with this strangely childlike notion of a loving God or else with a theoretical vacuum.

And if we take it seriously, we are going to find that this simple notion of a loving God does not make for an easy philosophy.

If we postulate that our capacity to love, this urge to grow and evolve, is somehow "breathed into" us by God, then we must ask to what end. Why does God want us to grow? What are we growing toward? Where is the end point, the goal of evolution? What is it that God wants of us? It is not my intention here to become involved in theological niceties, and I hope the scholarly will forgive me if I cut through all the ifs, ands, and buts of proper speculative theology. For no matter how much we may like to pussyfoot around it, all of us who postulate a loving God and really think about it eventually come to a single terrifying idea: God wants us to become Himself (or Herself or Itself). We are growing toward godhood. God is the goal of evolution. It is God who is the source of the evolutionary force and God who is the destination. That is what we mean when we say that He is the Alpha and the Omega, the beginning and the end.

When I said that this is a terrifying idea I was speaking mildly. It is a very old idea, but, by the millions, we run away from it in sheer panic. For no idea ever came to the mind of man which places upon us such a burden. It is the single most demanding idea in the history of mankind. Not because it is difficult to conceive; to the contrary, it is the essence of simplicity. But because if we believe it, it then demands from us all that we can possibly give, all that we have. It is one thing to believe in a nice old God who will take good care of us from a lofty position of power which we ourselves could never begin to attain. It is quite another to believe in a God who has it in mind for us precisely that we should attain His position, His power, His wisdom, His identity. Were we to believe it possible for man to become God, this belief by its very nature would place upon us an obligation to attempt to attain the possible. But we do not want this obligation. We don't want to have to work that hard. We don't want God's responsibility. We don't want the responsibility of having to think all the time. As long as we can believe that godhood is an impossible attainment for ourselves, we don't have to worry about our spiritual growth, we don't have to push ourselves to higher and higher levels of consciousness and loving activity; we can relax and just be human. If God's in his heaven and we're down here, and never the twain shall meet, we can let Him have all the responsibility for evolution and the directorship of the universe. We can do our bit toward assuring ourselves a comfortable old age, hopefully complete with healthy, happy and grateful children and grandchildren; but beyond that we need not bother ourselves. These goals are difficult enough to achieve, and hardly to be disparaged. Nonetheless, as soon as we believe it is possible for man to become God, we can really never rest for long, never say, "OK, my job is finished, my work is done." We must constantly push ourselves to greater and greater wisdom, greater and greater effectiveness. By this belief we will have trapped ourselves, at least until death, on an effortful treadmill of self-improvement and spiritual growth. God's responsibility must be our own. It is no wonder that the belief in the possibility of Godhead is repugnant.

The idea that God is actively nurturing us so that we might grow up to be like Him brings us face to face with our own laziness.

Entropy and Original Sin

Being about spiritual growth, this book is inevitably about the other side of the same coin: the impediments to spiritual growth. Ultimately there is only the one impediment, and that is laziness. If we overcome laziness, all the other impediments will be overcome. If we do not overcome laziness, none of the others will be hurdled. So this is also a book about laziness. In examining discipline we were considering the laziness of attempting to avoid necessary suffering, or taking the easy way out. In examining love we were also examining the fact that nonlove is the unwillingness to extend one's self. Laziness is love's opposite. Spiritual growth is effortful, as we have been reminded again and again. We are now at a position from which we can examine the nature of laziness in perspective and realize that laziness is the force of entropy as it manifests itself in the lives of all of us.

For many years I found the notion of original sin meaningless, even objectionable. Sexuality did not strike me as partic-

ularly sinful. Nor my various other appetites. I would quite
frequently indulge myself by overeating an excellent meal,
and while I might suffer pangs of indigestion, I certainly did
not suffer any pangs of guilt. I perceived sin in the world:
cheating, prejudice, torture, brutality. But I failed to perceive
any inherent sinfulness in infants, nor could I find it rational
to believe that young children were cursed because their
ancestors had eaten from the fruit of the tree of the knowledge
of good and evil. Gradually, however, I became increasingly
aware of the ubiquitous nature of laziness. In the struggle to
help my patients grow, I found that my chief enemy was
invariably their laziness. And I became aware in myself of a
similar reluctance to extend myself to new areas of thought,
responsibility and maturation. One thing I clearly had in common with all mankind was my laziness. It was at this point
that the serpent-and-the-apple story suddenly made sense.

The key issue lies in what is missing. The story suggests
that God was in the habit of "walking in the garden in the
cool of the day" and that there were open channels of communication between Him and man. But if this was so, then
why was it that Adam and Eve, separately or together, before
or after the serpent's urging, did not say to God, "We're
curious as to why You don't want us to eat any of the fruit of
the tree of the knowledge of good and evil. We really like it
here, and we don't want to seem ungrateful, but Your law on
this matter doesn't make much sense to us, and we'd really
appreciate it if you explained it to us"? But of course they did
not say this. Instead they went ahead and broke God's law
without ever understanding the reason behind the law, without taking the effort to challenge God directly, question his
authority or even communicate with Him on a reasonably
adult level. They listened to the serpent, but they failed to
get God's side of the story before they acted.

Why this failure? Why was no step taken between the
temptation and the action? It is this missing step that is the
essence of sin. The step missing is the step of debate. Adam
and Eve could have set up a debate between the serpent and

God, but in failing to do so they failed to obtain God's side of the question. The debate between the serpent and God is symbolic of the dialogue between good and evil which can and should occur within the minds of human beings. Our failure to conduct—or to conduct fully and wholeheartedly— this internal debate between good and evil is the cause of those evil actions that constitute sin. In debating the wisdom of a proposed course of action, human beings routinely fail to obtain God's side of the issue. They fail to consult or listen to the God within them, the knowledge of rightness which inherently resides within the minds of all mankind. We make this failure because we are lazy. It is work to hold these internal debates. They require time and energy just to conduct them. And if we take them seriously—if we seriously listen to this "God within us"—we usually find ourselves being urged to take the more difficult path, the path of more effort rather than less. To conduct the debate is to open ourselves to suffering and struggle. Each and every one of us, more or less frequently, will hold back from this work, will also seek to avoid this painful step. Like Adam and Eve, and every one of our ancestors before us, we are all lazy.

So original sin does exist; it is our laziness. It is very real. It exists in each and every one of us—infants, children, adolescents, mature adults, the elderly; the wise or the stupid; the lame or the whole. Some of us may be less lazy than others, but we are all lazy to some extent. No matter how energetic, ambitious or even wise we may be, if we truly look into ourselves we will find laziness lurking at some level. It is the force of entropy within us, pushing us down and holding us all back from our spiritual evolution.

Some readers may say to themselves, "But I'm not lazy. I work sixty hours a week at my job. In the evenings and on the weekends, even though I'm tired, I extend myself to go out with my spouse, take the children to the zoo, help with the housework, do any number of chores. Sometimes it seems that's all I do—work, work, work." I can sympathize with these readers but can persist only in pointing out that they will find laziness within themselves if they look for it. For laziness takes forms other than that related to the bare number of hours spent on the job or devoted to one's responsibilities to others. A major form that laziness takes is fear. The myth of Adam and Eve can again be used to illustrate this. One might say, for instance, that it was not laziness that prevented Adam and Eve from questioning God as to the reasons behind His law but fear—fear in the face of the awesomeness of God, fear of the wrath of God. But while all fear is not laziness, much fear is exactly that. Much of our fear is fear of a change in the status quo, a fear that we might lose what we have if we venture forth from where we are now. In the section on discipline I spoke of the fact that people find new information distinctly threatening, because if they incorporate it they will have to do a good deal of work to revise their maps of reality, and they instinctively seek to avoid that work. Consequently, more often than not they will fight against the new information rather than for its assimilation. Their resistance is motivated by fear, yes, but the basis of their fear is laziness; it is the fear of the work they would have to do. Similarly, in the section on love I spoke of the risks of extending ourselves into new territory, new commitments and responsibilities, new relationships and levels of existence. Here again the risk is of the loss of the status quo, and the fear is of the work involved in arriving at a new status quo. So it is quite probable that Adam and Eve were afraid of what might happen to them if they were to openly question God; instead they attempted to take the easy way out, the illegitimate shortcut of sneakiness, to achieve knowledge not worked for, and hope they could get away with it. But they did not. To question God may let us in for a lot of work. But a moral of the story is that it must be done.

Psychotherapists know that although patients come to us seeking change of one kind or another, they are actually terrified of change—of the work of change. It is because of this terror or laziness that the vast majority of patients—perhaps nine out of ten—who begin the process of psychotherapy, drop out of therapy long before the process has been completed. The majority of these drop-outs (or cop-outs) occur during the first few sessions or first few months of treatment. The dynamics are often clearest in the cases of those married patients who become aware during the first few sessions of therapy that their marriages are dreadfully disordered or destructive, and hence that the path to mental health will lie either through divorce or else through an enormously difficult and painful process of completely restructuring a marriage. Actually, these patients often have this awareness subliminally before they even seek psychotherapy, and the first few sessions of therapy only serve to confirm what they already knew and dreaded. In any case, they become overwhelmed by fear of facing the seemingly impossible difficulties of living alone or apparently equally impossible difficulties of working for months and years with their mates toward radically improved relationships. So they stop treatment, sometimes after two or three sessions, sometimes after ten or twenty. They may stop with some such excuse as "We've decided we made a mistake when we thought we had the money for treatment" or they may stop honestly with an open acknowledgment: "I'm afraid of what therapy might do to my marriage. I know it's a cop-out. Maybe someday I'll have the guts to come back." At any rate, they settle for the maintenance of a miserable status quo in preference to the tremendous amount of effort they realize will be required to work their way out of their particular traps.

In the earlier stages of spiritual growth, individuals are mostly unaware of their own laziness, although they may give it lip service by saying such things as "Of course, like everybody else, I have my lazy moments." This is because the lazy part of the self, like the devil that it may actually be, is unscrupulous and specializes in treacherous disguise. It cloaks its own laziness in all manner of rationalizations, which the more growing part of the self is still too weak to see through easily or to combat. Thus a person will say to the suggestion that he or she gain some new knowledge in a certain area,

"That area's been studied by a lot of people and they've not come up with any answers" or "I know a man who was into that stuff and he was an alcoholic who committed suicide" or "I'm too old a dog to learn new tricks" or "You're trying to manipulate me into becoming a carbon copy of yourself and that's not what psychotherapists are supposed to do." All of these responses and many more are cover-ups of patients' or students' laziness, designed to disguise it not so much from the therapist or teacher as from themselves. For to recognize laziness for what it is and acknowledge it in oneself is the beginning of its curtailment.

For these reasons, those who are in the relatively more advanced stages of spiritual growth are the very ones most aware of their own laziness. It is the least lazy who know themselves to be sluggish. In my personal struggle for maturity I am gradually becoming more aware of new insights, which tend, as if of themselves, to want to slip away from me. Or I glimpse new, constructive avenues of thought on which my steps, seemingly of their own accord, start to drag. I suspect that most of the time these valuable thoughts do slip away unnoticed and that I wander from these valuable avenues without knowing what I'm doing. But when I do become conscious of the fact that I am dragging my feet, I am compelled to exert the will to quicken my pace in the very direction I am avoiding. The fight against entropy never ends.

We all have a sick self and a healthy self. No matter how neurotic or even psychotic we may be, even if we seem to be totally fearful and completely rigid, there is still a part of us, however small, that wants us to grow, that likes change and development, that is attracted to the new and the unknown, and that is willing to do the work and take the risks involved in spiritual evolution. And no matter how seemingly healthy and spiritually evolved we are, there is still a part of us, however small, that does not want us to exert ourselves, that clings to the old and familiar, fearful of any change or effort, desiring comfort at any cost and absence of pain at any price, even if the penalty be ineffectiveness, stagnation or regression. In some of us our healthy self seems pathetically small, wholly dominated by the laziness and fearfulness of our monumental sick self. Others of us may be rapidly growing, our dominant healthy self reaching eagerly upward in the struggle to evolve toward godhood; the healthy self, however, must always be vigilant against the laziness of the sick self that still lurks within us. In this one respect we human beings are all equal. Within each and every one of us there are two selves, one sick and one healthy—the life urge and the death urge, if you will. Each of us represents the whole human race; within each of us is the instinct for godhood and the hope for mankind, and within each of us is the original sin of laziness, the ever-present force of entropy pushing us back to childhood, to the womb and to the swamps from which we have evolved.

The Problem of Evil

Having suggested that laziness is original sin and that laziness in the form of our sick self might even be the devil, it is relevant to round out the picture by making some remarks about the nature of evil. The problem of evil is perhaps the greatest of all theological problems. Yet, as with so many other "religious" issues, the science of psychology has acted, with a few minor exceptions, as if evil did not exist. Potentially, however, psychology has much to contribute to the subject. I hope that I will be able to make part of such a contribution in a later work of some length. For the moment, since it is only peripheral to the theme of this book, I will limit myself to briefly stating four conclusions I have reached concerning the nature of evil.

First, I have come to conclude that evil is real. It is not the figment of the imagination of a primitive religious mind feebly attempting to explain the unknown. There really are people, and institutions made up of people, who respond with hatred in the presence of goodness and would destroy the good insofar as it is in their power to do so. They do this not with conscious malice but blindly, lacking awareness of their own evil—indeed, seeking to avoid any such awareness. As has been described of the devil in religious literature, they hate the light and instinctively will do anything to avoid it, including attempting to extinguish it. They will destroy the light in their own children and in all other beings subject to their power.

Evil people hate the light because it reveals themselves to themselves. They hate goodness because it reveals their badness; they hate love because it reveals their laziness. They will destroy the light, the goodness, the love in order to avoid the pain of such self-awareness. My second conclusion, then, is that evil is laziness carried to its ultimate, extraordinary extreme. As I have defined it, love is the antithesis of laziness. Ordinary laziness is a passive failure to love. Some ordinarily lazy people may not lift a finger to extend themselves unless they are compelled to do so. Their being is a manifestation of nonlove; still, they are not evil. Truly evil people, on the other hand, actively rather than passively avoid extending themselves. They will take any action in their power to protect their own laziness, to preserve the integrity of their sick self. Rather than nurturing others, they will actually destroy others in this cause. If necessary, they will even kill to escape the pain of their own spiritual growth. As the integrity of their sick self is threatened by the spiritual health of those around them, they will seek by all manner of means to crush and demolish the spiritual health that may exist near them. I define evil, then, as the exercise of political power—that is, the imposition of one's will upon others by overt or covert coercion—in order to avoid extending one's self for the purpose of nurturing spiritual growth. Ordinary laziness is nonlove; evil is antilove.

My third conclusion is that the existence of evil is inevitable, at least at this stage in human evolution. Given the force of entropy and the fact that humans possess free will, it is inevitable that laziness will be well contained in some and completely uncontained in others. As entropy, on the one hand, and the evolutionary flow of love, on the other, are opposing forces, it is only natural that these forces will be relatively in balance in most people, while a few at one extreme will manifest almost pure love, and a few at the other extreme pure entropy or evil. Since they are conflicting forces, it is also inevitable that those at the extremes will be locked in combat; it is as natural for evil to hate goodness as it is for goodness to hate evil.

Last, I have come to conclude that while entropy is an enormous force, in its most extreme form of human evil it is strangely ineffective as a social force. I myself have witnessed evil in action, viciously attacking and effectively destroying the spirits and minds of dozens of children. But evil backfires in the big picture of human evolution. For every soul it destroys—and there are many—it is instrumental in the salvation of others. Unwittingly, evil serves as a beacon to warn others away from its own shoals. Because most of us have been graced by an almost instinctive sense of horror at the outrageousness of evil, when we recognize its presence, our own personalities are honed by the awareness of its existence. Our consciousness of it is a signal to purify ourselves. It was evil, for instance, that raised Christ to the cross, thereby enabling us to see him from afar. Our personal involvement in the fight against evil in the world is one of the ways we grow.

The Evolution of Consciousness

The words "aware" and "awareness" have repeatedly cropped up throughout. Evil people resist the awareness of their own condition. A mark of the spiritually advanced is their awareness of their own laziness. People often are not aware of their own religion or world view, and in the course of their religious growth it is necessary for them to become aware of their own assumptions and tendencies toward bias. Through bracketing and the attention of love we grow more aware of our beloved and of the world. An essential part of discipline is the development of an awareness of our responsibility and power of choice. The capacity of awareness we assign to that portion of the mind we call conscious or consciousness. We are now at the point where we can define spiritual growth as the growth or evolution of consciousness.

The word "conscious" is derived from the Latin prefix *con*, meaning "with," and the word *scire*, meaning "to know." To be conscious means "to know with." But how are we to understand this "with"? To know with *what?* We have spoken of the fact that the unconscious part of our mind is the possessor of extraordinary knowledge. It knows more than we know, "we" being defined as our conscious self. And when we become aware of a new truth, it is because we recognize it to be true; we re-know that which we knew all along. Therefore, might we not conclude that to become conscious is to know *with* our unconscious? The development of consciousness is the development of awareness in our conscious mind of knowledge *along with* our unconscious mind, which already possesses that knowledge. It is a process of the conscious mind coming into synchrony with the unconscious. This should be no strange concept to psychotherapists, who frequently define their therapy as a process of "making the unconscious conscious" or enlarging the realm of consciousness in relation to the realm of unconsciousness.

But we still have not explained how it is that the unconscious possesses all this knowledge which we have not yet consciously learned. Here again the question is so basic that we have no scientific answer. Again we can only hypothesize. And again I know of no hypothesis as satisfactory as the postulation of a God who is intimately associated with us—so intimately that He is part of us. If you want to know the closest place to look for grace, it is within yourself. If you desire wisdom greater than your own, you can find it inside you. What this suggests is that the interface between God and man is at least in part the interface between our unconscious and our conscious. To put it plainly, our unconscious is God. God within us. We were part of God all the time. God has been with us all along, is now, and always will be.

How can this be? If the reader is horrified by the notion that our unconscious is God, he or she should recall that it is hardly a heretical concept, being in essence the same as the Christian concept of the Holy Ghost or Holy Spirit which resides in us all. I find it most helpful to understand this relationship between God and ourselves by thinking of our unconscious as a rhizome, or incredibly large and rich hidden root system, which nourishes the tiny plant of consciousness sprouting visibly from it. I am indebted for this analogy to Jung, who, describing himself as "a splinter of the infinite deity," went on to say:

> Life has always seemed to me like a plant that lives on its rhizome. Its true life is invisible, hidden in the rhizome. The part that appears above ground lasts only a single summer. Then it withers away—an ephemeral apparition. When we think of the unending growth and decay of life and civilization, we cannot escape the impression of abso-

lute nullity. Yet I have never lost a sense of something that lives and endures underneath the eternal flux. What we see is the blossom, which passes. The rhizome remains.*

Jung never went quite so far as to actually state that God existed in the unconscious, although his writings clearly pointed in that direction. What he did do was to divide the unconscious into the more superficial, individual "personal unconscious" and the deeper "collective unconscious" that is common to mankind. In my vision the collective unconscious is God; the conscious is man as individual; and the personal unconscious is the interface between them. Being this interface, it is inevitable that the personal unconscious should be a place of some turmoil, the scene of some struggle between God's will and the will of the individual. I have previously described the unconscious as a benign and loving realm. This I believe it to be. But dreams, though they contain messages of loving wisdom, also contain many signs of conflict; while they may be pleasantly self-renewing, they may also be tumultuous, frightening nightmares. Because of this tumultuousness, mental illness has been localized in the unconscious by most thinkers, as if the unconscious were the seat of psychopathology and symptoms were like subterranean demons that surface to bedevil the individual. As I have already said, my own view is the opposite. I believe that the conscious is the seat of psychopathology and that mental disorders are disorders of consciousness. It is because our conscious self resists our unconscious wisdom that we become ill. It is precisely because our consciousness is disordered that conflict occurs between it and the unconscious which seeks to heal it. In other words, mental illness occurs when the conscious will of the individual deviates substantially from the will of God, which is the individual's own unconscious will.

I have said that the ultimate goal of spiritual growth is for

* C. G. Jung, *Memories, Dreams, Reflections*, Aniela Jaffe, ed. (New York: Vintage Books, 1965), p. 4.

the individual to become as one with God. It is to know with God. Since the unconscious is God all along, we may further define the goal of spiritual growth to be the attainment of godhood by the conscious self. It is for the individual to become totally, wholly God. Does this mean that the goal is for the conscious to merge with the unconscious, so that all is unconsciousness? Hardly. We now come to the point of it all. The point is to become God while preserving consciousness. If the bud of consciousness that grows from the rhizome of the unconscious God can become itself God, then God will have assumed a new life form. This is the meaning of our individual existence. We are born that we might become, as a conscious individual, a new life form of God.

The conscious is the executive part of our total being. It is the conscious that makes decisions and translates them into action. Were we to become all unconscious, we would be indeed like the newborn infant, one with God but incapable of any action that might make the presence of God felt in the world. As I have mentioned, there is a regressive quality to the mystical thought of some Hindu or Buddhist theology, in which the status of the infant without ego boundaries is compared to Nirvana and the goal of entering Nirvana seems similar to the goal of returning to the womb. The goal of theology presented here, and that of most mystics, is exactly the opposite. It is not to become an egoless, unconscious babe. Rather it is to develop a mature, conscious ego which then can become the ego of God. If as adults, walking around on two legs, capable of making independent choices that influence the world, we can identify our mature free will with that of God, then God will have assumed through our conscious ego a new and potent life form. We will have become God's agent, his arm, so to speak, and therefore part of Him. And insofar as we might then through our conscious decisions be able to influence the world according to His will our lives themselves will become the agents of God's grace. We ourselves will then have become one form of the grace of God, working on His behalf among mankind, creating love where love did not exist before, pulling our fellow creatures up to our own level of awareness, pushing the plane of human evolution forward.

The Nature of Power

We have now come to the point where we can understand the nature of power. It is a much misunderstood subject. One reason for the misunderstanding is that there are two kinds of power—political and spiritual. Religious mythology takes pains to draw the distinction between the two. Prior to the birth of Buddha, for instance, the soothsayers informed his father that Buddha would grow up to become the most powerful king in the land or else a poor man who would be the greatest spiritual leader the world had ever known. Either or, but not both. And Christ was offered by Satan "all the kingdoms of the world and the glory of them." But he rejected this alternative in favor of dying, seemingly impotent, upon the cross.

Political power is the capacity to coerce others, overtly or covertly, to do one's will. This capacity resides in a position, such as a kingship or presidency, or else in money. It does not reside in the person who occupies the position or possesses the money. Consequently political power is unrelated to goodness or wisdom. Very stupid and very evil people have walked as kings upon the earth. Spiritual power, however, resides entirely within the individual and has nothing to do with the capacity to coerce others. People of great spiritual power may be wealthy and may upon occasion occupy political positions of leadership, but they are as likely to be poor and lacking in political authority. Then, what is the capacity of spiritual power if not the capacity to coerce? It is the capacity to make decisions with maximum awareness. It is consciousness.

Most people most of the time make decisions with little awareness of what they are doing. They take action with little understanding of their own motives and without beginning to know the ramifications of their choices. Do we really know what we are doing when we accept or reject a potential client? When we hit a child, promote a subordinate, flirt with an acquaintance? Anyone who has worked for long in the political arena knows that actions taken with the best intentions will often backfire and prove harmful in the end; or that people with scurrilous motives may promote a seemingly wicked cause that ultimately turns out to be constructive. So also in the area of child-raising. Is it any better to do the right thing for the wrong reasons than the wrong thing for the right reasons? We are often most in the dark when we are the most certain, and the most enlightened when we are the most confused.

What are we to do, adrift in a sea of ignorance? Some are nihilistic and say, "Nothing." They propose only that we should continue to drift, as if no course could possibly be charted in such a vast sea which would bring us to any true clarity or meaningful destination. But others, sufficiently aware to know that they are lost, dare to hope that they can work themselves out of ignorance through developing even greater awareness. They are correct. It is possible. But such greater awareness does not come to them in a single blinding flash of enlightenment. It comes slowly, piece by piece, and each piece must be worked for by the patient effort of study and observation of everything, including themselves. They are humble students. The path of spiritual growth is a path of lifelong learning.

If this path is followed long and earnestly enough, the pieces of knowledge begin to fall into place. Gradually things begin to make sense. There are blind alleys, disappointments, concepts arrived at only to be discarded. But gradually it is possible for us to come to a deeper and deeper understanding of what our existence is all about. And gradually we can come to the place where we actually know what we are doing. We can come to power.

The experience of spiritual power is basically a joyful one. There is a joy that comes with mastery. Indeed, there is no greater satisfaction than that of being an expert, of really knowing what we are doing. Those who have grown the most spiritually are those who are the experts in living. And there is yet another joy, even greater. It is the joy of communion with God. For when we truly know what we are doing, we are participating in the omniscience of God. With total awareness of the nature of a situation, of our motives for acting upon it, and of the results and ramifications of our action, we have attained that level of awareness that we normally expect only of God. Our conscious self has succeeded in coming into alignment with the mind of God. We know with God.

Yet those who have attained this stage of spiritual growth, this state of great awareness, are invariably possessed by a joyful humility. For one of their very awarenesses is the awareness that their unusual wisdom has its origin in their unconscious. They are aware of their connection to the rhizome and aware that their knowledge flows to them from the rhizome through the connection. Their efforts at learning are only efforts to open the connection, and they are aware that the rhizome, their unconscious, is not theirs alone but all mankind's, all life's, God's. Invariably when asked the source of their knowledge and power, the truly powerful will reply: "It is not my power. What little power I have is but a minute expression of a far greater power. I am merely a conduit. It is not my power at all." I have said that this humility is joyful. That is because, with their awareness of their connectedness to God, the truly powerful experience a diminution in their sense of self. "Let thy will, not mine, be done. Make me your instrument," is their only desire. Such a loss of self brings with it always a kind of calm ecstasy, not unlike the experience of being in love. Aware of their intimate connectedness to God, they experience a surcease of loneliness. There is communion.

Joyful though it is, the experience of spiritual power is also terrifying. For the greater one's awareness, the more difficult it is to take action. I mentioned this fact at the conclusion of the first section when I gave the analogy of two generals, each having to make the decision of whether or not to commit a division to battle. The one who regards his division simply and solely as a unit of strategy may sleep easily after having made his decision. But for the other, with his awareness of each of the lives of the men under his command, the decision will be agonizing. We are all generals. Whatever action we take may influence the course of civilization. The decision whether to praise or punish a single child may have vast consequences. It is easy to act with the awareness of limited data and let the chips fall as they may. The greater our awareness, however, the more and more data we must assimilate and integrate into our decision-making. The more we know, the more complex decisions become. Yet the more and more we know, the more it begins to become possible to predict just where the chips will fall. If we assume the responsibility of attempting to predict accurately just where each chip will fall, we are likely to feel so overwhelmed by the complexity of the task as to sink into inaction. But, then, inaction is itself a form of action, and while doing nothing might be the best course of action under certain circumstances, in others it may be disastrous and destructive. So spiritual power is not simply awareness; it is the capacity to maintain one's ability to still make decisions with greater and greater awareness. And god-like power is the power to make decisions with total awareness. But unlike the popular notion of it, omniscience does not make decision-making easier; rather, it becomes ever more difficult. The closer one comes to godhood, the more one feels sympathy for God. To participate in God's omniscience is also to share His agony.

There is another problem with power: aloneness.* Here there is a similarity, in at least one dimension, between spiritual and political power. Someone who is approaching the peak of spiritual evolution is like someone at the peak of political power. There is no one above to whom to pass the buck; no one to blame; no one to tell you how to do it. There may not even be anyone on the same level to share the agony or the responsibility. Others may advise, but the decision is yours alone. You alone are responsible. In another dimension, the aloneness of enormous spiritual power is even greater than that of political power. Since their level of awareness is seldom as high as their exalted positions, the politically powerful almost always have their spiritual equals with whom they can communicate. So presidents and kings will have their friends and cronies. But the person who has evolved to the highest level of awareness, of spiritual power, will likely have no one in his or her circle of acquaintances with whom to share such depth of understanding. One of the most poignant themes of the Gospels is Christ's continual sense of frustration on finding that there was no one who could really understand him. No matter how hard he tried, how much he extended himself, he could not lift the minds of even his own disciples to his level. The wisest followed him but could not catch up with him, and all his love could not relieve him of the necessity to lead by walking ahead, utterly alone. This kind of aloneness is "shared" by all who travel the farthest on the journey of spiritual growth. It is such a burden that it simply could not be borne were it not for the fact that as we outdistance our fellow humans our relationship to God inevitably becomes correspondingly closer. In the communion of growing con-

* I make a distinction between aloneness and loneliness. Loneliness is the unavailability of people to communicate with on any level. Powerful people are surrounded by others only too eager to communicate with them; hence they are seldom lonely and may even yearn for loneliness. Aloneness, however, is the unavailability of someone to communicate with at your level of awareness.

sciousness, of knowing with God, there is enough joy to sustain us.

Grace and Mental Illness: The Myth of Orestes

A number of seemingly disparate statements have been made about the nature of mental health and illness; "Neurosis is always a substitute for legitimate suffering"; "Mental health is dedication to reality at all costs"; and "Mental illness occurs when the conscious will of the individual substantially deviates from the will of God, which is his or her own unconscious will." Let us now examine the issue of mental illness more closely and unite these elements into a coherent whole.

We live our lives in a real world. To live them well it is necessary that we come to understand the reality of the world as best we can. But such understanding does not come easily. Many aspects of the reality of the world and of our relationship to the world are painful to us. We can understand them only through effort and suffering. All of us, to a greater or lesser extent, attempt to avoid this effort and suffering. We ignore painful aspects of reality by thrusting certain unpleasant facts out of our awareness. In other words, we attempt to defend our consciousness, our awareness, against reality. We do this by a variety of means which psychiatrists call defense mechanisms. All of us employ such defenses, thereby limiting our awareness. If in our laziness and fear of suffering we massively defend our awareness, then it will come to pass that our understanding of the world will bear little or no relation to reality. Because our actions are based on our understanding, our behavior will then become unrealistic. When this occurs to a sufficient degree our fellow citizens will recognize that we are "out of touch with reality," and will deem us mentally ill even though we ourselves are most likely convinced of our sanity.* But long before matters have proceeded to this extreme, and we have been served notice of our illness by our fellow citizens, we are served notice by our unconscious of our increasing maladjustment. Such notice is served by our unconscious through a variety of means: bad dreams, anxiety attacks, depressions, and other symptoms. Although our conscious mind has denied reality, our unconscious, which is omniscient, knows the true score and attempts to help us out by stimulating, through symptom formation, our conscious mind to the awareness that something is wrong. In other words, the painful and unwanted symptoms of mental illness are manifestations of grace. They are the products of a "powerful force originating outside of consciousness which nurtures our spiritual growth."

I have already pointed out in the brief discussion of depression, toward the end of the first section on discipline, that depressive symptoms are a sign to the suffering individual that all is not right with him or her and major adjustments need to be made. Many of the case histories I have used to demonstrate other principles can also be used to illustrate this one: that the unpleasant symptoms of mental illness serve to notify people that they have taken the wrong path, that their spirits are not growing and are in grave jeopardy. But let me briefly describe one more case to specifically demonstrate the role of symptoms.

Betsy was a twenty-two-year-old woman, lovely and intelligent but with a demure almost virginal quality to her, who

---

* I recognize that this schema of mental illness is somewhat oversimplified. It does not, for instance, take into account physical or biochemical factors which may be of large and even predominant significance in certain cases. I also recognize that it is possible for individuals to be so much more in touch with reality than their fellow citizens that they will be deemed "insane" by a "sick society." Nonetheless, the schema presented here holds true in the vast majority of instances of mental illness.

came to see me for severe anxiety attacks. She was the only child of Catholic working-class parents who had scrimped and saved to send her to college. After one year of college, however, despite the fact that she had done well academically, she decided to drop out and marry the boy next door, a mechanic. She took a job as a clerk in a supermarket. All went well for two years. But then, suddenly, came the anxiety attacks. Out of the blue. They were totally unpredictable—except that when they did occur she was always out of her apartment somewhere without her husband. They might happen when she was shopping, when she was at her job in the supermarket, or simply when she was walking down the street. The intensity of the panic she felt at these times was overwhelming. She would have to drop whatever she was doing and would literally run back to her apartment or else to the garage where her husband worked. Only when she was with him or at home would the panic subside. Because of the attacks she had to quit her job.

When tranquilizers given her by her general practitioner failed to stop or even touch the intensity of her panic attacks Betsy came to see me. "I don't know what's wrong with me," she wailed. "Everything in my life's wonderful. My husband is good to me. We love each other very much. I enjoyed my job. Now everything's awful. I don't know why this has happened to me. I feel I'm maybe going crazy. Please help me. Please help me so that things can be nice like they used to be." But of course Betsy discovered in our work together that things were not so "nice" the way they used to be. First, slowly and painfully, it emerged that while her husband was good to her, various things about him irritated her. His manners were uncouth. His range of interests were narrow. All he wanted to do for entertainment was watch TV. He bored her. Then she began to recognize that working as a cashier in a supermarket also bored her. So we began to ask why she had left college for such an unstimulating existence. "Well, I got more and more uncomfortable there," she acknowledged.

"The kids were into drugs and sex a lot. I didn't feel right about it. They questioned me, not just the boys who wanted to have sex with me, but even my girl friends. They thought I was naïve. I found I was even beginning to question myself, to question the church and even some of my parents' values. I guess I got scared." In therapy Betsy now started to proceed with the process of questioning that she had run away from by leaving college. Ultimately she returned to college. Fortunately, in this instance, her husband proved willing to grow with her and went to college himself. Their horizons rapidly broadened. And of course her anxiety attacks ceased.

There are several ways to look at this rather typical case. Betsy's anxiety attacks were clearly a form of agoraphobia (literally, fear of the marketplace, but usually fear of open spaces), and for her represented a fear of freedom. She had them when she was outside, unhindered by her husband, free to move about and relate with others. Fear of freedom was the essence of her mental illness. Some might say that the anxiety attacks, representing her fear of freedom, were her illness. But I have found it more useful and enlightening to look at things another way. For Betsy's fear of freedom long predated her anxiety attacks. It was because of this fear that she had left college and had begun the process of constricting her development. In my judgment Betsy was ill at that time, three years before her symptoms began. Yet she was not aware of her illness or of the damage she was doing to herself by her self-constriction. It was her symptoms, these anxiety attacks which she did not want and had not asked for, which she felt had "cursed" her "out of the blue," that made her finally aware of her illness and forced her to set out upon the path of self-correction and growth. I believe that this pattern holds true for most mental illness. The symptoms and the illness are not the same thing. The illness exists long before the symptoms. Rather than being the illness, the symptoms are the beginning of its cure. The fact that they are unwanted makes them all the more a phenomenon of grace—a gift of

God, a message from the unconscious, if you will, to initiate self-examination and repair.

As is common with grace, most reject this gift and do not heed the message. They do this in a variety of ways, all of which represent an attempt to avoid the responsibility for their illness. They try to ignore the symptoms by pretending that they are not really symptoms, that everyone gets "these little attacks from time to time." They try to work around them by quitting jobs, stopping driving, moving to a new town, avoiding certain activities. They attempt to rid themselves of the symptoms by pain-killers, by little pills they've gotten from the doctor or by anesthetizing themselves with alcohol and other drugs. Even if they do accept the fact that they have symptoms, they will usually, in many subtle ways, blame the world outside them—uncaring relatives, false friends, greedy corporations, a sick society, and even fate— for their condition. Only those few who accept responsibility for their symptoms, who realize that their symptoms are a manifestation of a disorder in their own soul, heed the message of their unconscious and accept its grace. They accept their own inadequacy and the pain of the work necessary to heal themselves. But to them, as to Betsy and all the others willing to face the pain of psychotherapy, comes great reward. It was of them that Christ spoke in the first of the beatitudes: "Blessed are the poor in spirit, for theirs is the Kingdom of Heaven."*

What I am saying here of the relationship between grace and mental illness is beautifully embodied in the great Greek myth of Orestes and the Furies.† Orestes was a grandson of

---

* Matthew 5:3.

† There are many different versions of this myth, with substantial differences between them. No one version is the correct one. The version given here is mostly condensed from Edith Hamilton's *Mythology* (New York: Mentor Books, New American Library, 1958). I was led to this myth through Rollo May's use of it in his book *Love and Will* and that of T. S. Eliot in his play *The Family Reunion*.

Atreus, a man who had viciously attempted to prove himself more powerful than the gods. Because of his crime against them, the gods punished Atreus by placing a curse upon all his descendants. As part of the enactment of this curse upon the House of Atreus, Orestes' mother, Clytemnestra, murdered his father and her husband, Agamemnon. This crime in turn brought down the curse upon Orestes' head, because by the Greek code of honor a son was obliged, above all else, to slay his father's murderer. Yet the greatest sin a Greek could commit was the sin of matricide. Orestes agonized over his dilemma. Finally he did what he seemingly had to do and killed his mother. For this sin the gods then punished Orestes by visiting upon him the Furies, three ghastly harpies who could be seen and heard only by him and who tormented him night and day with their cackling criticism and frightening appearance.

Pursued wherever he went by the Furies, Orestes wandered about the land seeking to atone for his crime. After many years of lonely reflection and self-abrogation Orestes requested the gods to relieve him of the curse on the House of Atreus and its visitations upon him through the Furies, stating his belief that he had succeeded in atoning for the murder of his mother. A trial was held by the gods. Speaking in Orestes' defense, Apollo argued that he had engineered the whole situation that had placed Orestes in the position in which he had no choice but to kill his mother, and therefore Orestes really could not be held responsible. At this point Orestes jumped up and contradicted his own defender, stating, "It was I, not Apollo, that murdered my mother!" The gods were amazed. Never before had a member of the House of Atreus assumed such total responsibility for himself and not blamed the gods. Eventually the gods decided the trial in Orestes' favor, and not only relieved him of the curse upon the House of Atreus but also transformed the Furies into the Eumenides, loving spirits who through their wise counsel enabled Orestes to obtain continuing good fortune.

The meaning of this myth is not obscure. The Eumenides,

or "benignant ones," are also referred to as the "bearers of grace." The hallucinatory Furies, who could be perceived only by Orestes, represent his symptoms, the private hell of mental illness. The transformation of the Furies into the Eumenides is the transformation of mental illness into good fortune, of which we have been speaking. This transformation occurred by virtue of the fact that Orestes was willing to accept responsibility for his mental illness. While he ultimately sought to be relieved of them, he did not see the Furies as an unjust punishment or perceive himself to be a victim of society or of anything else. Being an inevitable result of the original curse upon the House of Atreus, the Furies also symbolize the fact that mental illness is a family affair, created in one by one's parents and grandparents as the sins of the father are visited upon the children. But Orestes did not blame his family—his parents or his grandfather—as he well might have. Nor did he blame the gods or "fate." Instead he accepted his condition as one of his own making and undertook the effort to heal it. It was a lengthy process, just as most therapy tends to be lengthy. But as a result he was healed, and through this healing process of his own effort, the very things that had once caused him agony became the same things that brought him wisdom.

All experienced psychotherapists have seen this myth acted out in their own practices and have actually witnessed the transformation of the Furies into the Eumenides within the minds and lives of their more successful patients. It is not an easy transformation. As soon as they realize that they will ultimately be required by the process of psychotherapy to assume total responsibility for their condition and its cure, most patients, no matter how eager for therapy they initially appeared to be, will drop out. They choose rather to be sick and have the gods to blame than to be well with no one to blame ever again. Of the minority who stay in therapy most must still be taught to assume total responsibility for themselves as a part of their healing. This teaching—"training" might be a more accurate word—is a painstaking affair as the therapist methodically confronts patients with their avoidance of responsibility again and again and again, session after session, month after month, and often year after year. Frequently, like stubborn children, they will kick and scream all the way as they are led to the notion of total responsibility for themselves. Eventually, however, they arrive. It is only the rare patient who enters therapy with a willingness to assume total responsibility from the beginning. Therapy in such cases, while it still may require a year or two, is relatively brief, relatively smooth, and frequently a very pleasant process for both patient and therapist. In any case, whether relatively easy or difficult and prolonged, the transformation of the Furies into the Eumenides does occur.

Those who have faced their mental illness, accepted total responsibility for it, and made the necessary changes in themselves to overcome it, find themselves not only cured and free from the curses of their childhood and ancestry but also find themselves living in a new and different world. What they once perceived as problems they now perceive as opportunities. What were once loathsome barriers are now welcome challenges. Thoughts previously unwanted become helpful insights; feelings previously disowned become sources of energy and guidance. Occurrences that once seemed to be burdens now seem to be gifts, including the very symptoms from which they have recovered. "My depression and my anxiety attacks were the best things that ever happened to me," they will routinely say at the termination of successful therapy. Even if they emerge from therapy without a belief in God, such successful patients still generally do so with a very real sense that they have been touched by grace.

Resistance to Grace

Orestes did not go to a psychotherapist; he healed himself. And even had there been expert psychiatrists in ancient Greece, he still would have had to heal himself. For, as has been mentioned, psychotherapy is only a tool—a discipline. It is up to the patient to choose or reject the tool, and once chosen, it is the patient who determines how much to use the tool and to what end. There are people who will overcome all manner of obstacles—for example, insufficient funds, previous disastrous experiences with psychiatrists or psychotherapists, disapproving relatives, cold and rejecting clinics—to obtain therapy and every last ounce of its possible benefit. Others, however, will reject therapy even if it is offered them on a silver platter, or else, even if they do become engaged in a therapeutic relationship, will sit in it like a bump on a log, extracting from it almost nothing no matter how great the therapist's skill and effort and love. While at the conclusion of a successful case I am tempted to feel that I have cured the patient, I know the reality of the situation is that I have been no more than a catalyst—and fortunate to be that. Since ultimately people heal themselves with or without the tool of psychotherapy, why is it that so few do and so many do not? Since the path of spiritual growth, albeit difficult, is open to all, why do so few choose to travel it?

It was to this question that Christ was addressing himself when he said, "Many are called, but few are chosen."* But why is it that the few are chosen, and what is it that distinguishes those few from the many? The answer that most psychotherapists are accustomed to give is based on a concept of

* Matthew 22:14; see also Matthew 20:16.

differing severity of psychopathology. In other words, they believe that while most people are sick, some are sicker than others, and the sicker one is the more difficult it is for that one to be healed. Moreover, the severity of one's mental illness is directly determined by the severity and the earliness of the parental deprivation that one experienced in childhood. Specifically, individuals with psychoses are thought to have experienced extremely poor parenting in the first nine months of life; their resulting illness can be ameliorated by this or that form of treatment, but it is almost impossible to cure. Individuals with character disorders are thought to have experienced adequate care as infants but very poor care during the period between roughly nine months and two years of age, with the result that they are less sick than psychotics but still quite sick indeed and very difficult to cure. Individuals with neuroses are thought to have received adequate parenting in their very early childhood but then to have suffered from poor parenting sometime after the age of two but usually beginning before the age of five or six. Neurotics are therefore thought to be less sick than either character-disordered people or psychotics, and consequently much easier to treat and cure.

There is, I believe, a good deal of truth to this schema, and it forms a body of psychiatric theory that is quite useful to practitioners in a number of ways. It should not be blithely criticized. Nonetheless, it fails to tell the whole story. Among other things, it denigrates the vast importance of parenting in late childhood and adolescence. There is good reason to believe that poor parenting in these later years can produce mental illness in and of itself, and that good parenting during the later years can heal many and perhaps all of the wounds caused by earlier poor parenting. Moreover, while the schema has predictive value in a statistical sense—neurotics are, on the average, easier to treat than character-disordered persons, and those with character disorders are, on the average, easier to treat than psychotics—it fails to predict very well the course of growth in an individual case. Thus, for example, the most rapid course of a completely successful analysis I have ever conducted was with a man who came to me with a major psychosis and whose therapy was concluded nine months later. On the other hand, I worked for three years with a woman who clearly had "only" a neurosis and achieved just only minimal improvement.

Among the factors that the schema of the differing severity of mental illness fails to take into account is an ephemeral something in the individual patient which might be called a "will to grow." It is possible for an individual to be extremely ill and yet at the same time possess an extremely strong "will to grow," in which case healing will occur. On the other hand, a person who is only mildly ill, as best we can define psychiatric illness, but who lacks the will to grow, will not budge an inch from an unhealthy position. I therefore believe that the patient's will to grow is the one crucial determinant of success or failure in psychotherapy. Yet it is a factor that is not at all understood or even recognized by contemporary psychiatric theory.

Although I am recognizing the extreme importance of this will to grow, I am not sure how much I will be able to contribute to its understanding, since the concept brings us once again to the edge of mystery. It will be immediately apparent that the will to grow is in essence the same phenomenon as love. Love is the will to extend oneself for spiritual growth. Genuinely loving people are, by definition, growing people. I have spoken about how the capacity to love is nurtured in one by loving parenting, but I have also noted that parental nurturing alone fails to account for the existence of this capacity in all people. The reader will remember that the second section of this book concluded with four questions about love, two of which we are now considering: why some people fail to respond to treatment by the best and most loving therapists, and why some people transcend the most loveless childhoods, with or without the help of psychotherapy, to become themselves loving persons. The reader will also remember I stated then that I doubted that I would be able to answer these questions to anyone's complete satisfaction. I suggested, however, that some light could be thrown on these questions by consideration of the concept of grace.

I have come to believe and have tried to demonstrate that people's capacity to love, and hence their will to grow, is nurtured not only by the love of their parents during childhood but also throughout their lives by grace, or God's love. This is a powerful force external to their consciousness which operates through the agency of their own unconscious as well as through the agency of loving persons other than their parents and through additional ways which we do not understand. It is because of grace that it is possible for people to transcend the traumas of loveless parenting and become themselves loving individuals who have risen far above their parents on the scale of human evolution. Why, then, do only some people spiritually grow and evolve beyond the circumstances of their parentage? I believe that grace is available to everyone, that we are all cloaked in the love of God, no one less nobly than another. The only answer I can give, therefore, is that most of us choose not to heed the call of grace and to reject its assistance. Christ's assertion "Many are called, but few are chosen" I would translate to mean "All of us are called by and to grace, but few of us choose to listen to the call."

The question, then, becomes: Why is it that so few of us choose to heed the call of grace? Why do most of us actually resist grace? We spoke earlier of grace providing us with a certain unconscious resistance to illness. How is it, then, that we seem to possess an almost equal resistance to health? The answer to this question has, in fact, already been given. It is our laziness, the original sin of entropy with which we have all been cursed. Just as grace is the ultimate source of the force that pushes us to ascend the ladder of human evolution, so it is entropy that causes us to resist that force, to stay at the comfortable, easy rung where we now are or even to descend to less and less demanding forms of existence. We have talked at length about how difficult it is to discipline ourselves, to genuinely love, to spiritually grow. It is only natural that we should shrink from the difficulty. While we have dealt with the basics of the problem of entropy or laziness, there is one aspect of the problem that deserves, once again, particular mention: the issue of power.

Psychiatrists and many laymen are familiar with the fact that psychiatric problems occur with remarkable frequency in individuals shortly after promotion to positions of higher power and responsibility. The military psychiatrist, who is particularly familiar with this problem of "promotion neurosis," is also aware that the problem does not occur with even greater frequency, because vast numbers of soldiers are successful in resisting their promotions in the first place. There are a great many low-ranking career noncommissioned officers who simply do not want to become top sergeants, first sergeants or sergeant majors. And there are also large numbers of intelligent noncommissioned officers who would rather die than become officers and who, often repeatedly, reject offers of officer training for which, by virtue of their intelligence and stability, they would seem to be well qualified.

And so it is with spiritual growth as well as in professional life. For the call to grace is a promotion, a call to a position of higher responsibility and power. To be aware of grace, to personally experience its constant presence, to know one's nearness to God, is to know and continually experience an inner tranquillity and peace that few possess. On the other hand, this knowledge and awareness brings with it an enormous responsibility. For to experience one's closeness to God is also to experience the obligation to be God, to be the agent of His power and love. The call to grace is a call to a life of effortful caring, to a life of service and whatever sacrifice seems required. It is a call out of spiritual childhood into adulthood, a call to be a parent unto mankind. T. S. Eliot described the matter well in the Christmas sermon he had Thomas Becket deliver in the play *Murder in the Cathedral:*

> But think for a while on the meaning of this word "peace." Does it seem strange to you that the angels should have announced Peace, when ceaselessly the world has been

stricken with War and the fear of War? Does it seem to you that the angelic voices were mistaken, and that the promise was a disappointment and a cheat?

Reflect now, how our Lord Himself spoke of Peace. He said to His disciples "My peace I leave with you, my peace I give unto you." Did He mean peace as we think of it: the kingdom of England at peace with its neighbours, the barons at peace with the King, the householder counting over his peaceful gains, the swept hearth, his best wine for a friend at the table, his wife singing to the children? Those men His disciples knew no such things: they went forth to journey afar, to suffer by land and sea, to know torture, imprisonment, disappointment, to suffer death by martyrdom. What then did He mean? If you ask that, remember then that He said also, "Not as the world gives, give I unto you." So then, He gave to His disciples peace, but not peace as the world gives.*

So with the peace of grace come agonizing responsibilities, duties, obligations. It is not remarkable that so many well-qualified sergeants have no desire to assume the mantle of an officer. And it is no wonder that patients in psychotherapy have little taste for the power that accompanies genuine mental health. A young woman who had been in therapy with me for a year for a pervasive depression, and who had come to learn a good deal about the psychopathology of her relatives, was exultant one day about a family situation that she had handled with wisdom, equanimity and facility. "I really felt good about it," she said. "I wish I could feel that way more often." I told her that she could, pointing out to her that the reason she had felt so well was that for the first time in dealing with her family she was in a position of power, being aware of all their distorted communications and the devious ways in which they attempted to manipulate her into fulfilling their unrealistic de-

* *The Complete Poems and Plays, 1909–1950* (New York: Harcourt Brace, 1952), pp. 198–99.

mands, and therefore she was able to be on top of the situation. I told her that as she was able to extend this type of awareness to other situations she would find herself increasingly on "top of things", and therefore experiencing that good feeling more and more frequently. She looked at me with the beginning of a sense of horror. "But that would require me to be thinking all the time!" she said. I agreed with her that it was through a lot of thinking that her power would evolve and be maintained, and that she would be rid of the feeling of powerlessness at the root of her depression. She became furious. "I don't want to have to think all the goddamn time," she roared. "I didn't come here for my life to be made more difficult. I want to be able to just relax and enjoy myself. You expect me to be some sort of god or something!" Sad to say, it was shortly afterward that this potentially brilliant woman terminated treatment, far short of being healed, terrified of the demands that mental health would require of her.

It may sound strange to laymen, but psychotherapists are familiar with the fact that people are routinely terrified by mental health. A major part of the task of psychotherapy is not only to bring patients to the experience of mental health but also, through a mixture of consolation, reassurance and sternness, to prevent them from running away from that experience once they have arrived at it. One aspect of this fearfulness is rather legitimate and, by itself, not unhealthy: the fear that if one becomes powerful one might misuse power. Saint Augustine wrote, *"Dilige et quod vis fac,"* meaning "If you are loving and diligent, you may do whatever you want."* If people progress far enough in psychotherapy they will eventually leave behind the feeling that they cannot cope with a merciless and overwhelming world and will one day suddenly realize that they have it in their power to do whatever they want. The realization of this freedom is frightening. "If I can do whatever I want," they will think, "what is to prevent me from making

* 1 Jn. 7. *Patrologia Latina*, 35, 2033.

gross mistakes, from committing crimes, from being immoral, from abusing my freedom and power? Is my diligence and my love alone sufficient to govern me?"

If the realization of one's power and freedom is experienced as a call to grace, as it often is, then the response will also be, "O Lord, I fear I am not worthy of your trust in me." This fearfulness is, of course, itself an integral part of one's diligence and love, and therefore useful in the self-governance that prevents the abuse of power. For this reason it is not to be cast aside; but it should not be so monumental as to prevent a person from heeding the call to grace and assuming the power of which he or she is capable. Some who have been called to grace may wrestle for years with their fearfulness before they are able to transcend it so as to accept their own godliness. When this fearfulness and sense of unworthiness is so great as to consistently prevent the assumption of power, it is a neurotic problem, and dealing with it may be a central issue or even the central issue in one's psychotherapy.

But for most people the fear that they might abuse the power is not the central issue in their resistance to grace. It is not the "Do what you want" part of Saint Augustine's maxim that causes them indigestion but the "Be diligent" part. Most of us are like children or young adolescents; we believe that the freedom and power of adulthood is our due, but we have little taste for adult responsibility and self-discipline. Much as we feel oppressed by our parents—or by society or fate—we actually seem to need to have powers above us to blame for our condition. To rise to a position of such power that we have no one to blame except ourselves is a fearful state of affairs. As has already been mentioned, were it not for God's presence with us in that exalted position, we would be terrified by our aloneness. Still, many have so little capacity to tolerate the aloneness of power that they reject God's presence rather than experience themselves as the sole master of their ship. Most people want peace without the aloneness of power. And they want the self-confidence of adulthood without having to grow up.

We have spoken in various ways about how difficult it is to

grow up. A very few march unambivalently and unhesitatingly into adulthood, ever eager for new and greater responsibilities. Most drag their feet and in fact never become more than partial adults, always shrinking from the demands of total adulthood. So it is with spiritual growth, which is inseparable from the process of psychological maturation. For the call to grace in its ultimate form is a summons to be one with God, to assume peership with God. Hence it is a call to total adulthood. We are accustomed to imagining the experience of conversion or sudden call to grace as an "Oh, joy!" phenomenon. In my experience, more often than not it is, at least partially, an "Oh, shit" phenomenon. At the moment we finally listen to the call we may say, "Oh, thank you, Lord"; or we may say, "O Lord, I am not worthy"; or we may say, "O Lord, do I have to?"

So the fact that "many are called but few are chosen" is easily explainable in view of the difficulties inherent in responding to the call to grace. The question we are left with, then, is not why people fail to accept psychotherapy, or fail to benefit from it even in the best hands, or why humans routinely resist grace; the force of entropy makes it only natural that they should do so. Rather, the question is the opposite: How is it that a few do heed the call that is so difficult? What distinguishes the few from the many? I am unable to answer this question. These people may come from wealthy, cultured backgrounds or from impoverished, superstitious ones. They may have experienced basically loving parenting, but they are as likely to have experienced profound deprivation of parental affection or genuine concern. They may enter psychotherapy because of minor difficulties of adjustment or with overwhelming mental illness. They may be old or young. They may heed the call to grace suddenly and with apparent ease. Or they may fight and curse against it, only gradually and painfully giving way to it, inch by inch. Consequently, with experience over the years, I have actually become less rather than more selective in determining with whom I will attempt therapy. I apologize to those I have excluded from therapy as a result of my ignorance. For I have learned that in the earlier stages of the psychotherapeutic process I have absolutely no ability to predict which of my patients will fail to respond to therapy, which will respond with significant but still partial growth, and which will, miraculously, grow all the way to the state of grace. Christ himself spoke of the unpredictability of grace when he said to Nicodemus: "Just as you can hear the wind but can't tell where it comes from or where it will go next, so it is with the Spirit. We do not know on whom he will next bestow this life from heaven."* Much as we have been able to say about the phenomenon of grace, in the end we are left having to acknowledge its mysterious nature.

The Welcoming of Grace

And we are left again facing paradox. Throughout this book I have been writing of spiritual growth as if it were an orderly, predictable process. It has been implied that spiritual growth may be learned as one might learn a field of knowledge through a Ph.D. program; if you pay your tuition and work hard enough, of course you will succeed and get your degree. I have interpreted Christ's saying "Many are called but few are chosen" to mean that very few choose to heed the call of grace because of the difficulties involved. By this interpretation I have indicated that whether or not we become blessed by grace is a matter of our choice. Essentially, I have been saying that grace is earned. And I know this to be true.

At the same time, however, I know that that's not the way it is at all. We do not come to grace; grace comes to us. Try as we might to obtain grace, it may yet elude us. We may seek it not,

* John 3:8. This translation is taken from the Living Bible because it seems to me superior to the King James version.

yet it will find us. Consciously we may avidly desire the spiritual life but then discover all manner of stumbling blocks in our way. Or we may have seemingly little taste for the spiritual life and yet find ourselves vigorously called to it in spite of ourselves. While on one level we do choose whether or not to heed the call of grace, on another it seems clear that God is the one who does the choosing. The common experience of those who have achieved a state of grace, on whom "this new life from heaven" has been bestowed, is one of amazement at their condition. They do not feel that they have earned it. While they may have a realistic awareness of the particular goodness of their nature, they do not ascribe their nature to their own will; rather, they distinctly feel that the goodness of their nature has been created by hands wiser and more skilled than their own. Those who are the closest to grace are the most aware of the mysterious character of the gift they have been given.

How do we resolve this paradox? We don't. Perhaps the best that we can say is that while we cannot will ourselves to grace, we can by will open ourselves to its miraculous coming. We can prepare ourselves to be fertile ground, a welcoming place. If we can make ourselves into totally disciplined, wholly loving individuals, then, even though we may be ignorant of theology and give no thought to God, we will have prepared ourselves well for the coming of grace. Conversely, the study of theology is a relatively poor method of preparation and, by itself, completely useless. Nonetheless, I have written this section because I do believe that the awareness of the existence of grace can be of considerable assistance to those who have chosen to travel the difficult path of spiritual growth. For this awareness will facilitate their journey in at least three ways: it will help them to take advantage of grace along the way; it will give them a surer sense of direction; and it will provide encouragement.

The paradox that we both choose grace and are chosen by grace is the essence of the phenomenon of serendipity. Serendipity was defined as "the gift of finding valuable or agreeable things not sought for." Buddha found enlightenment only when he stopped seeking for it—when he let it come to him. On the other hand, who can doubt that enlightenment came to him precisely because he had devoted at least sixteen years of his life seeking it, sixteen years in preparation? He had to both seek for it and not seek for it. The Furies were transformed into the Bearers of Grace also precisely because Orestes both worked to gain the favor of the gods and at the same time did not expect the gods to make his way easy for him. It was through this same paradoxical mixture of seeking and not seeking that he obtained the gift of serendipity and the blessings of grace.

This same phenomenon is routinely demonstrated by the manner in which patients utilize dreams in psychotherapy. Some patients, aware of the fact that dreams contain answers to their problems, will avidly seek these answers by deliberately, mechanically and with considerable effort, recording each and every one of their dreams in complete detail, and will literally bring to their sessions reams of dreams. But their dreams are of little help to them. Indeed, all this dream material may be a hindrance to their therapy. For one thing, there is not enough therapy time to analyze all these dreams. For another, this voluminous dream material may serve to prevent work in more fruitful areas of analysis. And then it is likely that all this material will be singularly obscure. Such patients must be taught to stop searching after their dreams, to let their dreams come to them, to let their unconscious make the choice of which dreams should enter consciousness. This teaching itself may be quite difficult, demanding as it does that the patient give up a certain amount of control and assume a more passive relationship in his or her own mind. But once a patient learns to make no conscious effort to clutch at dreams, the remembered dream material decreases in quantity, but it dramatically increases in quality. The result is that the patient's dreams—these gifts from the unconscious now no longer sought for—elegantly facilitate the healing process that is desired. If we look at the other side of the coin, however, we find that there are many patients who enter psychotherapy with absolutely no awareness or understanding of the immense value that dreams can be to them. Consequently they discard from consciousness all dream material as worthless and unimportant. These patients must first be taught to remember their dreams and then how to appreciate and perceive the treasure within them. To utilize dreams effectively we must work to be aware of their value and to take advantage of them when they come to us, and we must also work sometimes at not seeking or expecting them. We must let them be true gifts.

So it is with grace. We have already seen that dreams are but one form or way in which the gifts of grace are given to us. The same paradoxical approach should be employed toward all the other forms: sudden insights, premonitions and a whole host of synchronistic, serendipitous events. And to all love. Everyone wants to be loved. But first we must make ourselves lovable. We must prepare ourselves to be loved. We do this by becoming ourselves loving, disciplined human beings. If we seek to be loved—if we expect to be loved—this cannot be accomplished; we will be dependent and grasping, not genuinely loving. But when we nurture ourselves and others without a primary concern of finding reward, then we will have become lovable, and the reward of being loved, which we have not sought, will find us. So it is with human love and so it is with God's love.

A major purpose of this section on grace has been to assist those on the journey of spiritual growth to learn the capacity of serendipity. And let us redefine serendipity not as a gift itself but as a learned capacity to recognize and utilize the gifts of grace which are given to us from beyond the realm of our conscious will. With this capacity, we will find that our journey of spiritual growth is guided by the invisible hand and unimaginable wisdom of God with infinitely greater accuracy than that of which our unaided conscious will is capable. So guided, the journey becomes ever faster.

One way or another, these concepts have been set forth before—by Buddha, by Christ, by Lao-tse, among many others. The originality of this book results from the fact that I have arrived at their same meaning through the particular individual byways of my twentieth-century life. If you require greater understanding than these modern footnotes have to offer, then by all means proceed or return to the ancient texts. Seek greater understanding, but do not expect greater detail. There are many who, by virtue of their passivity, dependency, fear and laziness, seek to be shown every inch of the way and have it demonstrated to them that each step will be safe and worth their while. This cannot be done. For the journey of spiritual growth requires courage and initiative and independence of thought and action. While the words of the prophets and the assistance of grace are available, the journey must still be traveled alone. No teacher can carry you there. There are no preset formulas. Rituals are only learning aids, they are not the learning. Eating organic food, saying five Hail Mary's before breakfast, praying facing east or west, or going to church on Sunday will not take you to your destination. No words can be said, no teaching can be taught that will relieve spiritual travelers from the necessity of picking their own ways, working out with effort and anxiety their own paths through the unique circumstances of their own lives toward the identification of their individual selves with God.

Even when we truly understand these matters, the journey of spiritual growth is still so lonely and difficult that we often become discouraged. The fact that we live in a scientific age, while helpful in some respects, serves in others to foster discouragement. We believe in the mechanical principles of the universe; not in miracles. Through our science we have come to learn that our dwelling place is but a single planet of a single star lost amid one galaxy among many. And just as we seem lost amid the enormity of the external universe, so science has also led us to develop an image of ourselves as being helplessly determined and governed by internal forces not subject to our will—by chemical molecules in our brain and conflicts in our unconscious that compel us to feel and to behave in certain ways when we are not even aware of what we are doing. So the replacement of our human myths by scientific information has caused us to suffer a sense of personal meaninglessness. Of what possible significance could we be, as individuals or even as a race, buffeted about by internal chemical and psychological forces we do not understand, invisible in a universe whose dimensions are so large that even our science cannot measure them?

Yet it is that same science that has in certain ways assisted me to perceive the reality of the phenomenon of grace. I have attempted to transmit that perception. For once we perceive the reality of grace, our understanding of ourselves as meaningless and insignificant is shattered. The fact that there exists beyond ourselves and our conscious will a powerful force that nurtures our growth and evolution is enough to turn our notions of self-insignificance topsy-turvy. For the existence of this force (once we perceive it) indicates with incontrovertible certainty that our human spiritual growth is of the utmost importance to something greater than ourselves. This something we call God. The existence of grace is *prima facie* evidence not only of the reality of God but also of the reality that God's will is devoted to the growth of the individual human spirit. What once seemed to be a fairy tale turns out to be the reality. We live our lives in the eye of God, and not at the periphery but at the center of His vision, His concern. It is probable that the universe as we know it is but a single stepping-stone toward the entrance to the Kingdom of God. But we are hardly lost in the universe. To the contrary, the reality of grace indicates humanity to be at the center of the universe. This time and space exists for us to travel through. When my patients lose sight of their significance and are disheartened by the effort of the work we are doing, I sometimes tell them that the human race is in the midst of making an evolutionary leap. "Whether or not we succeed in that leap," I say to them, "is your personal responsibility." And mine. The universe, this stepping-stone, has been laid down to prepare a way for us. But we ourselves must step across it, one by one. Through grace we are helped not to stumble and through grace we know that we are being welcomed. What more can we ask?

Afterword

In the time since its initial publication, I have been fortunate enough to receive many letters from readers of *The Road Less Traveled*. They have been extraordinary letters. Intelligent and articulate without exception, they have also been extremely loving. As well as expressing appreciation, most of them have contained additional gifts: appropriate poetry, useful quotes from other authors, nuggets of wisdom and tales of personal experience. These letters have enriched my life. It has become clear to me that there is a whole network—far more vast than I had dared to believe—of people across the country who have quietly been proceeding for long distances along the less traveled road of spiritual growth. They have thanked me for diminishing their sense of aloneness on the journey. I thank them for the same service.

A few readers have questioned my faith in the efficacy of psychotherapy. I did suggest that the quality of psychotherapists varies widely. And I continue to believe that most of those who fail to benefit from work with a competent therapist do so because they lack the taste and will for the rigors of that work. However I did neglect to specify that a small minority of people—perhaps five percent—have psychiatric problems of a nature that does not respond to psychotherapy and that may even be made worse by the deep introspection involved.

Anyone who has succeeded in thoroughly reading and understanding this book is highly unlikely to belong to that five percent. And in any case, it is the responsibility of a competent therapist to carefully and sometimes gradually discern those few patients who should not be led into psychoanalytic work and to lead them instead toward other forms of treatment that can be quite beneficial.

But who is a competent psychotherapist? Several readers of *The Road Less Traveled* who moved in the direction of seeking psychotherapy have written to inquire how one should go about choosing the right therapist, distinguishing between the competent and the incompetent. My first piece of advice is to take the choice seriously. It is one of the most important decisions you can make in your lifetime. Psychotherapy is a major investment, not only of your money but even more of your valuable time and energy. It is what stockbrokers would call a high-risk investment. If the choice is right, it will pay off handsomely in spiritual dividends you could not even have dreamed of. While it is not likely you will be actually harmed if you make the wrong choice, you will, however, waste most of the valuable money, time and energy you have put into it.

So don't hesitate to shop around. And don't hesitate to trust your feelings or intuition. Usually on the basis of a single interview with a therapist, you will be able to pick up either good or bad "vibes." If the vibes are bad, pay your single fee and move on to another. Such feelings are usually intangible, but they may emanate from small tangible clues. At the time I entered therapy in 1966, I was very concerned and critical about the morality of America's involvement in the Vietnam War. In his waiting room my therapist had copies of *Ramparts* and the *New York Review of Books*, both liberal journals with antiwar editorial policies. I had begun to pick up good vibes before I had ever set eyes on him.

But more important than your therapist's political leanings, age or sex is whether he or she is a genuinely caring person. This too you can often sense quickly, although the therapist should not fall all over you with kindly reassurances and snap commitments. If therapists are caring, they will also be cautious, disciplined and usually reserved, but it should be possible for you to intuit whether the reserve cloaks warmth or coldness.

Since therapists will be interviewing you to see whether they want you for a patient, it is wholly appropriate for you to be interviewing them in return. If it is relevant to you, don't hold back from asking what the therapist's feelings are about such issues as women's liberation or homosexuality or religion. You are entitled to honest, open and careful answers. In regard to other types of questions—such as how long therapy might last or whether your skin rash is psychosomatic— you are usually well off to trust a therapist who says that he or she does not know. In fact, educated and successful people in any profession who admit ignorance are generally the most expert and trustworthy.

A therapist's ability bears very little relationship to any credentials he or she might have. Love and courage and wisdom cannot be certified by academic degrees. For instance, "board-certified" psychiatrists, the therapists with the most credentials, undergo sufficiently rigorous training so that one can be relatively certain of not falling into the hands of a charlatan. But a psychiatrist is not necessarily any better a therapist than a psychologist, a social worker or a minister— or even as good. Indeed two of the very greatest therapists I know have never even graduated from college.

Word of mouth is often the best way to get started on your search for a psychotherapist. If you have some friend you respect who has been pleased with the services of a particular therapist, why not begin on that recommendation? Another way, particularly advisable if your symptoms are severe or you have physical difficulties as well, would be to start with a psychiatrist. By virtue of their medical training, psychiatrists are usually the most expensive therapists, but they are also in the best position to understand all the angles of your situation. At the end of the hour, after the psychiatrist has had a chance to learn the dimensions of your problem, you can ask him or her to refer you to a less expensive nonmedical therapist if appropriate. The best psychiatrists will usually be quite willing to tell you which lay practitioners in the community are particularly competent. Of course, if the doctor gives you good vibes and is willing to take you on as a patient, you can stick with him or her.

If you are financially strapped and have no medical insurance coverage for outpatient psychotherapy, your only option may be to seek assistance at a government- or hospital-supported psychiatric or mental health clinic. There a fee will be set according to your means, and you can rest pretty well assured that you will not fall into the hands of a quack. On the other hand, psychotherapy at clinics has a tendency to be superficial, and your capacity to choose your own therapist may be quite limited. Nonetheless, it often works out very well.

These brief guidelines have perhaps not been as specific as readers might like. But the central message is that since psychotherapy requires an intense and psychologically intimate relationship between two human beings, nothing can relieve you of the responsibility for personally choosing the particular human being whom you can trust to be your guide. The best therapist for one person may not be the best for another. Each person, therapist and patient, is unique, and you must rely on your own unique intuitive judgment. Because there is some risk involved, I wish you luck. And because the act of entering psychotherapy with all that it involves is an act of courage, you have my admiration.

M. Scott Peck
Bliss Road
New Preston, Conn. 06777

March, 1979

Publisher's Note

In his classic work *The Road Less Traveled*, Dr. M. Scott Peck has led millions of readers on a rewarding journey of psychological and spiritual growth. In his profound and powerful new book, *The Different Drum: Community Making and Peace*, Dr. Peck challenges us to take the next essential step along the path of personal fulfillment in the creative experience of community. For it is only through community that we can achieve health and wholeness in our individual lives. It is only through community that we can learn to love ourselves, and to live in understanding and peace with all the other peoples of the world.

The experience of true community is a unique way of communicating with others, of sharing our deepest thoughts and feelings without fear or guilt. Writing with the immediacy and insight gained from his pioneering work in creating communities in every part of the country, Dr. Peck describes the exhilarating process by which we can join together, whatever our cultural backgrounds and religious beliefs, overcome our defenses and prejudices, and transcend our differences. With fascinating stories and case histories from his own personal experiences, he reveals that the steps we must take toward achieving community are surprisingly similar to the steps necessary to achieve maturity in our human growth. The rules Dr. Peck outlines for building community are very clear, but hardly undemanding of us human beings. As his book states, "there can be no vulnerability without risk; there can be no community without vulnerability; and there can be no peace (and ultimately life) without community."

A powerful new force for both individual and social change, community can and must be created among small groups of people, then in our churches, our business organizations and our governmental institutions, and ultimately among all peoples and nations if we are to achieve the best of which we are capable and ensure our survival as human beings. Dr. Peck's book is simultaneously the most important and most creative signpost pointing the way toward a future for humanity.

About the Author

Educated at Harvard (B.A.) and Case Western Reserve (M.D.), Dr. M. Scott Peck has served in administrative posts in the government during his career as a psychotherapist. He is currently Medical Director of the New Milford Hospital Mental Health Clinic and a psychiatrist in private practice in New Milford, Connecticut.